Batman, Superman, and Philosophy

Popular Culture and Philosophy® Series Editor: George A. Reisch

For full details of all Popular Culture and Philosophy® books, visit www.opencourtbooks.com.

Popular Culture and Philosophy®

Batman, Superman, and Philosophy

Badass or Boyscout?

Edited by
NICOLAS MICHAUD

OPEN COURT
Chicago

Volume 100 in the series, Popular Culture and Philosophy ®, edited by George A. Reisch

To find out more about Open Court books, call toll-free 1-800-815-2280, or visit our website at www.opencourtbooks.com.

Open Court Publishing Company is a division of Carus Publishing Company, dba Cricket Media.

Copyright © 2016 by Carus Publishing Company, dba Cricket Media

First printing 2016

Printed and bound in the United States of America.

ISBN: 978-0-8126-9918-0

This book is also available as an e-book..

Library of Congress Comtrol Number: 2016935516

Contents

It's About Damn Time

Finally, we can put the question of who's better, Batman or Superman, to rest!

Right?

Wrong.

Now, it seems that no matter what movie comes out, what comic is written, or what cartoon livens our Saturday morning, enthusiasts will be arguing the superiority of one or the other until Doomsday, pardon the pun. The refrain of those arguments will continue to reverberate long afterwards . . .

"Superman can destroy a planet with his fists!"

"Well Batman is a Billionaire!"

"Who needs money when you can shoot lasers from your eyes?"

"People who will buy kryptonite gauntlets to pummel your ass!"

And on and on it goes.

But there's something fans know that the rest of the world doesn't get: this argument isn't really about who's stronger, smarter, or handsomer . . . What the fans know is that what we're really arguing about is: *Who's the better hero?* And what we mean by that is, "Who should we try to be like?" And *that* is the question that matters to me, and to the philosophers who have come together here. What does it mean to be a hero, and, of the two, who is the better example of our best selves?

Since the day I saw Tim Burton's *Batman*, I wanted to be like the Caped Crusader. That fact might explain why I remain, to this day, grumpy, brooding, and not particularly well-adjusted. But, the fact is I also learned a lot from Batman . . . I learned about sacrifice, hard work, and what it means to never give up. And then, only a few years later, Superman died, and I learned what it means to give everything, absolutely everything, for the people you love, and for people you don't even know.

To the people who really know these characters, it's fun to argue about who would win in a fight, but what we all really worry about is which one is the best example of who we should be, how we should raise our children, and how we should look into the future . . . Because those two men are very different, both great heroes, but they follow very different paths. So, is it better to be hopeful in the face of great adversity, to believe that humanity can, and *will*, succeed? Or should we be cynical, and watch ourselves and others because everyone is really just one lab accident away from being a super villain?

So, to try to answer that question, we have invited some of the brightest philosophical minds to throw down not just on who's the better fighter . . . but who's the better *hero*.

And, holy argument, do they disagree. It will be up to you, the real experts to decide who comes out on top. Have fun, and remember, the fate of the world hangs in the balance . . .

Who should we be, Batman or Superman?

You decide.

Battle of the Billennium

1
Where Have All the Supermen Gone?

A.G. HOLDIER

When the definitive history of superhero movies is finally written, the year 2008 will undoubtedly go down as the second most important year in the development of the genre. Perhaps you remember: coming on the heels of years of disappointing sequels (including, among other things, Tobey Maguire's hip-thrusting in 2007's *Spider-Man 3*), many comic-book fans were skeptical that we would ever see Hollywood portray our mythical heroes with consistent skill and respect. Our hopes had been raised by Christopher Nolan's *Batman Begins* and Bryan Singer's work with the X-Men franchise, but would we ever truly see a superb superhero universe at the movie theater?

No one was asking that question in the summer of 2008 after Robert Downey Jr. first embodied the witty bravado of Iron Man and Heath Ledger made *The Dark Knight*'s Joker come more alive on-screen than anyone had yet thought possible. But as huge box-office success was seen for superhero movies that were simultaneously resonating well with comic-book fans, the most shocking development of all came in a short, ninety-second video clip that played after the credits of Louis Leterrier's *The Incredible Hulk* when RDJ's Tony Stark sauntered into a bar at the end of *the wrong movie*, doing something common to comic books, but unprecedented on the big screen—Iron Man was "crossing over" with the Hulk.

Close to a decade later, the explosion of the Marvel Cinematic Universe (MCU) has been formidable, ultimately producing one of the most lucrative films of all time—2012's

The Avengers—and there are no plans to slow down. The creation of a consistent, multi-movie fictional world, fueled by ten-picture deals that ensure familiar actors and actresses will maintain their on-screen personas to keep the story going, now strikes us as normal—but before the game-changing year of 2008, no one dared to hope for such a project.

. . . And that's the second-most important year.

Because while cross-overs between fan-favorites (but to-that-point not widely known characters) like Thor or Black Widow may have been clever, and the MCU is slowly crafting a beautifully complex fictional universe, the idea pales in comparison to what 2016 had in store.

For a new cross-over was coming; the gods were soon to meet; in 2016, Batman and Superman would share the screen.

And while many were excited to see a cinematic answer to the most classic of comics-based arguments—"In a fight between Batman and Superman, who would win?"—this long-awaited encounter gave us the opportunity here to drill down even further into the roots of the question and focus on something more fundamental: what is it about these two titanic characters that sees us so frequently pit them against each other, even while they are both on the same heroic side? Does anyone really win when Batman and Superman battle it out? In short, why must the Caped Crusader and the Last Son of Krypton fight at all?

Final Crisis: God Is Dead

Like a mustachioed version of the mysterious Phantom Stranger, our guide along the path to an answer takes the form of a late-nineteenth-century German philosopher named Friedrich Nietzsche. Like many a superhero, Nietzsche came from very humble beginnings and saw the death of his father, a Lutheran pastor, at a young age; this, among other things, led to Nietzsche losing his faith once he grew up. However, Nietzsche was a philosopher who saw that many of his fellow atheists were far too much like Batman's Two-Face for his intellectual comfort, pretending to be atheists on one hand, while continuing to cling to beliefs that only make sense if God actually exists. As Nietzsche had one character lament in his most famous work, *Thus Spake Zarathustra*:

"God is dead. God remains dead. And we have killed him. How shall we comfort ourselves, the murderers of all murderers? . . . Is not the greatness of this deed too great for us? Must we ourselves not become gods simply to appear worthy of it?"

Essentially, as Nietzsche sees it, the Final Crisis has come; the philosophical radion bullet has been fired—God has fallen and everything has changed. No longer can we look to a loving cosmic deity for protection or pretend that "all God's people" really matter; instead, the only god for us is whoever turns out to be the strongest—in all likelihood, someone like Darkseid.

Nietzsche's name for this new Godless cosmic rule is the "will to power," so, because we actually exist "beyond good and evil," then the only thing that determines what "should" be done is the strength of strong individuals; if all really are one in Darkseid, then whatever Darkseid says goes. As Nietzsche wrote in his provocatively-titled 1888 work *The Anti-Christ*:

What is good? All that heightens the feeling of power, the will to power, power itself in man. What is bad? All that proceeds from weakness. What is happiness? The feeling that power increases—that a resistance is overcome.

Anything else—any notion that values like self-sacrifice, humility, or generosity were "good"—Nietzsche called "slave morality" and blamed on generations of sneaky weaklings convincing whole cultures of religious lies in order to unfairly raise the weak above those who are truly powerful—as if Jimmy Olson could somehow trick Darkseid's parademons into worshiping a photographer rather than their rightful god. The only proper thing to do according to Nietzsche's system is for the strong man to take his place at the top of the world.

Behold, I Teach You the *Overman*!

But what does this all have to do with Batman fighting Superman? The key lies in the final crucial element of Nietzsche's philosophy (something that clearly resonated in Clark Kent's solar-powered ears): the concept of the *Übermensch*. To Nietzsche, the *Übermensch* would be the true pinnacle of human existence, both physically and mentally superior to all other human beings and able to bend existence itself to his will. Being the strongest specimen, the *Übermensch* would be able to create his own rules of morality and society, making him as far above normal men as humans are above apes. This could, therefore, give meaning to the entirety of the human species: that we could create something so much better than ourselves. "Man is a rope, tied between beast and overman [*Übermensch*]—a rope over an abyss," Nietzsche would write, "what is great in man is that he is a bridge and not an end." Ultimately, Nietzsche was hoping for a superhero.

This word—*Übermensch*—that Nietzsche coined is not always translated as "overman," but can also be rendered into English as the more familiar-sounding "Superman."

Does this mean that Superman is Nietzsche's *Übermensch*, physically and mentally capable of more than any other being on the planet? At first glance, Supes certainly appears to match the description—but is that enough? On second thought, after studying Nietzsche's concept more clearly, could it turn out to be that the actually Earth-born (and Earth-bound) Batman is the real example of human perfection? After all: Batman is the genuine product of nothing but human grit and ingenuity— could Bats be the real overman?

Perhaps this is at the root of their eternal struggle: which hero is the true Hero? After we consider each one in turn, we may find that neither one actually qualifies . . . but they are each something else, something iconic, maybe something even more important.

All-Star "Apollo"

It might seem easy to grant Superman the title of "superman": if Nietzsche's *Übermensch* is thought to be the very pinnacle of physical prowess, with powers to control the universe in ways unlike any mere human being, the alien Kal-El certainly seems to fit the bill. Add to that the religious imagery that has always surrounded the figure—ranging from the Christ parallels in *Man of Steel* all the way back to Siegel and Shuster co-opting the very name of God himself ("El" in Hebrew) for their character—and we appear to have a convincing candidate for Nietzsche's God-replacement. But the Man of Tomorrow deserves a more careful analysis.

On the one hand, Nietzsche would be captivated by Superman's range of abilities, particularly their way of taking the best of human abilities (such as strength or speed) and cranking their power up off the charts. To borrow another line from Nietzsche, Superman's abilities tend to "remain faithful to the Earth," with no hint of mystical or magical empowerment (even though he can see the "halo" of a living creature's soul in *Birthright*)—his talents are biological. By absorbing the power of the sun to accomplish the impossible, Superman proves to be the very embodiment of the will to power. And although the *Übermensch* is explicitly a development out of humanity (and not, say, Kryptonian biology), many of the most beloved stories in the Superman canon play with the idea that simple men and women could one day become like Kal-El; whether we consider the liquid DNA from *All-Star Superman*, the character "Steel" in *Reign of the Supermen!*, or the time-traveling rocket from *Red Son*, there is a well-established thread in Superman's story that the Last Son of Krypton is leading us to follow in his footsteps.

On the other hand, not everything about the Man of Steel would impress the philosopher of the *Übermensch*, for the very idea of "Clark Kent" might disqualify Superman from being the *superman*. Despite having the ability to travel throughout the stars, Superman restricts himself (generally) to a single planet, where he not only foregoes (apart from in several Elseworlds titles) setting up his own kingdom to rule the unpowered peasants, but goes so far as to allow himself to live as a subservient commoner: a model of Nietzsche's "slave morality" if ever there was one. The mere fact that Superman has a "mild-mannered alter-ego" would turn Nietzsche's stomach, for no true *Übermensch* would ever hide his absolute superiority.

Instead of the superman, we might consider Superman as a good example of a different one of Nietzsche's ideas: the Apollonian creative force that gives aesthetics structure and focus. In his first book, *The Birth of Tragedy*, Nietzsche lays out a philosophy of art (looking primarily at music, though the idea can be applied to all art) that recognizes the Greek god Apollo as the embodiment of the harmony and logic that is required for a musical composition to make sense. Nietzsche saw the Apollonian force as something "simple, transparent, and beautiful," standing clear in the light of day to promote cheerfulness, an illusion that shields us from the passionate chaos that fuels a true work of art while still allowing us to experience its beauty. Found primarily in logical lyrics and dialogue, the Apollonian force filters the emotional experience of an audience into an orderly structure that can be understood. As a time-honored defender of "truth, justice, and the American way"—particularly in stories like Frank Miller's *The Dark Knight Returns*—Superman, in all of his solar-powered glory, is indeed a solid candidate for the latest embodiment of Apollo, the Greek god of the sun.

A Dionysius in the Family

So, if the Man of Steel isn't Nietzsche's superman, perhaps his perpetual clash with the Dark Knight stems from a subconscious recognition that he doesn't deserve his name. Is it possible that Batman could be the real *Übermensch*—the real superman?

Certainly, in this debate, Bruce Wayne's Batman has one strength that Superman lacks: he is genuinely human. (In Chapter 21 of this volume, Suzie Gibson argues that Batman fulfills Nietzsche's concept of the *Übermensch*, since he is not an immortal but a deeply mortal being.) Because Nietzsche was quite clear that the connection of the *Übermensch* to the Earth is biological and not merely chosen, Batman accomplishes this in a way that Superman cannot. Unlike Superman, Batman relies on nothing else but himself to be the source of his power. In a world without a yellow sun, the Son of Metropolis would fall while the Guardian of Gotham uses the shadows to grow even stronger, for it was only ever due to his own effort and determination—that is to say, his *will*—that Batman was a hero in the first place. And the possibility (however slim) of a real human being actually becoming a superhero like Batman would impress Nietzsche in a way that Superman never could, for it sounds much more like the eventual birth of the *Übermensch* towards which humanity can aspire.

On top of that, Batman grapples explicitly with Nietzschean motivations, turning the tragic death of his parents into fuel for his revenge; "What makes one heroic?" Nietzsche asks in *The Gay Science*, "To approach at the same time one's highest suffering and one's highest hope." Consider Wayne's internal monologue in the early pages of Miller's *Year One* (mirrored on screen in *Batman Begins*) where he muses on both the loss of his parents and his boyhood fear of bats before combining both to overcome each by the sheer force of his will. Thinking ahead to the many nights of broken bones and gunshot wounds that he would sustain, Batman certainly lives by the old adage "what does not kill me makes me stronger"—an adage first coined by Friedrich Nietzsche.

However, that very fact—that he *is* repeatedly broken—reminds us that Batman is still a human being underneath his cape and cowl. While he is undoubtedly an impressive specimen of strength and skill, the Caped Crusader does not really display "a new health, stronger . . . more audacious, and gayer than any previous health," as Nietzsche describes it in *The Gay Science*. Moreover, Batman certainly does not love himself in the way that the rightfully proud *Übermensch* should and is constantly plagued by suppressed feelings of emotional self-loathing (as shown particularly well in Morrison's *Arkham Asylum*); as he says in the middle of his fight with a hypnotized Superman in Loeb's *Hush*, "Even more than the Kryptonite, he's got one big weakness. Deep down, Clark's essentially a good person . . . and deep down, I'm not." This doubt and lack of pride means that Batman also fails to make the grade of the *Übermensch*.

But, like Superman, we can find a different home for Batman inside Nietzsche's philosophy: the parallel creative force of the Dionysian from *The Birth of Tragedy*. Functioning as the opposite pole to the Apollonian, the Dionysian gives art its passion and depth, using the musical melody and other emotional cues to fuel the fires of creativity and "convince us of the eternal joy of existence." This art-force is the very embodiment of chaos and emotion (Dionysius himself was the Greek god of wine, revelry, and a passionate existence) and cuts across all strata of culture to unify humanity in a primordial state. Anyone can enjoy art, just as anyone could be Batman, provided they grapple honestly with the deep, dark emotions that give him the strength to continue existing. Batman may not be the *Übermensch*, but his ability to transform his own pain into a beautiful expression of a meaningful life means that he is something far more important.

The Tragedy of the Superhero

In his book *Supergods: What Masked Vigilantes, Miraculous Mutants, and a Sun God from Smallville Can Teach Us about Being Human*, Grant Morrison analyzed the 1930s origin of Batman and Superman as the near-simultaneous emergence of yin and yang:

> Batman was born of the deliberate reversal of everything in the Superman dynamic: Superman was an alien with incredible powers; Batman was a human being with no superhuman abilities. Superman's costume was brightly colored; Batman's was grayscale and somber with mocking flashes of yellow. . . . Superman was of the day; Batman was of the night and shadows. Superman was rational, Apollonian; Batman was Dionysian.

And Morrison, who has made a name for himself as one of the premier writers in comics, has certainly emphasized this dichotomy in his sporadic (and award-winning) Superman and Batman stories—most notably in the pages of *JLA*, which he has worked with off-and-on since 1996, that constantly sees these titans standing side-by-side, using their respective strengths to complement their respective weaknesses.

Which should come as no surprise: if Superman is the embodiment of Nietzsche's Apollonian force and Batman is his Dionysian counterpart, then they will function at their best when they function together. This was the very goal of *The Birth of Tragedy*: to understand the power of the Apollonian-Dionysian connection, using the strengths of rationality to better experience the wild, drunken passions of life within the aesthetic experience. As Nietzsche proclaimed towards the end of the book:

> . . . the intricate relation of the Apollonian and the Dionysian in tragedy may really be symbolized by a fraternal union of the two deities. Dionysius speaks the language of Apollo; and Apollo, finally the language of Dionysius; and so the highest goal of tragedy and of all art is attained.

So, the best kind of art (the likes of which Nietzsche did not think had been seen since the days of Greek tragedy) will be that which allows the chaos and madness of Dionysian existence to be displayed with Apollonian clarity and understanding.

Perhaps it is in the comic book, that postmodern art form that combines emotional illustration with logical prose in a mashup of the best of both Dionysius and Apollo, where we catch a glimmer of a rebirth of art unlike anything seen since the days of Nietzsche's beloved Greek tragedies—complete with our own incarnations of the same iconic gods.

The Dark Knight (Eternally) Returns

Why, then, do Superman and Batman fight? Looking at them through the lens of Nietzsche's aesthetics, their roles as the twin poles between which all art emerges begins to give us an answer: despite their partnerships, their team-ups, and their friendship, these two superheroes are, at their core, fundamentally and diametrically opposed. They do not fight over who is the real overman, but rather as an inescapable expression of their deepest character traits. Like the moon chasing the sun, Dionysian emotion offsets Apollonian light: conflict is inevitable—but never final. Even in their most famous battle at the climax of *The Dark Knight Returns*, though Batman certainly wins the day, both he and Superman survive to continue protecting the people under their watch, albeit in their own unique ways.

Which is why 2016 held such promise for the future of superhero films: though both of these cultural icons have performed well at the box office in years past, that year saw their first meeting on the big screen—and, from the looks of the contracts that are still being signed, *Batman v Superman: Dawn of Justice* is poised to be the genesis of another complex fictional universe. Though only time will tell what sort of day will rise after that *Dawn,* it is a safe bet that it will be a popular one.

Because no matter who your personal favorite is in this grudge match of ultimate proportions, there is one thing that we can count on when the shining Man of Steel and the brooding Dark Knight square off against each other: we are in for a treat.

That is to say: who wins when Batman fights Superman? We do.

ROUND ONE

DECISION — SUPERMAN!

The Son Shines Bright

2
Sure We're Criminals

DANIEL MALLOY

> You were the one who laughed . . . that scary laugh of yours . . . "Sure
> we're criminals," you said. "We've always been criminals. We have to
> be criminals."
>
> —SUPERMAN, quoting Batman, *The Dark Knight Returns*

A criminal is someone who breaks the law.
Batman and Superman are vigilantes, which is against the law.
Therefore, Batman and Superman are criminals.

But . . .
Breaking the law doesn't make you a bad person. Some of
history's most prominent respected figures have been criminals: Socrates, Jesus, Henry David Thoreau, Gandhi, and
Martin Luther King, Jr., to name a few. But history's vindica-
tion of these figures doesn't mean that law breaking isn't
wrong. These people were civil disobedients, which is its own
special category of criminal.

For all we may admire them, the law breaking of the Dark
Knight and the Metropolis Marvel isn't comparable to civil disobedience. Batman and Superman aren't civil disobedients.
They don't break the law because it's unjust. In fact, they usually break the law to enforce the law. This makes them not only
criminals, but hypocrites as well.

The distinct relations Batman and Superman have to the
law shed light on political obligation; that is, the duty to obey
the law. Even though both heroes maintain connections to law
enforcement, and both are criminals, their attitudes toward the

law differ. Superman is respectful, and strives to comply with authorities. Disobedience doesn't come naturally to the Man of Tomorrow. For Batman, on the other hand, law enforcement authorities are tools in his war on crime. Like any tool, they are to be used when needed and laid aside when they aren't. Compliance or non-compliance, obedience or disobedience, is a matter of strategy for the Dark Knight, not morality. Superman's attitude of politeness without being slavishly bound by the law is an example everyone should follow—even Batman.

Bruce Wayne: Fugitive

In 399 B.C.E., the philosopher Socrates was tried and convicted of impiety and corrupting the youth of Athens. He was sentenced to death. According to an account from his student Plato (around 428–348 B.C.E.), while Socrates was awaiting his execution a friend, Crito, came to him and offered to help him escape. Socrates refused, arguing that he had an obligation to obey the law, even when it was wrong.

How different from the actions of the Caped Crusader when he was framed and arrested for murder! (*Bruce Wayne—Murderer?*) Bruce Wayne escaped before even going to trial. Rather than attempt to solve the crime, he spent most of the next year running away—from the crime, from himself, from his "family" (*Bruce Wayne—Fugitive*). Far from respecting the law, Batman disregarded it. It was an obstacle to his war on crime, so he ignored it.

Batman, like Socrates, was innocent of the crime in question. But there are plenty of other crimes the Caped Crusader commits on a regular basis: vigilantism, assault and battery, breaking and entering, obstruction of justice, littering—and that's just his typical Wednesday.

If we do have duties to obey the law, it's worrying to think that they aren't influenced by the goodness or badness of the laws. As Plato's Socrates argues, we have a duty to obey the law, even if the law is wrong. Theories of political obligation thus have to confront two questions. First, do we have a duty to obey the law? And second, if we do, does it extend to all laws, even bad ones? In the cases of both Socrates and Batman, their objections aren't to the existence of the laws—Batman has no issues with the laws against murder, for instance—but with certain applications of them.

Superman in Handcuffs

One of the most striking images from Zach Snyder's *Man of Steel* (2013) is the moment Superman surrenders himself to the American government. Superman is put in handcuffs. Knowing what we do about Superman, it's obvious that he remains in handcuffs because he chooses to—and only because he chooses to. When he breaks the cuffs, he shows no sign of effort or even awareness that he has done so. He breaks out of the handcuffs as easily as you or I might break a spider's web. Just like remaining in the cuffs, if Superman obeys the law, it's solely because he chooses to, which is the core of the "consent theory" of political obligation.

Consent theory holds that political obligations are like the obligations that arise from making promises. Once I have made a promise, I have a duty to keep it, regardless of the content of the promise. If I promise to do something I don't want to, or that will seriously inconvenience me, well, that's just tough, isn't it? But the actual obligation depends on the initial promise. In the same way, my duty to obey the law is based on my initial consent. I have to obey the law because I've agreed to.

A basic form of consent theory appears in Plato's *Crito*, but the theory gained a great deal of support much later, in the seventeenth century, when it found defenders in philosophers like Thomas Hobbes (1588–1679) and John Locke (1632–1704). Hobbes and Locke present an interesting contrast, because although they both argue that the obligation to obey the law flows from consent, they set entirely different limits to this obligation. Each says that consent can't exist in a vacuum—we consent to obey laws for some *reason*. Just as we don't make a promise without knowing what we're promising, we don't consent to obey the law without at least some inkling of what the content—or limits—of the law will be.

What the law can and can't do is restricted by what the law's for. For example, if the purpose of law is to prevent people from hurting each other, then laws against smoking, gambling, and driving without a seatbelt are illegitimate, because those actions don't hurt anyone else. The law is designed for a particular purpose and our consent is dependent on the laws serving that purpose.

As Hobbes sees it, our consent is based on a concern for our own security. So long as a ruler (or sovereign, as Hobbes calls it) can ensure security and maintain order, we're obliged to obey whatever laws are in place. This may sound reasonable, but Hobbes assigns to his sovereign virtually unlimited authority— he goes so far as to call the sovereign a "mortal god." For an example of Hobbes's mortal god, think of Darkseid. Under the rule of Darkseid, the inhabitants of Apokolips don't have good lives— they're enslaved and abused in ways that are virtually unimaginable. But Apokolips without Darkseid's iron fist on the reins wouldn't necessarily be better. Perhaps, with someone else in charge, it would be (seriously, it could also be worse—Desaad would be a far crueler ruler than Darkseid). But while life could be better without Darkseid, it's undeniable that he provides a degree of security. So, according to Hobbes, the inhabitants of Apokolips are bound to obey his laws. The fact that they're basically slaves doesn't change things—it just means that the first bit of security they got was from Darkseid himself. They agreed to obey, and he agreed not to obliterate them—unless he feels like it.

Locke, on the other hand, argued for a much more restricted concept of political obligation. As Locke understands it, we don't agree to be ruled simply to gain security, but to protect all of our *natural* rights. Since the purpose of government is to protect natural rights, a government that violates those rights is no longer legitimate, and so we're not obligated to obey it. Darkseid, from Locke's perspective, is an illegitimate ruler and violating his laws, even openly rebelling against them, is morally permissible—perhaps even required.

The consent theory has to be modified slightly when dealing with beings like Superman and even Batman, though. After all, there aren't many threats to their security or rights. Both are living threats to others' security: Batman's attitude and Superman's abilities make them both potential violations of other people's rights. With Superman's senses, no one other than the most security conscious citizens of Metropolis has any guarantee of privacy. So, why would Superman and Batman agree to obey the laws? We can set aside Batman, as he plainly doesn't. Why would Superman? I think he agrees to obey the laws, even to wear handcuffs, so that people will trust him. Complying with the law is part of how Superman demonstrates that he's one of the good guys.

The *Red Son* Problem

There's one problem with consent theory that's obvious from the start: most people living under a set of laws haven't agreed to obey them. And I don't just mean those living under non-democratic governments. Even the citizens of democracies rarely make promises or swear oaths to obey the law of the land, whatever it may be. Few US citizens have sworn oaths to uphold the Constitution. The Pledge of Allegiance doesn't count. Aside from the fact that it never mentions either the Constitution or the laws, it's generally sworn by minors who can't take binding oaths.

Consent theorists have recognized this as a problem, and have found one way to deal with it: those living under a set of laws have given tacit consent to them. Asking for a promise would be insisting on explicit consent. Tacit consent could be given by participating in government, or taking part in the community, or even by not leaving. So, the Superman of Mark Millar's *Red Son* agreed to abide by the laws of the Soviet Union by choosing to reside there. As long as he doesn't leave, he's bound by the laws.

David Hume (1711–1776) pointed out the flaw in the reasoning that says simply living somewhere means you consent to the laws of that place. It isn't always easy to leave a place. It might be a simple matter for Superman to leave the Soviet Union, but most of the people living there couldn't leave. Even if there are no legal barriers—no laws against emigrating—there can still be innumerable and insurmountable obstacles to packing up your life and moving elsewhere. Even if we set aside practical concerns, like the time, inconvenience, and expense of establishing yourself in a new life elsewhere, obstacles still remain.

It wouldn't be all that inconvenient for Superman or Batman to pick up stakes and move. Batman has more money than God and Superman has a fortress at the North Pole that he visits semi-regularly. But even so, there are ties that keep them where they are. Leaving Metropolis seems like an easy thing for Superman to do, until you realize that leaving Metropolis means leaving Lois, Jimmy, and Perry behind. And as for Batman— Batman leaving Gotham? Permanently? The very idea is absurd. Even when Gotham was reduced to a wasteland in the *No Man's*

Land storyline, Batman stayed. So, tacit consent, and hence consent theory, doesn't justify political obligation.

Thanksgiving with the Kents

When the infant Kal-El crashed on the Kents' farm in Kansas, they had no obligation to take him in. At best, they had a duty to see that the boy was taken care of, but they could have done that by calling the proper authorities. Martha and Jonathan went above and beyond the call of duty by adopting the boy as their own and raising him in a loving environment. Clark Kent owes a debt of gratitude to his adoptive parents. It would be wrong of him not to acknowledge and honor it—by helping his parents when they need it, listening to their advice when they give it, and just generally being there for them.

A similar case can be made for the law. Anyone living under a system of law owes some benefits to it. Laws provide stability. Specific laws provide services, such as police and fire departments, roads, parks, utilities, and education. Those living under such laws owe a debt of gratitude to them for those benefits. The least the laws can ask in return is obedience.

But there are some people living under systems of law who don't seem to benefit from them. Bruce Wayne hasn't benefited from the law. When he needed the services of the police, they were nowhere to be found. Gotham's notoriously corrupt police force not only let Bruce's parents die, they then failed to catch their killer. What's more, Bruce is wealthy enough to afford any and all of the benefits provided by the law, even in the absence of law. His education was largely private. Being independently wealthy, he has no debt to the law, and therefore no obligation to obey it.

But this objection isn't nearly as strong as it appears. It rests on the existence of the Wayne fortune, which young Bruce inherited when his parents were killed. Inheritance is a legal procedure. So, Bruce's possession of the fortune is based on law. But the Waynes' wealth is also dependent on the existence of law. Without law, money and wealth can't be formalized or protected the way they are. Contracts, the basis of any economy, are inconceivable in the absence of law. Further, Wayne Enterprises exists, in part, because it has access to a pool of qualified workers—workers who have at least some level of education, often provided at public expense, and dictated by law.

So, even someone like Bruce Wayne, whom the law has failed spectacularly and who could do without public services, still owes a great deal to the law. Obedience is the bare minimum, and one that both Batman and Superman fail to provide—though Superman at least has the good grace to seem reluctant about it.

Thank You, Superman

Clark owes a debt of gratitude to his adoptive parents because of the benefits he received, but also because Martha and Jonathan didn't have to take him in. They made a choice, a choice that involved some sacrifices on their part, so that they could raise Clark and provide him with a good childhood.

But the law doesn't make choices. It doesn't sacrifice to provide the benefits it does. Martha and Jonathan made a choice to be Clark's parents, and that choice cost them. The law made no such choice and isn't capable of doing so. The Kents could become parents or not. But the law can't become something else. It isn't a person. It's a thing, an institution, a tool. It's an object constructed by human beings to perform certain functions. We don't thank light switches for turning on lights, or cars for taking us places—that's what they're *for*. The entire purpose of their existence is to perform those functions.

The law performs many different functions. It maintains order and seeks to establish justice and distribute resources fairly. These are all important and necessary for modern societies. But we owe no gratitude to the law for performing its various functions. It's only doing what it's designed to do. The gratitude theory has things backwards. Far from owing gratitude to the laws and institutions for the benefits they provide, thus making us their servants, laws and institutions exist to serve us. When they perform their functions well, we may approve of them—but we are never indebted to them. So there's no obligation to obey the law based on what the law provides us.

In fact, if we owe gratitude to anyone, it's to volunteer crime fighters—also known as vigilantes—like Batman and Superman. They don't have to do what they do. They break the law in order to do it, but they do it to uphold the law.

Daniel Malloy

He's Not Wearing Hockey Pads

The city of Gotham has been positively infested with masked vigilantes. Some of them have been linked to and even trained by Batman, like the various Robins and Batgirls. Some have been granted the Batman's seal of approval, like Orpheus, the briefly careered protector of the Hill. And some haven't been so fortunate, like Savant and (arguably) Anarky. And some go back and forth, like Catwoman and Huntress (Helena Bertinelli). The thing is, Batman claims for himself the right to decide who can patrol the streets of Gotham. If you want to be a masked vigilante in Gotham, you play by his rules. And, in fairness to Batman, the rules he holds other vigilantes to are the same ones he follows himself—no killing, for example. Thus, he treats them fairly.

But just the act of becoming a vigilante breaks the rules of fair play. Fair play or fairness theory says that we obey the law because we expect everyone else to do the same. I expect others not to steal from me, so I refrain from stealing from them. To do otherwise would be cheating. When Lex Luthor breaks the law, he gains an advantage that he isn't entitled to over the law-abiding, and disadvantages everyone else.

In an early scene in Christopher Nolan's *The Dark Knight* (2008), Batman stops a drug deal involving the Scarecrow and restrains some would-be copycat vigilantes. When one of the vigilantes demands to know what gives Batman the right to be a vigilante while denying to everyone else, the Dark Knight responds "I'm not wearing hockey pads."

How are we to understand this defense? Maybe Batman has the right because he is better trained and equipped than the copycats, and therefore less likely to be hurt or killed in pursuing his nighttime hobby. Or, perhaps Batman/Bruce Wayne can afford the kind of equipment necessary to be an effective force for good, and the copycats can't. Either way, Batman's response boils down to the claim that he's better at being a vigilante than the copycats—but that doesn't make his law-breaking right. The Joker is better at being a murdering psychopath than just about anyone else; that doesn't give him the right to be a murdering psychopath. If Batman thought through the implications of his answer, I doubt he would stand by it. "I'm not wearing hockey pads" basically means that might makes right. I can do this therefore I have a right to. The rules don't apply to me because I'm better at breaking them than you are. That's antithetical to everything that both Batman and Superman stand for.

Joker's Justice

You might object to the application of the fair play rule because Batman and Superman aren't breaking the rules to help themselves. On the contrary, they sacrifice a great deal to help others—in part by picking up the slack where law enforcement fails. Superman battles threats that the Metropolis Police Department simply can't handle, and Batman—well, Batman does whatever the hell he wants. Further, whatever advantage they're getting isn't over the law-abiding, but over other rule breakers. Batman's costume is designed to scare criminals—that superstitious and cowardly lot—not the good people of Gotham.

Two responses offer themselves immediately to this criticism. First, good intentions don't forgive bad actions. If I kill a person so that I can harvest her organs and save five or six others, my intention to save lives doesn't change the fact that I committed murder to do it. Just because Batman dresses as he does to scare criminals doesn't prevent him from scaring law-abiding citizens, clashing with honest cops, or inspiring other, less well-intentioned acts of vigilantism—to say nothing of how he inspires certain criminals, like the Joker, to entirely new heights of depravity.

There's also the problem that two wrongs don't make a right. Cliché, perhaps, but still true. The fact that some people break the law doesn't give everyone the right to. The threat represented by the Joker doesn't justify the threat of the Batman. That would undermine the entire concept of law. The fact that some people break the rules is the entire reason we have law enforcement in the first place. If you want to fight crime, there are legitimate, legal ways to do so—none of which involve dressing up like a bat.

But this first justification of Batman's and Superman's vigilantism is limited. It isn't about fair play but only a limited application of it—where you violate rules in order to hinder other rule breakers and help non-rule breakers. You could also object to the theory of fair play obligations itself. The most well-known such objection comes from philosopher Robert Nozick (1938–2002). In his *Anarchy, State, and Utopia*, Nozick asks us to imagine a scenario like this: imagine if Bruce Wayne wasn't Batman, and, instead, the Batman was a traditional position in Gotham. Each year, a citizen would be selected by lottery to be the Batman. Once a citizen's name came up, they would have to suit up and patrol the streets of Gotham, hunting down criminals and evildoers. There's no law about this; it's just the way things are done. The lottery is fair—every citizen has the exact same chance as every other citizen to be selected. And everyone benefits from having a Batman on patrol. Now imagine that one year the citizen selected to be Batman doesn't want to. Do they have an obligation to other Gothamites to put on the cowl?

Nozick argues that they don't. Just because their fellow citizens expect him to be the Batman doesn't oblige them to do it. And, argues Nozick, the benefits they might have gotten from having a Batman in the past likewise don't oblige them, because they didn't agree to the system in the first place. What others do can't oblige us to do the same without some further reasons, like a prior agreement. And, *vice versa*, if I obey the law because I expect others to, that doesn't mean that they have to meet my expectations.

Anyone with a Badge—or a Flag

Vigilantes like Batman and Superman usually only fight certain kinds of crime. This statement might lead us to think of the crimes of supervillains like the Joker or Lex Luthor, but the activities of Batman and Superman and others like them aren't that limited. They will all go after non-supervillain criminals, after all. In Batman's case, it seems like that's what he spends most of his time doing. The Arkham crowd he puts away are occasional diversions from his larger mission of combatting street crime—your everyday thieves, rapists, and murderers. But notice that all the criminals Batman and Superman go after haven't just violated the law; they have also done something that is morally wrong. You can hardly imagine Batman or Superman going after jaywalkers or double-parkers.

So perhaps we've confused our vigilantes. Maybe they're not enforcing the law at all. They're enforcing morality, and perhaps that's a completely unrelated concept to law. Perhaps there is no moral duty to obey the law at all. Perhaps on the question of legality, morality must remain silent. This is the approach offered by philosophical anarchists. They put forward two main reasons for thinking that this is the case.

There are objections to every defense of political obligations. Based on that fact, philosophical anarchists argue that there are no political obligations. The argument goes like this: the arguments defending political obligations fail. If we did have duties to obey the law, then we could defend them. We can't. So, we must not have duties to obey the law.

But this argument overextends itself. First, just because we don't agree on a defense of political obligations doesn't mean there isn't one. In fact, the existence of the debate over political obligations shows that we at least believe there's some truth to be had. Second, even if no defense of political obligations has been successful, it doesn't follow that no defense could be successful. It only follows that there's still work to do in finding a successful defense.

The second argument tries to show that no defense of political obligations could ever be successful. In his *In Defense of Anarchism*, philosophical anarchist Robert Paul Wolff argues that the notion of a political obligation would require anyone subject to a law to violate a duty they owe to themselves. Namely, every person is autonomous; we are capable of making free, rational choices about right and wrong. According to Wolff we have a duty to preserve this autonomy. By subjecting ourselves to law, we sacrifice it, particularly if we hold that we are morally bound to obey the law. By letting the law dictate what is right or wrong, we reduce ourselves to the level of children. Batman and Superman, in their refusal to abide by the rules, are showing us how to be adults. But then, so are the Joker and Lex Luthor.

The problem, for Wolff and other philosophical anarchists, isn't the idea that there are some things we shouldn't do—that can be granted easily. Lex and the Joker are evil people who should be stopped. The problem is about why we shouldn't act like Lex or the Joker. To explain this, Wolff introduces a distinction between conforming to the law and obeying it. A person conforms to the law when she acts as the law dictates, but only because she chooses to—a bit like how Superman can walk down the street, conforming to the law of gravity. On the other hand, a person who obeys the law acts as the law dictates because the law tells her to—like how most of us obey the law of gravity. For Wolff, the obedient person has given up her right and responsibility to make her own decisions. She will abide by whatever law happens to be in place. If Superman and Batman displayed this sort of obedience then when the President of the United States issued warrants for their arrests, they would have surrendered themselves—regardless of the fact that the President in question was Lex Luthor (*Superman/Batman: Public Enemies*).

Luthor's Laws

Lex Luthor was President of the United States. *Lex Luthor*. What's more, he seems to have won the office fairly. And Superman, ever the dutiful Boy Scout, did nothing to stop him, until the evidence of Luthor's crimes was glaringly obvious for all to see. Why wait? Because Superman believes in people and in institutions.

Batman, on the other hand, believes in his mission. In the name of that mission, he breaks the law and acknowledges no real legal constraints. His motto might well be the old Latin expression *inter arma enim silent leges*: in times of war the law falls silent. Batman is at war, and so disregards the law.

Superman doesn't have that luxury. With his abilities and public image, it would be an easy thing for him to become a dictator. Just as he has to hold back in combat against most of his enemies, Superman must restrain his public persona in the name of preserving the things he believes in. Obedience to the law, or at least public co-operation with it, is one of the ways Superman protects the public from himself. Were he to utterly disregard the law and other public institutions, then he would become what Luthor is convinced he already is: an alien overlord.

As is so often the case with these two, the difference comes down to one of attitude, rather than action. Superman and Batman both break laws, but Superman does so in a far more constrained way which endorses the legitimacy of the law. He acknowledges that we should obey the law, even if he doesn't always obey it himself. Batman, on the other hand, lives in a world without laws, where the only constraint on his actions or those of his compatriots are the rules he sets, and can change at will. Answerable to no one, Batman, in spite of his intentions, is a force of chaos.

3
Darwin in Metropolis

BEN SPRINGETT

KA-POW! By the time you've read these words, Superman has already defeated Batman in a thousand different ways. Not bad for an individual who has no powers at all on his home planet of Krypton.

When on Earth, Superman's Kryptonian DNA reacts to the radiation of our sun and gives him superpowers. Superman's life on Earth is a rare example of a really drastic change of environment for a creature. It's even rarer because the change actually benefits the creature, in this case "Superman," and those of us around him as well!

Now that Superman lives on Earth, not only is Superman more likely to survive in a fight with Batman, but *your own* survival will more likely benefit and continue with the help of Superman rather than Batman. Seriously, whether it's a giant asteroid, Darkseid, or evil Kryptonians endangering the planet, who would you rather have on your side, *the* Superman or a guy with a batarang and a grappling hook? If you live anywhere other than the hub of Gotham city, your life depends on choosing Superman over Batman.

Survival of the Fittest

Fitness is something that's applied to life forms like animals, humans or aliens—though it's usually humans and animals. Astrobiology (the study of aliens) is currently empty: we don't have any aliens—except in the DC Universe, when Superman comes to Earth.

Charles Darwin (1809–1882), the father of evolutionary biology, studied some of the animals on Earth to arrive at his conclusion that life gradually evolves over a long period of time ("survival of the fittest" was later attached to his ideas, which he welcomed). But what if life forms had been drastically different?

Let's start with a common question aimed at evolutionary biology: if the fittest always survive, why don't we actually see any creatures like Superman in the world—a being that simply couldn't be any better at surviving? Even sharks could do better by having torpedoes mounted on their sides. Why is the world full of zebras that get eaten, bumbling pandas and stupid humans? Why aren't there any individuals that can set objects on fire with their bare eyes like Superman can?

One answer is that evolution's main mechanism, natural selection, does just enough for creatures to get by. Holy terminology Batman! I'd better explain natural selection now!

Evolution and natural selection aren't the same. Over the millennia, creatures have drastically changed in the way they look and behave; the newer species we see today have descended from older species. That's evolution. Natural selection is thought to be the main mechanism by which evolution has occurred. Natural selection is not random. . . .

Take a colony of bats in a cave, about fifty female and fifty male. They *vary* from one another in the observable characteristics they have, which are known as "traits." Bats, who hunt mainly at night, get a sense of their surroundings by releasing sounds that bounce off objects in the environment and come back to them, which they are constantly listening to—a trait known as echolocation which tells a bat where surrounding objects are. Some of these hundred bats have really good echolocation, others don't. They don't all survive either. There's the greater likelihood that those who survive will reproduce and pass on the genes are responsible for their traits (such as accurate echolocation, for example)—this is known as *heredity*, which applies to all reproducing life forms.

Damian Wayne, Bruce Wayne's only son,[1] has half the genetic make-up of his father. This means he'll carry many of

---

[1] The idea of Batman's son was first introduced in *Batman: Son of a Demon* (1987) with Talia al Ghul as the mother. The son was later reinterpreted by Grant Morrison and named as Damian Wayne in Batman #655

the traits that Bruce was born with, such as his body shape and ability to think. For those individuals that aren't wiped out of existence—Damian Wayne, successful bats—there are still differences in their fitness levels. Individuals have different chances of going on to reproduce and pass on their genes. Those bats with particularly good echolocation will be more likely to successfully find a mate. There's also competition for mates and resources. Crucially, there's not enough of either to go around and many individuals will be wiped out every generation.

The traits the offspring have inherited are likely to help them to survive because they're likely to live in the same or similar environment. The traits that were successful one generation ago (echolocation for flying around dark caves) are likely to still help in survival. These helpful traits are known as adaptations to the environment. This is the other sense of fitness: these offspring "fit" into their environment well. Mutations in the genetic code can change the trait an individual has. One possible mutation might allow a bat to have echolocation that reflects what's going on in the environment more accurately (some mutations in the genetic code are favorable, resulting in the greater likelihood that those with the mutation will survive than those without the mutation). This mutation will help that bat with the mutation to survive and so it'll be more likely to reproduce.

"Survival of the fittest" can just mean the ability to survive and reproduce. Perhaps we can measure the fitness of an individual literally by the number of offspring an individual has. So we can see that one quick answer to the question of who is fitter gives the answer of Batman—since he has one child (Damian Wayne), whereas Superman has none, according to most mainstream storylines (this would even out if we take account of *Superman Returns*, where he has one child with Lois Lane). But fitness can instead be thought of in terms of an individual's ability to reproduce, rather than actually counting their children. This view takes fitness as a "dispositional" concept. Superman *could* survive and reproduce much more than Batman, should he desire. Can evolutionary biology tell us anything else about who's superior?

(2006). In this later version, Talia al Ghul drugged Batman to produce the son.

From Galápagos to Gotham City

Darwin did most of his work theorizing about the animals on Earth, based on trips he made collecting evidence of different lifeforms adapting to their environment. He collected evidence from around the world (many crucial finds occurred on the Galápagos Islands off the coast of Ecuador). He found out about the vampire bat from Chile and saw massive fossils, indicating life forms that no longer are. Darwin was left unsure why creatures aren't made better than they are.

Is it the case that all we can do is look at the animals of our world? Our world could've turned out very differently to the way it actually is now. Batman doesn't exist but we think that somebody like him could exist. For all we know, there could even be an alien whose genetics allows them to manipulate the environment around them and fly without wings. Both Gotham City and Metropolis contain individuals who may be informative for evolutionary biology. DC Comics presents a thought experiment that Darwin didn't have access to. Evolutionary biology could also help in establishing ways in which one superhero might be superior to another.

Batman is a way of picturing the fittest possible man (who doesn't violate the laws of physics) who could exist. He's the perfect thought experiment for vamping up the fitness levels of a human as a man that's constantly challenged by villains who want to end his life. In other words, every time he manages to survive, he demonstrates his fitness. In trying to kill him, villains test Batman both mentally and physically.

From Metropolis to the Morphospace!

Evolutionary biologists would be amazed if they landed in Metropolis and witnessed Superman battling Lex Luthor and saving the USA from being plunged under the sea level (one of Luthor's many mad plans). Unlike Batman, Superman carries out feats no other animal or human possibly could. We can easily conclude that Superman's fitness is on a whole other level from both Batman and everyone else too.

The first thing that would be noticeable to any evolutionary biologist, were they to compare Clark Kent and Bruce Wayne, would be that both have a humanoid shape (or both have a Kryptonian shape). The term for the observable bodily structure of an individual or animal is its "morphology." Batman and Superman have similar looking bodily structures but very different abilities. There's something about Superman's body that reacts differently to the environment. Superman, a *Kryptonian*, has a natural ability to fly and a strength that transcends the abilities of any individual of the human species on Earth. Batman, a member of *Homo sapiens* and mere mortal, relies on multiple skills: photographic memory, fighting styles, cunning intelligence and technological prowess that natural selection would surely favor over most, if not all, other members of the human species.

Evolutionary biologists make use, in their imagination, of a gigantic space that contains all of the bodily blueprints of nature. Just think how different the human body is from that of a horse, a unicorn, a squid, Gorilla Grodd, a cat or Krypto the Dog. The giant imaginary space that contains every possible animal in every possible configuration is known to biologists as the Morphological space, or Morphospace. The Morphospace doesn't respect copyright laws. It contains every possible version of every individual. Exactly as he is, Bruce Wayne's already there. There's also a version of Bruce Wayne with four arms. The Morphospace can tell us about the historical routes evolution takes in constructing a creature's morphology. To get to *Homo erectus* (an upright human), evolution worked with an animal that walked on all four limbs. Is it possible to get to a humanoid shaped creature with special powers ranging from heat vision and flight with no visible means of flying? We have no idea how the evolution of life has occurred on Krypton and if Superman can't exist—if his morphology is impossible to achieve—then he can't be fitter than Batman! Batfans will tell us to leave the debate there—Batman has a more plausible existence. We'll proceed with our argument, but we'll need to just assume that Superman could exist and that he has a place on the Morphospace. Maybe biology could also find a way of bending the laws of physics. Assuming that Superman does have a place on the Morphospace, and evolution could reach such a creature through natural selection, then we can draw the following evolutionary points:

- Batman is engaged in arms races with his enemies. Consider the development of gadgetry between Batman and his enemies. Batman is always increasing his arsenal, often in response to the gadgetry or increasing powers of his enemies. Superman is not in any arms race at all. Not being in an arms race is usually suggestive of a species having far surpassed all competition. In this case, the creature can't be any better at surviving than it already is!

- Superman can survive in more different habitats than Batman.

- Superman has only one weakness whereas Batman has multiple vulnerabilities.

- Superman is obviously fitter than Batman. Superman has clear superiority over Batman in the area that really matters—the ability to stay alive!

Superman is unanimously fitter than Batman, but does this make Superman a superior superhero? In terms of superherodom, you might think it's a draw. Both are equally trying to do good, right?

Altruism of the Superhero

Darwin was puzzled by those that sacrificed themselves for others, since it didn't have an obvious explanation in terms of natural selection—where is the heredity advantage in the nobleness of dying for others, and thereby not reproducing? It's even more puzzling for evolutionary biologists to find the emerging behavior of superheroes who dedicate their lives to helping others (Batman's personal pledge to defend Gotham City and Superman's constantly helping those around the world).

Doing something to benefit others at a cost to oneself, measured in terms of fitness is defined as biologically altruistic behavior. Examples of altruism:

- Meerkats make alarm calls to fellow meerkats to signal predators on the scene, at the risk of being eaten themselves.

- **The brilliant Oskar Schindler saved the lives of over one thousand Jewish people during the holocaust at the risk of his life and at a cost of his entire business.**

Both Batman and Superman are trying to do good for others and often at a cost to their own wellbeing. For example, they regularly put themselves at the risk of death and suffer injury. Though Superman is fitter than Batman, Batman is more altruistic. Remember that altruism is defined as behavior which increases the fitness of others and decreases your own fitness. It's hard for Superman, who has such invulnerability, to reduce his fitness, which altruism requires. So the concept of altruism doesn't do justice to Superman's behavior. He doesn't qualify for being very altruistic on the technicality that he can't reduce his own fitness and yet he does more good than Batman. Superman helps many more people. Maybe Superman's a creature that has transcended the usual concepts of evolutionary biology like altruism. This would make Superman a different kind of superhero to Batman.

Batfans will tell us to leave it there: Batman is more altruistic so he's the better superhero. That would end the debate much too prematurely. Darwin's attempted solution to the existence of altruistic behavior was to say that natural selection must be occurring for the good of the group, rather than just the individuals and their specific adaptations to their environment. Wouldn't it benefit a group to have a completely selfless hero amongst them? The group would be more likely to survive over other groups without such a hero. Wouldn't that selfless hero also have to be actually effective at helping the group? And what if the hero was really good at helping a group even though it cost him nothing? The group would be even better at surviving.

Effectively a Superhero

What good is a clumsy superhero? Once someone has an intention to do significant good they become a real hero. A *super-hero* ought to be judged on how effective they are in realizing their good intentions. Imagine if Oskar Schindler (1908–1974) was totally incompetent, and he didn't even manage to save a single life but in trying to save lives he got himself and others killed. As good as his intention was, clearly the heroics would be curbed. There's a place on the Morphospace for Captain Clumsy (whose mission is world peace), someone who intends to help others but actually causes more damage and harm to others than if he hadn't got involved. Mr. Minimal also has a place on the Morphospace. He spends all day sitting on buses pressing the bell for people when he gets a sense that they want to get off at the next stop. He's *really* effective at doing things like this. But help like this is totally insignificant. Captain Clumsy and Mr. Minimal have never been realized as superheroes, despite their good intentions. A great superhero achieves both qualities—effectiveness in achieving significant moral aims. Superman is much more effective in helping significantly more individuals. This sets Superman far apart from Batman. Superman is effective in taking responsibility for a much larger group than Batman. How large a group are we talking here?

Saving the Planet Daily!

Natural selection is now thought to occur at different levels, from the genes that build bodies, to individual traits that allow capabilities, to groups of individuals. In an abstract sense, natural selection can apply at the level of planets. Planets can vary from one another if one has Batman residing on it, and Superman residing on another.

The entire planet will be more likely to survive various potential endings (such as nuclear self-destruction, meteorites, or alien invasions) if we have a world with Superman rather than Batman whose job is mostly confined to a single city. This is where the fitness of many other creatures comes to depend upon one other individual, in this case, that of a superhero. Perhaps we can re-use "Superhero" (with a capital "S") as a technical term in evolutionary biology for a creature who intentionally increases the fitness of many others, regardless of whether they're being technically altruistic or not (reducing their own fitness).

The fitness of many individuals in Gotham City depends upon the actions of Batman. The fitness of every creature in the world depends upon the actions of Superman. Superman is the greater Superhero in the sense of being himself fitter and having more dependents on his actions. It's important that a Superhero is actually effective in his actions! Batman can't effectively deal with the responsibility of looking after such a large group.

Batman is no doubt a great Superhero. One slogan on the internet cites something you'll never hear Batman say: "Save Me Superman!" This is probably the case, but embarrassingly for Batman, he's contained within the set of individuals that Superman saves.

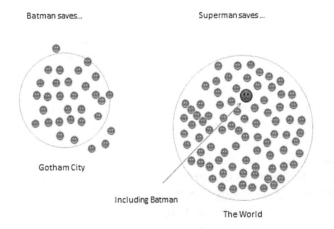

Batman saves...   Superman saves...

Gotham City

Including Batman

The World

Batman frankly can't avoid this, because Superman increases the level of fitness of the human species as a whole and Bruce Wayne is a member of the human species. Stephen Jay Gould (1941–2002) was another eminent evolutionary biologist who had a particular view of evolution that has generated reams of philosophical commentary.

Gould pointed out that extinction of the species is one of the most common features of evolution. Ninety-nine percent of all species that have ever existed have gone extinct. Humans are pretty lucky to still be around at the moment. They could disappear at any instant and nobody would miss us, nor would we be likely to ever return if evolution was to start all over again from scratch. Looking at the world through Gould's goggles, Batman's activities (at the level of the species) start to look insignificant. At best, he can only marginally increase the fitness of our species. The definition of Superhero we gave earlier was that they should effectively help many others. By noticing an increase in the fitness of a *species* (rather than just a large group of individuals) we have a real way to measure how effective a Superhero is. Superman raises the bar on being a Superhero by significantly increasing the fitness of our species. A Superhero responsible for a species needs to be able to avoid as many endings as possible and it's clear that Superman can avoid more endings than Batman can.

Gould had a particular view on the evolution of life as constantly hit by real catastrophes throughout history that aggravate the extent to which extinction occurs (such as asteroids, starvation, or viruses). In the DC Universe, there are further potential catastrophes that we can't rule out with certainty in real life, such as alien invasion and destruction of the planet. Superman can defend us well against many of these potential extinctions to our species and thereby helps to significantly raise the fitness of our species. There's a sense in which Batman can increase the fitness of the species as a whole, if Wayne Enterprises plunges finances into viral research. He'll be much less prepared for the many and varied catastrophes that could hit Earth and our species as a whole though. To that end, Superman is a superior Superhero according to evolutionary biology, because Superman increases the fitness of the human species.

Let's put this all as an argument. Philosophers love arguments. Not the sort that Arnold Wesker gets in with Scarface. An argument is stated with premises, which, if true, help us to reach a conclusion:

> **Premise 1.** From a Darwinian perspective, "Superhero" can be used as a term to define an individual who effectively increases the fitness of many others.
>
> **Premise 2.** When one Superhero, X, saves more lives than another Superhero, Y, X is a superior Superhero to Y.
>
> **Premise 3.** By increasing the fitness of the species, Superman will always increase the fitness of significantly more individuals (and save more lives) than Batman.
>
> ───
>
> **Conclusion.** Superman is a superior Superhero to Batman.

Who can save the species? You have a choice to make. The fitness of the species and your own personal fitness depend on your choosing Superman over Batman. You can choose Batman because he's more like the rest of us humans. But you might not be able to enjoy that choice for much longer. . . .

If a catastrophe faces Earth and we're wiped out, then our fitness level is reduced to zero. While Superman is around and our planet is kept safe, then the fitness level of our species is kept safe too.

Why Save Us?

There's one final concern we should think about in terms of the evolution of Superheroes. A view that has been unfortunately attached to Darwin's theory of evolution is the view that the fitter should survive and see their power increase and the less fit should see their power diminish and die out. This is known as Social Darwinism. Social Darwinism is problematic for many reasons. Even if it was the case that everybody is just out for themselves, there's nothing that says that this should happen or that we should continue to behave in this way.

And it's not true that everybody is just out for themselves. Superman is a crucial counterexample to Social Darwinism, not seeking to increase his own super-fitness and undermine the less fit. He doesn't live by the policy of Social Darwinism. We love Superheroes like Superman who direct their efforts to saving others. Our fascination with these Superheroes shows that we're not really Social Darwinists after all—we hope that the more fit will help out the less fit. Reducing your fitness in order to help others is the sign of a hero. An individual can reach a point of having so much fitness, like Superman, that their fitness can't be reduced, and we see them as apparently not very altruistic. But Superman is working for the good of a much larger group—our Earth.

Why does Superman save us? As Richard Dawkins, another evolutionary biologist, constantly repeats: once we have a certain level of conscious awareness, we don't have to live by the rules of evolution. We can even begin to guide the evolutionary process itself. Being able to set our own goals and values in life is the beginning of superherodom.

Superman and Batman *both* have the intention to do good. They pass the first crucial criterion of being a hero. Next criterion: effectiveness. This is where Batman and Superman are worlds apart. Superman's effectiveness as a Superhero is what allows him to be a better protector of the Earth. A *world* with Superman working for it is more likely to survive than one without. Given our insecure place in the universe, Superman is better for us than Batman as we proceed into a future potentially ridden with catastrophes.

4
A Cape and a Code

Scott Farrell

No epic tale of adventure would be complete without a knight in shining armor, would it? Once upon a time, as a storyteller might say, such knightly characters were expected to pull swords from stones or delve into dragons' lairs. You can find knights in today's adventure stories too, but now you'll generally see them soaring through the sky in a bright red cape, or stalking the shadowy city streets by moonlight.

It's true—Superman and Batman have their literary roots in the knightly romances of the Middle Ages. Just look at the language and symbolism that surround the two of them: Batman is referred to as both the "Dark Knight" and the "Caped Crusader." Superman is nicknamed the "Man of Steel," calling to mind a champion clad in gleaming metal armor, and he wears an S-shaped emblem on his chest reminiscent of the shield a knight would carry into battle.

Without a doubt, there are lots of subtle (and not-so-subtle) indications that the creators of Superman and Batman used imagery and terminology associated with knighthood to frame these superheroes. But medieval warriors knew it took more than a sword and a metal suit to make a person a knight. It required a heroic philosophy, a code of honor. And for medieval knights, that was the code of chivalry.

So, if Superman and Batman are to be cast into the roles of the "knights" of the twenty-first century, can we say that either of them lives up to the philosophy of chivalry? When compared side by side, which of them would earn the title of "most chivalrous superhero"?

Truth, Justice, and the Medieval Way

The word "chivalry" gets a lot of bad press (it's generally followed by the phrase "... is dead!"), and is often used to indicate a heightened (if somewhat old-fashioned) sense of good manners and fair play. Most superhero fans would probably accept the term "chivalrous" in reference to George Reeves's portrayal of Superman from the black-and-white 1950s serial, or Adam West's squeaky-clean image of Batman from the notorious TV show. But in the post-Frank Miller world where superhero tales are colored in gritty shades of moral ambiguity, seeking "chivalry" among the exploits of Superman and Batman might seem as anachronistic as a radio advertisement for Ovaltine.

To launch our chivalric comparison of the Man of Steel and the Dark Knight, we must go back to the original meaning of the word, *chevalerie*, or "the way of the mounted warrior." It was a concept first developed in the feudal culture of Europe in the Middle Ages. Among the medieval military elite, the virtues of chivalry included courtoisie (or "courtly behavior") as well as loyalty, courage, generosity, prowess, and franchise (defined by medieval historian Maurice Keen in his book "Chivalry" as "the free and frank bearing that is a visible testimony to the combination of good birth and virtue").

Although some medieval knights authored philosophical treatises on the knightly code, it isn't real-life knights, but fictional ones from the legends of King Arthur that we think of when we consider the code of chivalry today. And there's a good reason for that. Like a medieval Justice League, Knights of the Round Table such as Lancelot, Gawain, Bedevere, and the rest provided exciting, dramatic narratives of heroism in action in a way that's far more engaging than even the most eloquent sermon on chivalric morality. Though full of action and adventure, those stories also include plenty of thoughts on how to live by a code of honor amongst all the jousting and sword combat.

One author who gave serious consideration to the pursuit of chivalry was C.S. Lewis, best known as the creator of the fantasy series "The Chronicles of Narnia." In an essay titled "The Necessity Of Chivalry," (written in 1940—a time when duty, honor, and sacrifice were very much on the minds of people in England) Lewis delved into the medieval legends of the

Knights of the Round Table to come up with the defining qualities of chivalry, the principles that someone of "knightly virtue" should be expected to embody.

Lewis began by explaining that chivalry places a "double demand" on human nature, and a person who aspires to the ideals of knighthood must be capable of being both "stern" and "meek." In his own words:

> The knight is a man of blood and iron, a man familiar with the sight of smashed faces and the ragged stumps of lopped-off limbs; he is also a demure, almost a maidenlike, guest in hall, a gentle, modest, unobtrusive man.

Let's start with this concept as a way of evaluating our modern knights, Superman and Batman. Both of them demonstrate a sort of dual nature, but for them, it is not a metaphoric duality. Their superhero identities, contrasted with their everyday alter-egos allow us to see both sides of their personalities in a literal manner.

Superman is a character of bold, confident action in fighting villains, often vanquishing his foes with a wink and a witty quip. Clark Kent, on the other hand, is meek and wallflowerish, and can't even bring himself to ask a woman he admires out on a date. The dichotomy is summed up by Lois Lane herself, in the television show *Smallville*. In the fourth season episode "Gone," she says to Clark:

> don't get you. Half the time you're all "Yes, Ma," and "Yes, Pa." And the other half, you are the most overconfident guy I've ever met.

Even in her younger days, Lois seems perceptive enough to detect the two sides of young Clark Kent/Kal-El's nature: the gentle, respectful son raised with old-fashioned country values on a Smallville farm, and the mighty, invincible hero who will win her heart as he saves the world over and over again. (With such a stark contrast in the internal value structures of Clark and Superman, perhaps we can forgive Lois for being deceived for so long by a simple pair of black-framed glasses.)

Bruce Wayne and Batman present a similar double-sided character. Batman is the very embodiment of a "Spartan" lifestyle. He endures extreme degrees of physical abuse and deprivation as a means of training and preparing himself for his quest to clean up Gotham City. Bruce Wayne, in stark contrast, is a refined gentleman's gentleman, a trust-fund child raised with a taste for the finer things in life, and it's hard to imagine him denying himself (or any of his friends) any sort of creature comfort, no matter how extravagant or indulgent it might be.

We see this side of Bruce come out in the 2005 movie *Batman Begins*, when he celebrates his return to Gotham (after extended travels abroad) by arriving at one of the city's finest hotels in a sleek Italian sports car, wearing an Armani suit, with a supermodel on each arm. When the ladies grow bored by the political talk at the dinner table and go wading in the hotel fountain, rather than making a scene and arguing with the maître d', Bruce handles the situation by purchasing the hotel on the spot and "setting some new rules about the pool area." It's almost hard to believe this is the same man who, not so long ago, was languishing in solitary confinement in a prison hellhole, and nearly freezing to death trudging up a glacier to prove his dedication to Henri Ducard in order to gain access to the League of Shadows.

So, both Superman and Batman possess the "dual nature" that Lewis views as the basis of the spirit of chivalry. But a knight is not merely a hero with a split personality. Chivalry includes the expectation that those dual qualities will drive a hero to action in a very specific way.

Holy Two-Face, Batman!

Although chivalry maybe found in a display of contrasting values, such as valor and humility, or ruggedness and courtesy, Lewis goes on to explain that a person of knightly character must know how to balance those contrasts. Chivalry, he says, is not a license to seek the half-way point between two extremes at all times; a knight is not a man of infinite moderation. "He is not a compromise or a happy mean between ferocity and meekness; he is fierce to the nth degree and meek to the nth," Lewis explains.

Does one of our superheroes demonstrate an advantage in this regard? Is either Batman or Superman fierce *and* gentle "to the nth degree" when such action becomes necessary?

It would be hard to argue that Batman isn't willing go to extremes. Consider the exchange between Batman and the Joker in the 2008 movie *The Dark Knight*. When the Joker's taken into custody, Commissioner Gordon attempts to question him in an interrogation room to find out where he's holding DA Harvey Dent hostage. But Gordon, restrained by police procedural rules, can't get any information out of him. Gordon then unlocks the Joker's handcuffs and steps out "for a cup of coffee." Through the room's one-way mirror, police investigators watch as the lights come up, revealing Batman lurking in one of the darkened corners of the room. Batman (after jamming a chair in front of the door, ensuring that no one can re-enter the room to intervene) proceeds to employ a level of brutal violence that would never be sanctioned by the Gotham police department. When you're resorting to tactics that make even corrupt cops wince, you're definitely into "extreme" territory.

We've also seen Superman go "to the nth degree" in his efforts to thwart the plans of the arch-villains he's pitted against. In 1978's *Superman: The Movie*, Lex Luthor launches a scheme to increase the value of a worthless strip of California desert real estate he's acquired by using a nuclear missile to activate the San Andreas fault and send the western half of the state into the Pacific Ocean. Even though Superman pushes himself to the limits of his super speed and strength, he isn't able to stop Lois Lane (in California on assignment from the *Daily Planet*) from being crushed in a newly opened crevasse. When he eventually finds her mangled body, Superman roars with anger and proceeds to use his superpowers to actually turn back time (despite the fact that he was expressly forbidden to do this by his father, Jor-El) and prevent the whole incident from ever happening. Making the planet turn backwards should certainly qualify as taking things "to the nth degree."

On the other side of the coin, Superman and Batman are both capable of being mild, gentle, and compassionate to the same degree of extremity. In *Batman Begins*, the Caped Crusader takes a moment out of a clandestine mission to give a piece of his high tech (and probably very costly) surveillance gear to a boy living in a tenement in the Narrows, who laments that "the other kids won't believe me" when he says he saw the Batman. Similarly, in *Superman: The Movie*, the Man of Steel finds time, between foiling a jewelry heist and preventing Air Force One from crashing in a thunderstorm, to swoop down and get a little girl's cat, Fluffy, out of a tree.

Clearly both Superman and Batman are willing to take things to extremes—in terms of gentleness and ferocity—when necessary. Neither has earned any advantage in our quest to see which has the more knightly characteristics. But each of these heroes has their own rationales and motives, and it's the internal battles they fight which may provide us with some insight about who is the more chivalrous of the two.

It's a Bird, It's a Plane, It's a Knight

Traditionally, superheroes like Superman and Batman make the job of fighting crime seem natural. No one in the 1940s or 1950s really gave much thought as to why Superman put himself in front of bullets, or Batman lurked in the shadows to apprehend thugs. That was just . . . what they did.

But more recently, in the television shows *Smallville* and *Gotham*, and the reboot movies *Batman Begins* and *Man of Steel*, writers have delved into the backgrounds of the heroes, letting fans explore their psychology along with their adventures. As these superhero origin tales play out, we begin to see one common theme emerge: Becoming a superhero doesn't happen by accident.

Batman's quest to clean up Gotham's culture of crime began as a child, when his parents were murdered in cold blood by a robber in an alley. The original Batman comic presented the entire incident, from botched robbery to the Caped Crusader silhouetted in the moonlight, in just a few panels on two pages. But the recent versions of the story have elaborated the emotional complexities of a man who uses his own phobias of bats and dark places as a drive to make criminals feel the same paralyzing terror he experienced as he watched a killer gun down his beloved parents.

For young Master Wayne, it's clear that being brave and strong didn't come naturally. In Frank Miller's 1986 comic book mini-series *Batman: The Dark Knight Returns*, Bruce Wayne recounts a time when he was young and chased a rabbit into a cavern beneath the manor house (which would eventually become the Batcave) where he confronted something truly horrifying. Surrounded by a swarm of bats, Bruce saw a massive, demonic bat-creature that he describes as, "untouched by love or joy . . . glaring, hating."

Was this creature real, or just a product of young Bruce's terrified imagination? We're never quite sure, but what is clear is that after the death of his parents, Bruce returned to this moment of intense fright to establish an iron-clad inner determination never to let himself be overcome by fear again. Had he done "what comes naturally," he would surely have instinctively, and quite reasonably tried to cure himself of that fear (probably with years of regular visits to an expensive psychotherapist). Instead, he did a very non-instinctive thing: he made a deliberate choice to become "the fiercest survivor . . . the purest warrior" by seizing that petrifying sense of dread and forging it into strength and courage.

Superman's story involves a different type of personal transformation. Kal-El arrives on Earth as an infant, and is raised by Jonathan and Martha Kent, who embody simple, Midwestern values of friendliness, humility, and hard work. As their adopted son grows, however, they begin to see that he is very different: strong, fast, and essentially immune to physical harm. He is a teenager who could, quite literally, conquer the world if he gave up his farmboy façade and used his powers to their full extent.

In just about every Superman story there's a scene in which Clark's adoptive father, Jonathan Kent, explains why the Last Son of Krypton must practice self-restraint. In the 1978 movie, for instance, after Clark has perplexed some of the local football jocks by running ahead of their truck at supersonic speed, making it seem like he's in two places at once, Pa sits him down for an important conversation:

> "Been showing off a bit, haven't you?" Mr. Kent asks.
> Clark explains, "I didn't mean to show off. It's just that . . . guys like Brad, I just want to tear them apart."

When Jonathan urges Clark to consider working towards a higher purpose rather than merely impressing Lana Lang by scoring touchdowns and intimidating the school bully with his powers, Clark asks, "Is it 'showing off' if someone's doing the things he's capable of doing? Is a bird showing off when it flies?"

For Superman, the struggle is not to overcome fear and dread, but to restrain superiority, to avoid the assumption that might makes right, and that supreme might is the ultimate justification for any action. The only person on Earth who has the ability to prevent Superman from becoming a global tyrant is himself.

Both Superman and Batman have to make deliberate choices in internalizing their virtuous qualities, and, according to C.S. Lewis, that is a true hallmark of living by the code of chivalry. As Lewis explains, it's our natural, human tendency to be either "stern" (like invincible Kal-El) or "meek" (like terrified Bruce Wayne). But those two qualities are truly exclusive of one another. That is why, he says: "(The knight) is a work not of nature, but of art; of that art which has human beings, instead of canvas or marble, for its medium. Knightly character is . . . something that needs to be achieved, not something that can be relied upon to happen."

Making the meek man bold (like Bruce Wayne) and making the powerful man compassionate (like Kal-El) are two very different concepts. How difficult is it for the urbane and soft-spoken man to find valor in himself in times of crisis, rather than acting like a helpless milksop? Lewis, himself a veteran of the trenches of World War I, reported that he observed many young Englishmen of gentle spirit rise to the call of heroism that was expected of them in military service. It may take a deliberate effort for an upper-crust socialite to overcome his docile tendencies, but there is a cultural expectation, and even reward (in the form of medals of valor, and the respect of a grateful public) for doing so.

The converse, however, is more problematic in Lewis's view. What incentive does a tyrant have to restrain his desire for conquest and subjugation? A mighty warrior can win celebrated victories in battle, but if he can't (or won't) sheath his sword when the fighting is done, then in the end he's no hero. From the Viking sagas, to the triumphant generals of the Roman empire, to Achilles, the Greek champion of the Trojan war, Lewis points to many historical and mythical examples of great warriors who fell short of the standard of chivalry because they knew "nothing of the demand that the brave should also be modest and merciful."

The Last Son of Krypton . . . Can Be Kind of a Jerk

Here it is, the most telling aspect of chivalry: creating a conqueror who can make room for the virtues of charity and compassion. What would Superman be without the restraints of chivalry to soften his character?

We get a peek at the answer in the *Smallville* second-season episode "Red," in which Clark buys a high-school class ring set with a gem of red kryptonite, an extraterrestrial substance that (for Kryptonians) removes all sense of inhibition. Wearing the ring, he begins treating the girls in his life (Lana, and the episode's minor love interest, Jessie) like playthings; he torments and humiliates a blind man; and he defies several figures of authority (a federal marshal, a bouncer in the Wild Coyote tavern, and a few good Samaritans) with his super strength, speed, and heat vision. He uses his X-ray eyesight to get an intimate look at classmate Chloe Sullivan, then brags about it to his friend Pete. ("Did you know Chloe has a birthmark on her cheek?" Clark asks. When Pete replies, "No, she doesn't," Clark smirks, "Not that cheek.")

In the course of the episode, Clark physically assaults his father, steals a car and a motorcycle, and announces his intentions to drop out of high school and use his superpowers to make himself rich. It's only Pete's quick thinking (and his coincidental access to a shard of green kryptonite) that allows him to get the affecting ring away from Clark, restoring his gentle personality and preventing him from going down a path that seems headed for world domination.

This is not an extraordinary dynamic, according to Lewis, or even an unusual one. The young man who excels in high-school sports, who is elected Homecoming King, and who dates all the pretty cheerleaders, may be considered a sterling role model during his school career, and could be on a trajectory toward great achievements as an adult. But without kindness to put the brakes on his ambition and desire, such a man is more likely to wind up behind bars than receiving a medal of honor. "Such is heroism by nature," Lewis cautions. "Heroism that is outside the chivalrous tradition."

By looking at the principles of the code of chivalry, we've come upon a notable divergence between our two superhero knights. Although Bruce Wayne's struggles to face and over-come his personal demons of fear and inaction are admirable, it is Kal-El who travels the path of self-control that, in Lewis's philosophy, is most worthy of being called true chivalry.

There's no doubt that both Superman and Batman have rightfully earned their knightly nicknames, the Man of Steel and the Caped Crusader. Each of them brings together the "dual demands" of strength and gentleness, and each knows when to go to "the nth degree" of both ferocity and compassion. But it's Superman's willingness to make the hardest choice, the choice of restraint and benevolence against the lure of power and indulgence, that makes him not just a superhero, but the ideal modern embodiment of the knightly principles defined by the philosophy of chivalry.

5
How Heroes Argue

TIM LABAUVE

"ALERT! ALERT!
ALL MEMBERS REPORT TO THE HALL IMMEDIATELY!
THIS IS AN EMERGENCY!"

The call came over the Justice League's secret frequency, and Superman reported immediately. The Hall of Justice was now filling with the Earth's greatest defenders, each responding to the call of a populace in danger—the Joker has kidnapped a small family and is holding them hostage. Uncertain as to the best way to proceed, the group looks to their most respected members, Batman and Superman.

Towering over the seated members and stepping before them, Superman's stature and confidence are unmistakable. Soon, his deep and booming voice fills the room. The Hall of Justice, formerly buzzing with conversation, falls silent as all eyes rest on the Last Son of Krypton. In calm, even tones, this beacon of truth, justice, and the American way sets forth a plan that will hopefully prevent harm to all involved, including the dastardly villain.

"We must be patient and allow the police to handle this situation," he says, his calm voice and even demeanor reassuring the group.

"Our involvement here would only escalate the situation. I've spoken with the local police department and this is how we should proceed." As the most trusted and experienced of Earth's heroes, Superman's voice eases their fears, and the Justice League find themselves nodding in agreement. Setting his jaw and gazing one last time at his audience, he takes his seat and relinquishes the floor to Batman.

In rebuttal, the Dark Knight appeals to reason, reminding the Justice League of their duty to protect the innocent and punish the guilty.

"We must come down fast and hard, so that the Joker never knew what hit him!" He looks out over the group to assess their level of emotional involvement.

"How would you feel!" he wants to know, "if you *knew* there was something you could have done to prevent injustice, and you had done nothing?" Bristling with an inhuman fervor, Batman narrows his eyes, which seem to pierce the hearts of all present. Robin, Batman's protégé, silently wonders if Batman's passion is still driven by his quest to avenge the murder of his parents. He can't help but remember the untimely deaths of his own parents at the hands of criminals. Some members of the Justice League shout out in anger against the Joker, while others clench their jaws in silent defiance of villainy. Wonder Woman can't help but wipe a tear from her eye as Batman, shaking with passion, finds his chair.

Feeling as though the group is slipping through his fingers, Superman stands once again and raises his hands to calm the crowd. Someone hollers, "Let's go get 'im!" from somewhere in the Hall.

"Wait," Superman's voice booms, "You must listen to reason." He reminds the group of the last time the Joker had committed such a public crime and how he did so with the sole purpose of drawing Batman into a fight.

"He only wants to cause as much chaos as possible! It is safer for the citizens and their police force to handle this situation . . . please, you must understand this!" The crowd surges towards the door and Superman seems to have lost them, when he shouts one last time, "PLEASE! LISTEN TO ME!"

The movement stops and the room is silent except for the reverberation left behind by Superman's super-shout. "Listen to me," he pleads, his face pained with worry for the lives at stake. The crowd eyes the Man of Steel, as if finally remembering their trust in his character.

"We've worked side-by-side for years. I consider many of you to be my closest friends. Please . . . trust me."

There's a pause, as the mightiest champions of justice consider Superman's plea. Finally, a lone voice rises from the crowd, strong and clear.

"I'm with you," calls Wonder Woman, as she steps up next to him. "And so are we." This time it's Green Arrow and the Flash. Slowly, the world's greatest heroes move closer to its greatest protector, leaving the Dark Knight at the door.

"Thank you," says Superman, the stress lines fading from his face. Batman, choosing to take matters into his own hands, slinks alone from the hall, intent on bringing swift and painful justice upon his greatest foe.

All-Star Superman

In the end, Superman's ability to persuade wins the day and peace is restored. In the realm of superheroes, Superman is second to none. He is the prime superhero in our collective cultural consciousness. He is the prototype for comic-book superheroes. The defining traits of the superhero—everything from the secret identity, to the costume, to the hidden lair, to the villainous arch-nemesis—are fully realized in the Superman mythology. He shaped our understanding of what the superhero is. As a character, he also manages to embody a perfect balance of the classical persuasive methods of the Greeks. From an argumentative standpoint, his appeal is undeniable. Even when placed against such heavyweights as Batman, the appeal of the Superman mythology comes out on top.

Of Gods and Supermen

> For a city to live, a man had given his all and more.
> But it's too late. For this is the day . . .
> That a Superman died." ("Doomsday!")

These words, which conclude Dan Jurgens's ground-breaking story arc, *The Death of Superman*, echo those of German existentialist Friedrich Nietzsche (1844–1900). In his "Parable of the Madman," Nietzsche proudly declares that "God is dead . . . we have killed him." According to Nietzsche, the "death" of "God" is a result of irrelevance—humanity has evolved to a point where an all-powerful god is no longer a necessary arbiter of virtue and morality.

The fate of irrelevance is one that some would argue has been haunting the Man of Steel for years. As movie writer Max Landis (perhaps too joyously) explains in his parody film, *The Death and Return of Superman*, nobody cares about Superman. Enlisting the help of comedic effect and multiple celebrity cameos, the movie re-presents the events of Jurgens's comic. Landis makes the claim that killing off Superman was a last-ditch effort of publisher DC Comics to make a fifty-year-old character relevant again. Landis states that Superman's popularity stems solely from his primacy among superheroes: he was simply the *first*. Since then, the genre has spawned innumerable heroes with similar or even identical powers, and one power, according to Landis, even greater: "pathos."

Up, Up and to Sway!

"Pathos," as used in the art of rhetoric, is an appeal to the emotions of the audience. In short, it is used to stir up a desired emotion in order to convey a specific message to the audience. The concept of pathos was most famously explained by Aristotle (384–322 B.C.E.), the ancient Greek philosopher and student of Plato.

Aristotle's guide to argumentation, *On Rhetoric*, identifies three primary modes of persuasion used in argumentation, of which "pathos," or the emotional state of the listener, is one. The other two are: "logos," (literally "word") by which logic and facts are employed to convince the audience; and "ethos," by which the audience is swayed by the character of the speaker. A well-rounded rhetorician would employ all three in order to appeal to a wider audience and give a more complete argument. As heroes go, Superman is the fuller embodiment of Aristotle's argumentative ideal, displaying a greater balance of the three modes of persuasion, while Batman's appeal is limited to his logical nature and, primarily, his emotional connection with the reader.

A Batarang to the Heart

Pathos is an important part of any argument to be sure. As a mode of persuasion, it is certainly powerful. The brief episode that introduces this chapter shows Batman using the art of pathos to convince. By appealing to the emotions of his audience, he utilizes their already-present feelings of fear of loss, their deep-seated anger towards villains and even their love for justice and peace to stir them to action.

As heroes go, Batman could be considered the embodiment of pathos. He is utterly relatable. Lacking any super-powers, Batman is an anomaly amongst big-name superheroes. Working only with his anger and thirst for justice, Batman pushes the boundaries of human frailty to transform himself into something more than Bruce Wayne: he becomes a symbol of justice for the citizens of Gotham and an icon of fear for its criminal underworld.

Consider the most recent iteration of the Batman mythos presented in Christopher Nolan's *Dark Knight* trilogy. The Batman presented here is afraid of his own anger, of what he might do when offered the opportunity to enact revenge against the petty criminal who killed his parents. He is flawed. His poor decisions have the potential to hurt those about whom he cares the most. The memories of those whom he has lost are painful—they are "poison in his veins" (*Batman Begins*).

The feelings that drive the character of Batman are all-too-human. Every one of us experiences similar feelings of loss, of guilt, of anger, of weakness and futility. It inspires us to see a hero so similar to us who has channeled his frailty into a symbol that is "incorruptible . . . everlasting." We wonder if maybe we too could overcome adversity and become something greater. The pathos of Batman can draw us in and engage us in a way that is distinctly human.

Superman, meanwhile, isn't completely without pathos. While it's difficult for mere mortals to relate to a god-man walking among us, there are underlying themes of the Superman story that do touch a chord for each us. Bryan Singer's 2006 film, *Superman Returns*, presents the titular character as a wanderer, seeking his place in the universe. Themes of isolation, a yearning for belonging, and a love of family are found throughout the story. These are all common human experiences which can appeal to almost all audiences, especially the teen demographic, which has traditionally been the core audience of superhero movies. In the end, however, Batman's humanity gives him the edge over Superman when it comes to pathos.

Derailing the Pathos Train . . .

While pathos in the arts is a powerful tool, it can also be a dangerous tool when relied on exclusively. When a speaker, author or artist reaches into the very heart of her audience to stir up emotion, the *message* can be lost. As Aristotle relates his three modes of persuasion in *On Rhetoric*, he also identifies the three elements present in any argument: the speaker, the audience, and the *subject being argued*.

In today's media-obsessed culture, even Superman wouldn't be able to escape the onslaught of reality television. In fact, reality TV is a fine example of pathos-driven communication. These TV shows, designed to entertain, do more than just that: they help us to feel. Whether it's disappointment that our favorite celebrity fell on *Dancing with the Stars*, relief that our guy or girl made it through on *American Idol*, or confusion/elation at the hijinks of the Kardashians, we feel *something* that we believe is real. Sometimes we laugh, sometimes we cry, but there is never a dull moment. They contain pathos to the extreme, but very little of worth. Entertainment without substance. But reality TV is a fairly benign example of emotional communication removed from any real meaning.

How dangerous could a great political leader be, if his appeal to pathos was great enough to cause audiences to lose their concern for the issues at hand? Such a leader could lead armies into an unjust war; he could convince entire countries to tolerate genocide; his charisma could lead to the greatest atrocities humanity has ever seen. It could be argued that Adolf Hitler's rise to power and his subsequent atrocities in Nazi Germany were the result of his remarkable ability as a rhetorician. By appealing to the populace's fear and sense of national pride, he was able to lead a people in some of the greatest crimes in history, against all logic.

People, however, are more than a collection of emotions—we are "rational animals" after all. Even Batman's pathos-laden storylines are filled with the deductive reasoning of the world's greatest detective. So, arguments contain more than just an appeal to the heart of the audience, they also contain *facts*. For this, we turn to the all-powerful "logos."

. . . and Letting Logos Reign

As a mode of persuasion, "logos" refers to measurable phenomena and facts. For example, when shopping for a new Batmobile, the Dark Knight may be sold on information such as miles-per-gallon, top speed or heat-seeking missile capacity. This approach is based in the logos. It appeals to the intellect and is easily quantified.

Batman's approach to crime-fighting fits nicely into the "logos" category. His methodical preparation, his utility belt loaded with job-specific tools, his dependence on technology—all betray a logical approach. As a master detective, he's constantly on the hunt for evidence and clues to analyze in order to crack the case.

If you were to try to convince someone of Batman's superhero pedigree, however, you may not turn up enough evidence! As the truth element of argumentation, the logos looks towards factual analysis, and as a superhero, Superman could be said to exemplify this logos. Superman's superhero résumé is as complete as they come. Extraordinary origin story? Check. Secret identity? Check. Powers beyond measure? Check. Every aspect of the superhero mythos which audiences have come to expect are present and accounted for. As such, the Man of Tomorrow's appeal as a superhero can, from a logical standpoint, go unquestioned.

The problem with pure logos is that it tends to be inhuman. You can argue facts and figures, but without the human element, the argument can't and won't fly. Quantitative analysis does very little to touch the heart of an audience. It's the appeal to the humanity of a listener that will sway opinion and draw people in. This is the concept that drives Max Landis's premise regarding Superman's irrelevance. It is often said that Superman is "too powerful." In other words, "he's nothing like us: how can he have an interesting story if he's nothing like us?" Sure, between his alien origin story (depicted to great effect in Zack Snyder's film, *Man of Steel*), invulnerability, being more powerful than a locomotive, faster than a speeding bullet and able to leap—you know the rest—he's utterly unrelatable. This might be why it was important to "kill" Superman: at least this way he can die—he's unlike us in all things but death. That at least is something (finally) that we could share with Superman.

This Looks Like a Job for Ethos

While some find it easy to connect with their audience through emotion, or attempt to convince with facts, the final mode of persuasion, "ethos," is far more difficult to utilize. It depends not on emotional appeal or listing information, but instead on the very character of the speaker. Aristotle suggests that "character may almost be called the most effective means of persuasion (the speaker) possesses" (*On Rhetoric*, Book I, Part 2).

While Aristotle goes on to say that character should be communicated by what the speaker says, it is very often communicated by who the speaker is, or by what he has done. Even Batman would seem to agree that character can be indicated by your actions when he's pressed as to his identity: "It's not who I am underneath . . . but what I do . . . that defines me" (*Batman Begins*).

The Superman mythology delivers a more virtuous, inspirational character, driven by care and generosity towards those around him. He rescues kittens from trees, would help scouts light their campfire and even pummels supervillains who threaten his mother. We could potentially use him as our moral compass. He has surpassing ethos.

Batman, on the other hand, possesses a much darker character. His method of inspiration is fear. Working in the shadows, he's a criminal's worst nightmare, employing brutal interrogation tactics to extract information and delivering justice with his fists. He would not be invited to your kid's birthday party, much less to the United Nations' deliberations on nuclear disarmament.

By connecting itself to a speaker's character, an audience reveals something of itself through that identification. Our demand for and preference for a Batman-type story, dark and brooding, says something about our collective psychology. Similarly, a preference for Superman-type stories, which present a near-perfect superhuman "boy scout," would reveal something much different.

The stories that we write and the tales that we love speak about us—they expose us for who we really are. As Elliot S.

Maggin puts it in his beautiful introduction to Mark Waid's
Kingdom Come, "Super-hero stories . . . are today the most
coherent manifestation of the popular unconscious. They're stories not about gods, but about the way humans wish themselves to be; ought, in fact, to be." By latching onto a character
like Batman, who is deeply flawed, we expose and affirm our
own flawed human nature. When Superman is our guy, we
demonstrate our yearning for perfection.

I'm Mythos

You will give the people of Earth an ideal to strive towards. They will
race behind you; they will stumble, they will fall. But in time, they will
join you in the sun. In time, you will help them accomplish wonders.

This quote, taken from *Man of Steel,* echoes a sentiment from
Richard Donner's 1977 film, *Superman: The Movie:* "They could
be a great people . . . they wish to be. They only lack the
strength to show the way." The concept of Superman as an
example for humanity has become a major theme within that
character's mythos.

While hero stories routinely display feats of super-human
strength, unassisted flight and laser vision, there is another
power that Superman can claim to possess: strength of *virtue.*
The desire to do that which is best. Historically, he is driven by
"truth, justice, and the American way." What else is "truth" but
the aforementioned logos, and justice but the practical application of that truth? In short, Superman embodies the ideals of
truth, justice, virtue, and goodness. We hold such stories up as
a model. Superman could be described as an example of the
best possible version of ourselves.

When we break from a myth of virtue and truth, embracing
instead stories of weakness and vanity, we deny our true identity: a people who are intrinsically good and capable of wonders! In his magnum opus, *Kill Bill,* Quentin Tarantino
comments on Superman's identity:

Now, a staple of the superhero mythology is, there's the superhero
and there's the alter ego. Batman is actually Bruce Wayne. Spider-
Man is actually Peter Parker. When that character wakes up in the
morning, he's Peter Parker. He has to put on a costume to become

Spider-Man. And it is in that characteristic Superman stands alone. Superman didn't become Superman, Superman was born Superman. When Superman wakes up in the morning, he's Superman. His alter ego is Clark Kent. His outfit with the big red "S"—that's the blanket he was wrapped in as a baby when the Kents found him. Those are his clothes. What Kent wears—the glasses, the business suit—that's the costume. That's the costume Superman wears to blend in with us. (*Kill Bill Volume 2*)

As a race, human beings share in Superman's unique "alter ego" situation. Just as Superman disguises himself as Clark Kent, so too are we the stewards of truth, beauty, and goodness. Those ideals dwell within our flawed humanity. They emerge every time we choose to help someone in need, when we place someone else before ourselves, when we put our faith in one another. We are a "great people," we can "accomplish wonders," facts which have been demonstrated by great men and women throughout history. Sometimes it takes incredible acts of selflessness and fortitude in the name of those ideals to stir them up in us (witness the examples of moral heroes such as Martin Luther King Jr., Mahatma Gandhi, and Jesus of Nazareth).

The example of such *real* heroes is why a mythology based in virtue is critical for our society. Such moral heroes do not have the superhuman abilities of Superman, but they do demonstrate a near-perfection in the paths of peace, patience, love, and goodness. They help us to see the difference between how things are and how they ought to be. A mythology of virtue preserves and defends such transcendent truths (logos), appeals to our humanity (pathos), and transforms us into the "superheroes" we were meant to be (ethos). And that is why Superman not only does win, but *must* win. He shows us that, through following the path of virtue, each one of us is capable of greatness.

More Human than a Superman

6
The God We Need Now

CHRISTOPHER KETCHAM

When I was young, I got this idea that I could bring forth upon this Earth a real hero. In 1939 there was dust, there was war in Europe, and the Depression hadn't wound up yet. The end to the Depression came in 1942 after Pearl Harbor. I dug this writing up a while ago from an old trunk I thought about throwing away in a move to a smaller place. It's faded, like me, now—written long ago in 1939 when comics were my world and we needed a hero.

We Need a Hero

It hasn't been super for heroes in our twentieth century, especially today in 1939. This Depression keeps on keeping on, war is looming in Europe and the number one song on the radio is, "Brother can you spare a dime?" It seems that God, the one at least in the Bible, has gone, left us.

In God's place, Fascism, economics, and Communism have risen, replacing world religions at a frightening pace. Perhaps the one-God who was effective when the world was small like in the Middle East of Biblical times can't handle a world today that's this big. God doesn't seem to come down from the mount anymore and complain about our antics like in the days of Abraham. I think God is scared of what we have wrought. God has decided to sit out the twentieth century and let us blow ourselves up. We need help here. Here's what I propose. We need to select a new God to help us through these trying times. Hear me out.

Where Are the Heroes?

I ask you, where are the heroes, the larger than life Odysseus, the half Gods like Hercules born of a god and a human woman and the legions more of his kind that the Greeks had? Granted they were not much better than humans with their pettiness and sexual appetites. But they made for great stories and kept the Greeks on their toes. I know, they had Alexander and we have Hitler, but at least there were gods looking over Alexander's shoulder. We have nothing like those gods looking over Hitler's or Mussolini's, Stalin's, or Tojo's shoulder. Some think Roosevelt's like a god, but there are many who think that he's gone too far with his entitlement programs and public works projects.

I'm not saying that we need an omniscient and omnipotent God who acts like a puppeteer, selecting everyone's every move. That doesn't make sense, and all we would have is a tired God and confused people because there is an awful lot of free will out there now. What got us into this Depression and impending war in the first place—greedy people. A controlling God wouldn't let that happen unless the God were evil and every theologian, from René Descartes to the Catholic Church keeps telling us that God couldn't possibly be evil. However, what if the God we need is strong, but fair? Not controlling, mind you, but someone who works behind the scenes to show us that we are going about it all the wrong way.

I think we've been listening to the scientists for far too long. They've become like the gods now but with dull and boring scientific methods, not myths, monsters, dragons, heroes, and villains. They explain lightning, and gravity, and bullet trajectories with formulas and scientific papers. They don't hurl lightning bolts like Zeus, plunge Icarus from the skies, or throw javelins with the accuracy of an Achilles. They, the scientists, have stripped the magic, the transcendent properties of electricity, light, and weaponry down to formulas and theory.

Hope

There is hope. We wonder about the mystery years of Jesus from his birth until he began to preach his gospel. How did he get from poor carpenter to the Messiah? Yes, there are a few of us today who have been searching for one and the same who may be hiding among us. We still have a chance: don't forget, the Jews have never accepted the idea that Jesus is Messiah. So, if not everyone agrees about Jesus, then there must be room for another hero like him and maybe even some might call that person Messiah. I'm not holding much hope for another Messiah but I do believe there is room for at least one more hero.

Taking that on faith, I want to turn your attention to the mysterious life of one Clark Kent as a potential hero or even a god. Remember he appeared in a flash of light from the skies like the beacon that the three wise men used to guide them to Jesus's manger. Not the same, you say. Surely not, none but the mystics would claim that Jesus was an alien. We know that Clark Kent is different because he was not discovered by the scientists, Madison Avenue, Wall Street, or a Berlin propagandist. Two high-school students in Ohio, Jerry Siegel and Joe Shuster discovered him in 1933. We were starved for his coming . . . and what an impression he has made. The boys and DC Comics have published books of his mythology, his methods, and his gospel at numbers to rival the combined religious publications around the world.

Is not Clark Kent a Messiah for our times in the guise, not of a carpenter or shepherd, but a reporter appropriate for what we need now—he's what's been missing—a god-like creature with fantastic powers, bullet speed, locomotive strength, x-ray vision, the ability to fly, all gifts that anyone alive in the twentieth century covets? He's right for our time.

But is he the God we're looking for? I do have my doubts. Superman was born of science; it's derivative science fiction to be exact. His heroic powers are transcendental but not because his powers transcend human understanding as would a god's powers, but from the fact that he was born on a planet far different from our own where he would have been a normal child.

Times Change

Now I do agree that times have changed. We need a new kind of god. What worked in biblical times for shepherds and marketplace merchants will not work in a world burgeoning with new technologies and hundreds of diverse occupations. We would be laughed at if we had designed a Superman who rides around in slow chariots, hefting broad swords and spears and traversing the city on a brightly colored magic carpet. We gave him not the job of a warrior but that of a respectable newspaper man. Newspaper man? No, all wrong! Look at the times we're in. Here we've loved gangsters and bank robbers whom reporters and dime novels have made into demigods. In Germany, their propaganda machines have idolized the likes of Hitler who we know with his little bushy mustache and piercing eyes is no sweetheart. I'd like our next god to be more like Clyde Barrow or Jesse James, not a gumshoe reporter.

We know that Superman's image and persona has been compromised, not by his creators but by business. Superman started out that way, as a villain that is. You know high-school boys. When the boys sold their hero to DC comics in nineteen thirty-eight, DC redrew Superman as a good guy. This has happened before. What we know of as the New Testament of the Bible today grew out of discussions among the religious leaders of the time as to which books of gospel should be put permanently into the New Testament of the Bible. They ended up deciding that they wanted Jesus to be all good with few human failings. He couldn't possibly have had more than a platonic relationship with Mary Magdalene because that would ruin the whole celibacy thing for the priests. So, with the same idea in mind, the clerics at DC Comics decided that Superman had to be a good, maybe a too good guy. For example, what's with Superman's relationship with Lois Lane? My point is made.

It's all part of the same kind of propaganda machine. With people like Hitler, Stalin, and Tojo stirring up trouble around the world, the publishing synod has decreed that we need someone who is beyond reproach to be our new god. But why not a fireman or a doctor or a high-school teacher? Because he has to be near the developing story. Clark Kent has to be near enough to the news in order to foil the bad guys before they get wind of it. I guess that it makes sense for these times, but I still don't think he will be the God we'll want once all the Hitlers of today are gone. I think Superman will help us win the battle against this terrible Depression and if there is war he probably will serve us well. Things are changing rapidly. The God of Abraham got tired of trying to keep us from taking morality into our own hands. I fear that Superman is likely to suffer the same fate in the long run. I must keep searching for the god who will replace Superman. Someone has to do it; why shouldn't it be me?

We Can Do Better than That

Yeah, I wrote that when I was young and foolish in 1939. Later I read a lot and studied philosophy with an abbey monk who was teaching me Latin. He was fond of Descartes, Kant, and Aquinas. I'm now reading my youthful writing again at the dawn of the twenty-first century.

Such a long time ago, and a lot has happened since. The war came and went and I was a year too young to go to it when it ended. We won and killed all the bad guys without God coming to our rescue. We unleashed the atomic bomb and got into frozen fisticuffs first with Stalin, then Khrushchev, and real battles with Mao. We got MAD (mutual assured destruction) and our prophets now came from *both* science and Wall Street. I'm still looking for that messiah, that God that we can follow. Superman was good while he lasted, but he doesn't seem right for today. We, the America of today, aren't the squeaky clean arsenal of democracy we once were, saving the world from dictators. We lost some of that sheen when we left a demilitarized zone in Korea, and then abandoned Vietnam. We supported Sadam Hussein for trying to invade Iran whose Ayatollah kicked us out of town and kept our hostages for more than a year, and then we took Sadam down for invading Kuwait which is where we get a lot of our oil. No, our hand's aren't clean.

After I read my childish effort I realized that it's never left me. I still pine for someone whom we can worship, perhaps not in the theological sense, but someone we can turn to for some sort of salvation, but now, in today's world.

Do we need a reporter today? Probably not. With the Internet and super-searches, the information we need is at our fingertips, and if what we need we can't find there, our government snoops at the NSA can get it, well, at least for those in power.

Surely there's a place for Mother Teresa–type goodness, but in politics and business, the righteous rarely last long. Some get booted out for not being aggressive enough. Others are just self-righteous on the surface. They talk a good game but then get busted for improper tweets or find ways of skimming off the top. The crimes aren't as obvious any more as the bank robberies and mobster hits were when I was a kid. They're now back-room special-purpose vehicles that take money from legitimate enterprises, pay bribes that are necessary to secure an international football tournament, or they take the form of rogue traders who bet the world's economy on a housing bubble. What do I think we need today?

I want a god-like figure who's a bit nasty, maybe a player, you know what I mean? And he's got certain powers for sure but he gets pissed off at times, bends rules, hurls down lightning bolts (maybe lasers or grappling hooks), and quite often messes with our heads, sending us on horrid quests and missions to test our mettle. He's got to go toe to toe with the savage business people and political ideologues of today. He's not evil, mind you, but he is mysterious, handsome, a bit vengeful, dark even, and above all someone we cautiously admire but still in the back of our minds are wary of getting on his bad side. Got it? So let's figure out where he might come from. And for that I direct you back to the real mythology of gods, half-gods, and monsters.

Welcome (to) Hades

I take you back in the world of ancient Greece that has only just sprung its geometric cities from the hilltops and plains of its pastoral past. As their story-tellers and myth-weavers try to make sense of the new sciences of geometry, physics, and philosophy, they also grapple with how to co-exist with the grand mysteries of the land, nature, and the many gods who send wind and rain that both nourish their crops and drown hapless sailors. You see, there's no need to declare the dominance of science just yet in ancient Greece, because it can only tenuously explain some mysteries.

We still have mysteries today which is why I think ancient Greece can still help us to locate our next god. Case in point: how do you explain quantum mechanics? Even those who write the formulas and check them twice still don't know how it's possible for separate but quantumly entangled particles to do the same thing at the same time from across the room.

I suggest we must go back to the old gods of Greece. Greek gods were around for a whole lot longer than this present-day scientific revolution. We need to discover why. We could go back further to the half-lion-half man or cat-headed creature of Egyptian mythology but that's just too strange. We need something more realistic. The funny thing is, in Greece the gods looked like people. And they had all the same desires and were involved in the same indiscretions as mortal men and women. But they had powers beyond that of mortals. However, they weren't the all-knowing all-seeing, all-powerful, all-everywhere God of the Bible. No, they had select powers which they sometimes used in concert with each other, but petty jealousies and brooding memories of ancient slights often set them at odds with each other . . . for which humans were their pawns.

In a word, the gods were us with all our charms and warts, but grotesquely so. The randy Zeus with his many affairs and his efforts to cover these up so that his wife Hera wouldn't find out would ring true whether in ancient Greece or modern day Atlanta. Hera was no fool either; she knew what was going on and tried to make her rivals' lives miserable with her behind-the-back scheming. Why didn't she just divorce Zeus? Well, you see it just wasn't done on Olympus. We do have to be realistic in today's society where half of American marriages end in divorce.

We could go back to the earliest of the Greek gods, the Titans for a look-see. But like their names imply they were huge. We aren't looking for a Godzilla. Their descendants include Zeus, Poseidon, Hades, Phoebus Apollo, Pallas Athena, Hera, and others who looked just like us. Certainly we could choose Zeus but he was head of all gods and that is just a little bit close to the Bible 'one God' idea. We've been there, remember? Poseidon (Neptune) is the ruler of the sea and Apollo the god of light. Sorry, not quite right.

We've become so jaded that maybe we need someone who isn't the bright shining star we thought we needed at the dawn of World War II. I'm thinking that today we want something dark. How about Hades? He's the god of the underworld. No, Hades isn't a Satan, deceiver of the Bible. Remember that each god had to have a realm, sea, sky, light, or mountain. After drawing lots, the underworld fell to Hades. His name translates into rich; he has a cap which makes him invisible and he rarely leaves the underworld, his realm (Hamilton, *Mythology*, p. 26). His wife is Persephone, Queen of the underworld. And in the underworld there is Tartarus where Hades and Persephone rule (p. 41), but it's not only a place where the evil or wicked go to be punished. It's also the place where the good are rewarded for their goodness. A three-headed dog, Cerberus guards the entrance—any may enter; none can leave. And it takes an Indiana Jones–type to figure out where in hell Hades's palace is in Tartarus (p. 42).

So let's construct a creature of the dark who's as rich as hell (Hades), who lives for the most part hidden behind a protective maze that no one can penetrate and who seldom ventures into the upper world except perhaps at night. Why not a she? Why not both? And shouldn't they have a kid? But that's kind of morbid, you say. A kid in Tartarus? Well, it isn't the Hell of the Bible; it's the realm of the underworld where the dead hang out and there are plenty of them around. So, who should it be?

No Need to Guess, Now, Is There?

It can't be the ace reporter Superman. No, it's Batman, and boy Robin. They aren't related. Batwoman comes around sometimes but she isn't Batman's girlfriend. So it isn't quite the same as Hades and Persephone. But doesn't it have the ring of truth? Bruce Wayne, billionaire businessman with his huge mansion and subterranean fortress which he constructs and into which he and Batwoman and Robin alone can enter . . . But of course, so can Alfred Pennyworth, his trusted butler, and we all know Pennyworth is as selective of admission to the manse as Hades's three-headed dog Cerberus.

But Batman's no god, you say. I understand. Batman is a man of business and a Silicon Valley–type science geek who has unlimited resources to create the most wonderful and useful toys, tools, technology, and a stealthy cloak that's as invisible as a B-2 bomber without being . . . invisible. And he's as dark as they come, which of course is consistent with caves, bats, and bottomless sinkholes—the underworld.

Hades wasn't happy he drew the underworld. Batman isn't happy. He's sad, forced into the murky depths of darkness as a child when his parents are murdered before his eyes. And from this riddling depression, this post-traumatic stress he burns with a vengeance that rivals the fire stoked in the Biblical Hell. As a businessman he's as ruthless as is necessary and he dispatches the evil-doers of Gotham City with abandon. He's no goody-two-shoes like Superman. He's the industrialist, technologist and as such is a bit of a psychopath (as most company presidents are). He eschews the company of others to dwell in his own dark and brooding castle. He shows little emotion and empathy, preferring to exact his vengeance without the need for recognition. Nor has he remorse or guilt when he carries out his noble deeds which he does with reckless uninhibitedness and indomitable courage. He wreaks his will only against bad guys. Deep down inside we wonder whether put into a situation where evil is ambiguous he would still pursue vengeance without a second thought.

Sure, Superman has all the powers we might attribute to a Greek god and he also has weaknesses of Greek gods, but he's a being from another planet. While he's firmly in the pantheon that is science fiction, he's just that, fiction. Whereas every day we read about in the tabloids and see on the TV the Bruce Waynes of the world. Despite the stories that so-and-so is an alien or has three wives who are witches, we eat this stuff up. It's Bruce Wayne the billionaire with the mega-yacht and private jet fleet, driving around in his Bentley we gobble up as so much news. The paparazzi take pictures of him toasting the winner at the Pebble Beach Concours d'Elegance and then he disappears into a blacked-out limo to return to the bowels of his business to hone another deal that will beget the next big thing. He's the most interesting person on Earth. And he serves humanity, giving away millions or even billions to charities that put a flush in every potty or a veggie on every inner-city public-school child's plate. We worship him, praise him, but at the same time envy him.

So, it isn't Superman we envy. No, Superman we can't be. He's from Krypton and even if we went there we wouldn't absorb his super powers. But we hear from all the self-help gurus that we can all be billionaires like Bruce Wayne because the American dream guarantees that if we work hard enough we will get rich—we think, scheme, do, and dream the right things and because of that we will grow rich.

Bruce inherited his billions. Unlike some who squander their inheritance, Wayne put his to good use. He became like Charles Foster Kane from the movie *Citizen Kane* who inherited a great fortune but worked his money until he became the ruler of a vast newspaper publishing fortune reminiscent of Joseph Pulitzer (1847–1911). *Pow!* Take that, Superman. It's the billionaire who owns your newspaper who's the one we look up to now. The billionaire's our god, not Superman any more. Having money, big money is the thing, the only thing today.

And so it's Bruce Wayne, a.k.a. Batman, who has become our mythical hero. We teach our children to be like him, rich, philanthropic, and it's okay to be a bit eccentric at the same time as long as we're striving for more, ever more.

But is Bruce Wayne a god? Well, the Greek gods were like us, but they weren't. So are the very wealthy, you say. And this is true. The wealthy are human but they have such different lifestyles and we look up to them like gods. Read the tabloids, if you don't believe me.

We do make sacrifices to the *über*-rich like the Greeks did to their gods. The rich get special tax breaks we pay for and for which politicians' pockets are filled. If the rich don't like the tax break they have in Gotham City, they move their operations to another city. This is a bit like Zeus who threw a thunderbolt at your flock of sheep if you didn't give him a proper sacrifice. We write books on how to become a Bruce Wayne, how to think like a Bruce Wayne, and have reality TV shows to showcase the places that are like Wayne Mansion which they call Olympus or Xanadu. Sure, Superman is a nice guy but we all know in the end nice guys finish last.

So Superman, sorry, you've been knocked down a peg, from a perch you could only temporarily occupy. Certainly, when I was young we needed a super-being like Superman to punch Hitler in the nose, but Captain America, of course, did that first. Then Batman came along just a year after Superman in DC comics and he was thinking beyond the war, beyond science fiction. He knew that it was real technology that could enhance the human that was needed to retool the arsenal of democracy, not an alien who just happened along because his planet blew up.

I know many of you will not be happy with this turn of events, the turning out of Superman in favor of the Billionaire Batman. I can hear the scientists and futurists expound that the god-like realm of the industrialist, the Bruce Waynes, will also be usurped as was Superman. They see artificial intelligence in humanoid form becoming the new god.

I guess that I haven't completely left that kid of 1939. I still pine for the traditional hero, the god-like superhero that at least looks like one of us. But then again I think, let's look on the bright side. We need to leave a legacy for our grandkids to deal with. They'll need to battle their own human monsters and technological demons. I don't know about you, but my grandkids can't wait. They see in their future: androids, robots, and drones. They dream in cyberspace and while they're awake sit with fingers flying over keyboards in this world while their minds live in virtual worlds. Perhaps that's the future of theology for our grandkids. Cyber + god = cybergod who abides in and operates from a virtual realm.

Don't you think that you want someone who's dressed up with a cape or some other identifying feature you can point to and say: "hero"? I don't know how we would recognize a cybergod if it looked just like us. If we clone them, we then have hundreds of gods, and then aren't we back to the ancient Greeks or the Egyptians again where gods become watered down to the point where we need a different god for every new occasion?

Call me old-fashioned, but I say it's just one hero we need— and it's Batman.

7
How Batman Cowed a God

Patrick J. Reider

What if you took the soul of a man—his heart, thoughts, and intelligence—and placed it in the body of a god? One possible answer is explored in the mythos of Superman. What makes Superman intriguing is that he is not some mindless brute with god-like powers. He is above all, a being of virtue and uncompromising self-control.

Would a person like Superman know perfect happiness? According to some of the most venerated thinkers of the Eastern and Western traditions, true and lasting happiness is achieved by virtue alone. Surely the god-like embodiment of Superman's alien biology and virtues would ensure bliss—or would it?

Unlike Superman's alter ego Clark Kent, Batman's alter ego Bruce Wayne merely plays at living a life most city dwellers would call human. He's a fierce and exceedingly intelligent predator of the night consumed by a selfish need for vengeance. He personifies a pagan-like wrath that honors no law—he bends only to the call of private principles. What type of human weakness might a being of unfathomable power—a super-man—inadvertently expose to the keen analytic mind of an avenging dark knight? Would he discover that a superhuman being who cannot be overcome, who is loved and adored by most, and who awes the commoner, desires to be overcome? And if Superman cannot be overcome by force, by what other means would such a being wish to be dominated and thus diminished? More to the point, why would such a 'superman' harbor self-defeating desire?

Now imagine you were merely a man, albeit the Dark Avenger unbowed in the presence of a god, but just a man nonetheless. Imagine further that this god-like being whose physicality had no rational limit, secretly feared you, because in his heart of hearts, he was slave to morality that favors the weak and abhors the strong, while you did not.

In probing the morality of Superman and Batman, I will uncover a foreboding clash between contemporary values and a forgotten age of nobility, which is both terrible and awe-inspiring. The question "Which hero holds the moral high ground?" I will leave to the reader. The question I ask is less subtle, and a bit more knucklehead, for I want to know: Which morality holds a strategic advantage in a showdown?

The Dark Knight and Dark Delights

In the last several decades comic book heroes have transitioned from figures of carefree entertainment and wish fulfillment— "Gee golly, I wish I could punch out some Nazis and have super powers!"—to dark and psychologically rounded characters seeking to cope with deep human flaws. In exploring psychological limitations that endure even after the endowment of inhuman powers, we find new ways to explore the psyche or spirit of our age. So much so, that we can speak of Batman or Superman as telling symbols of human achievement, vanity, and potential. This way of talking about superheroes, despite all the trappings of pop culture, oddly enough parallels the discussion of Greek gods favored in the bygone age of elite classical education.

The more recent depiction of Batman that conforms to this view of superheroes is the "Dark Avenger"—a man so consumed by the self-centered desire for vengeance that his public persona, Bruce Wayne, is merely a thin disguise hiding a man who has little in common with the average liberal-minded citizen. This version of Batman respects no law. In order to catch his prey, he will break and enter, threaten a weak man, spy, steal information, hack, and more often than not, beat (rather severely) anyone who transgresses his sense of right. And if it helps him catch his prey, he will do these things to innocent individuals (well perhaps not severe beatings) as readily as the villain he seeks. In short, Batman is a criminal who has no regard for laws, but a very high regard for his own private principles and values. Above all the principles he sets before himself is one iron rule that defines him: a cold methodical vengeance towards those he, and he alone, judges to be a villain.

On the other hand, we have Superman, who is very different than the cold fiend known as the Dark Knight. And unlike Batman, Superman's alter-ego, Clark Kent, may very well be his "true" self. Unlike Batman, who underwent a formative change due to the violent death of his parents, Clark's life, even after becoming Superman, is morally oriented by his farmer parents, their rural values, and his hometown. Humility, self-sacrifice, empathy, hard work, restraint of emotion and physical indulgences are all consistent values expressed by Clark's parents. As Superman, Clark unfailingly embodies these values.

For the traditional moralist, Friedrich Wilhelm Nietzsche (1844–1900), a controversial German philosopher, made outright disturbing claims about the type of values Clark Kent personifies. He argues that the origins of contemporary Western values originated as a movement against the vibrant, action-oriented, capable, robust individuals who decided for themselves what was worth pursuing and what was to be avoided. These robust individuals were the first to consider their lives "good," and those who were unable to emulate such a life were considered "bad." Here, there is no heavy moral connotation to "good" and "bad." "Good" merely meant that which is perceived as genuinely life affirming—a sensuous, bold, and playful attitude towards life that enable action and nobility, while "bad' concerned anything that resists the productive impulses of life. Many of the current stories told about Wonder Woman, a fierce Amazonian warrior who lives according to regal, noble, and chivalrous principles loosely mirror this conception of the "good" person.

Nietzsche further argues that the more intelligent, so-called "bad' people (according to this old-world paradigm) resented, and later hated, the vibrant success of the self-proclaimed "good" men. In their vast and bitter intelligence, the cleverest of the "bad" men encouraged the masses to resent the so-called "good" people and their way of life. And in doing so, they claimed that a meek, humble, empathetic, and sensually restrained life was the truly good life. This caused a moral reversal in which the self-proclaimed "good" people became perceived as "bad."

The character Beowulf, in the animated move *Beowulf,* laments this shift in moral views when he states something like "Gone is the age of Heroes; with the new God, all we have left is crying martyrs." In a deliberate effort to provoke the reader, Nietzsche also offers a negative evaluation of this later moral outlook, which he calls "slave morality." Nietzsche calls it by this name, because the slave epitomizes the so-called "bad" person who resents the circumstances of his life, but is powerless to change it.

The clever and centuries-long struggle of reversing the original moral code of the aristocratic (meaning the most worthy) pagans to that of Christian ethics, according to Nietzsche, is the foundation of our contemporary morals. Regardless of whether we take Nietzsche's account to be true or false, it's clear that unlike Batman or Wonder Woman, the traditional account of Superman falls on the moral divide that Nietzsche calls "slave morality." For this reason, Superman is not Nietzsche's *Übermensch* (German for Over-human, Above-Human, or Superman), which personifies all the best traits of the original "good" men. Rather, Superman defends all the values that directly oppose these so called "good" men. In Nietzschian terms, Superman would the unwitting pawn of slave morality.

The Dark Knight and Dark Delights

Batman's primary drive is revenge. While his personal call to vengeance forbids him to kill, this self-imposed restraint does not seem to be a publicly agreed upon sense of right and wrong. Rather, it seems to be more of a personal choice to differentiate himself from those he hunts. As if to say, "See, I am not like you. Batman does not kill." If this is true, he may not have a deep and abiding respect for life, even though he refuses to kill under any circumstance.

In the animated movie *Under the Red Hood,* Batman refused to kill the man he believed murdered Robin. In a dramatic reunion with Robin (who is of course still alive), Robin is deeply hurt that Batman refused to kill his attempted murderer. Batman responds coldly to Robin (with whom Batman perhaps developed his deepest personal relationship), verging on the uncaring. Why? Because Batman obeys, conforms, submits, and compromises for only the wishes of Batman. It seems that an unyielding sense of pride (as opposed to a respect for life) keeps him from killing. Along with his pride, there also seems to come a sense of being more than that which he hunts, and perhaps even more than those he saves (though he would never admit as much, not even to himself). Surely such pride helps him be a single-minded, relentless, disciplined, and practiced hunter.

In the line of duty, a cop or a solider is occasionally forced to kill to save lives. Batman will not kill, even if killing the Joker, Bane, Scarecrow (or any other comic psychotic who makes modern serial killers seem unambitious) would save countless lives. Here again, his motivation does not appear to be respect for the sanctity of life, but a wish to avenge, to punish, and perhaps even torment his prey. The latter requires living beings, for one cannot punish the dead (or at least non-sorcerous types cannot).

Does Batman wish to save others from harm as a purely altruistic goal, or does he wish to thwart and punish those who have not harmed him directly, but remind him of the individual who killed his parents? The latter seems to be the case, for he has fetishized every violent criminal as a symbol of that which has harmed him, and in harming these surrogate transgressors, he obtains power over a world that deeply scarred him. Batman is both the wrathful aristocratic lord and the tragic victim.

Who Is Bruce Wayne to Batman?

What is Batman? He is a first-class detective, scientist, computer wiz, fighter, stealth expert, spy, escape artist, historian— whatever it takes to get his prey, he does it. These traits require a Herculean effort, discipline, and practice. Such a man would make the Olympic athlete, the devoted cancer researcher, or the fanatical political hacker seem lazy and unfocused. He will practice double-dealing until his fingers bleed, lay in filth as a bum for weeks, and crouch in the cold without moving for an entire night, if it would help him catch a crook. With unblinking eyes, he coldly analyzes any act of human butchery, deciphers any code, or breaks into any facility, in order to hunt and hunt an endless parade of prey—the cowardly criminals.

Such a man would have no room for what one would consider a "normal life." His alter ego Bruce Wayne must be something he plays at, like the psychopath who plays at having sympathies, understanding, and affection. While the psychopath is incapable of forming such emotional ties, Batman can form emotional attachments but generally chooses to avoid them. Yet, like many psychopaths, Batman is very adept at hiding his lack of real human connection and "normal" emotional responses.

Batman is an emotionally detached loner by necessity. How could anyone who possesses such a wide array of expertise (with no off-season) and commits nightly acts of vengeance function with an attachment to civilian life? How could such a person keep alive the unyielding desire for revenge without avoiding the simple pleasure that heals a heart? How does such a man find time to nurture the relationships that foster true caring? The simple answer is that he does not and cannot, if he wishes to remain Batman—a Dark Avenger who never quits, never complains, and never dreams of anything but the next hunt.

Such a life does not foster popular Western values that are associated with its Judeo-Christian morality. It's a pre-Christian value system. It is one of unyielding compromise, unabridged pride in ceaseless accomplishment, self-centered desire, and disregard for the laws of common men. None of these traits foster partnerships. Batman instead uses other superheroes as tools in his personal war.

Batman exemplifies the pagan-like wrath of Nietzsche's so-called "good men," who do not feel shame or remorse for their violent anger towards those who have harmed them or even those they dislike. Take for example the greatest of the ancient Greek Heroes, the pagan named Achilles. Out of spite, he drags the dead, defeated, and broken body of Hector, a once noble and powerful warrior, before the walls of Hector's home city. The pagan Greek and Roman aristocrat, of warrior heritage could be terrible to behold. What would such men be like if they lived today? Well, one possible outcome: the Dark Knight.

The values I have been discussing are aristocratic. They come from a privileged class that perceives itself to be entitled and deserving of pursuing its wishes. The thoughts and feelings of others are not even an afterthought. Such individuals serve their will and their wills alone. They pride themselves on their powers, both mental and physical. They disdain weakness, so much so that they cannot identify or understand how others could be weak or would allow themselves to be so.

Why the Billionaire Playboy?

Yes, Batman needs a cover and his family holdings to pursue his one-man war on villains. But instead of a playboy, why not be a billionaire hippie philanthropist? Why not be a billionaire holy man, a mild and timid person who is afraid of interacting with others, or an agoraphobic? Why not a billionaire volunteer teacher, Big Brother, soup kitchen worker, etcetera, etcetera? The easy answer is that Batman is not any of these things.

Yes, but he is not a playboy, right . . . or is he? Well, he does sleep with beautiful women, party, and indulge in extravagant luxuries. He does all of this without shame. Why? Because he is an aristocrat and holds the values of one. So while he may not be singularly driven by excitement for the parties and recreational activities his playboy persona projects, he does not find anything improper in performing or seeking out such pleasure.

None of the above commentary is intended to be an ethical evaluation of Batman from a particular standpoint. Its purpose is to define a character, one of many possible formulations of Batman seen over the decades, in order to contrast and clarify a completely different set of values consistently seen in the tales of Superman.

Superman or Clark Kent Superwimp?

Why would one of the most powerful and disciplined beings in the universe choose to remain Clark Kent, rather than the living embodiment of a noble Greek god of self-proclaimed virtue? One predominant theme of Superman's mythos is a profound desire to help the underdog, to protect the weak and powerless, and to curb the actions of the strong who would harm or hamper the flourishing of commoners. Clark champions these values, so much so that you wonder if he feels it a profound burden to be Superman. For whenever he chooses to be Clark Kent, he is passively permitting harm that could otherwise be adverted by Superman.

For those who live a simple country life, in which you have to worry and struggle to get by, excessive power, extravagant expressions of health, and endless vitality seem not only alien but unfair and improper. If one with the upbringing of Clark Kent did not use his god-like powers to singularly aid others, he would likely feel guilty and unworthy of being what he is by birth.

By being Clark Kent—a person of standards, but nonetheless a mild-mannered pushover, who's weak, simple, and slightly gullible, he unloads the great responsibility that Superman entails. Like Batman, Superman's alter ego could be different than it is. But unlike Batman, Superman appears to want to be his alter ego. He may even be more truly Clark than Superman. Again, why be a bungler when you can be a god amongst men? Why play at being mortal when you could just be Superman all the time? The answer is humility, guilt, and the unburdening of responsibility.

If Superman wants to be pushed around as Clark Kent, then would he also want to be abused as Superman? Here, I am *not* talking about a Lex Luthor or Darkseid harming Superman for some evil purpose and Superman enjoying it. Rather, I am talking about the secret way that some individuals like to be put in their place by their girlfriend or boyfriend, or the feeling of release one gets when someone else takes charge and, in doing so, proves herself to be more worthy of your responsibilities.

For the sake of argument, let's assume that, if Superman, a being of incredible discipline and restraint, had a moral flaw, it would be the desire to be bested by someone better than himself, to be no longer above or over humans, and to be free of what a good country boy must only see as improper and inhuman powers. Let's accept for a moment that Superman unconsciously wants to be the type of shabby, needy, and non-self-sufficient being that humans generally are. In short, let's read Superman as a god who is undone by his own morality—slave morality that yokes him with the weight of protecting worlds and forever separates him from the common man.

Wham, Bam, the Showdown

With the above interpretations of Batman and Superman in mind, the following exchange seems probable:

Glaring at Superman, Batman growls, "I gave you a plan. Follow it."

Superman replies, "No, I will attack. You know only I can take those types of hits and survive." As if to accentuate Superman's claim, the acidic sting of charred flesh wafted by. Superman glances towards the odor of Darkseid's latest victim. It was more a black and bloody smudge than a corpse.

Wanting Superman's undivided attention, Batman steps forward. His grim face mere inches from Superman's towering figure, ever beautiful and frightening, even when framed by the devastation of war. "Who are you to tell us mere mortals that we cannot endanger ourselves? Who are you to force yourself upon us as our protector?"

"That's not what I am saying." Superman could not hide the bitter sadness in his voice.

Locking eyes, Batman's growl turns into a cold statement of fact, "That is what you're doing. Now follow the plan or I'll take you out myself."

Batman's glare dares Superman to try something. Reluctantly Superman averts his gaze.

At that moment, Superman is overwhelmed by unexpected feelings: he feels normal, he feels like he's just a man, and above all, he feels happy. At last, he is no longer pretending. He truly is what Ma and Pa named him, Clark Kent—not a benevolent alien overlord, but just a shabby frail man, being put in his place by a superior . . .

Is there any wonder why a fierce and regal warrior like Wonder Woman romantically pursues Batman and not Superman? (Of course I'm ignoring the current story lines that have Superman and Wonder Women romantically entangled. I find this as likely as the Swedish bikini team pursuing the *Dumb and Dumber* characters.)

And why does Clark Kent have a thing for Lois Lane, an egotistical, manipulative, overly-confident, and cocky socialite?

Come on. Really . . . Do you need an answer?

8
Saints and Superheroes

DANIEL MALLOY

Riddle me this:

When is a good action not the right action?

Take a simple example: imagine you're walking down the street, going about your business, when you come upon a small, crying child. You ask what's wrong, and the child tells you that the family's pet cat is stuck in a tree and can't get down. Superman or Batman would, of course, leap into action to rescue the stranded feline. Will you?

You might; I might not. Maybe I'm afraid of heights or cats or trees or afraid of small children! The point is, while there's no doubt that it's a good thing if you rescue the cat, that doesn't mean it's a bad thing that I don't. I don't have to. I'm under no moral obligation to either the cat or the child to risk my life for the fleabag.

That's the riddle presented to moral philosophy by heroes like Superman and Batman. Of course their actions are good. Heroes don't behave badly. But, their actions go beyond what's morally required. We praise Superman or Batman for rushing into a burning building to save a puppy, but we'd hardly condemn Jimmy Olsen for staying safely outside snapping pictures. On the other hand, we would praise Jimmy if he rushed into the building, but we would condemn Superman or Batman if they didn't. The Metropolis Marvel and the Dark Knight are heroes, and so they have raised the bar for themselves in a way that Jimmy hasn't. Heroes are defined by doing good things that are not the right thing. And that is a strange thing.

Putting the "Hero" in Superhero

Technically, the riddle of how an action can be good but not required is called the problem of "supererogation." Supererogation is how we talk about actions that are good, but not right—the actions of heroes and saints. It presents a puzzle for moral philosophers because most moral philosophies hold that the good and the right are connected in a way that makes it impossible to have one without the other. Good actions should also be right actions.

Batman and Superman present a valuable opportunity for exploring this riddle because of the similarities and differences between them. What makes them different from one another is what elevates them to the level of "super" heroes—Superman is super because of his powers, Batman because of his determination, training, and intellect. But what makes them heroes seems to be the same. But what exactly is that? What makes a person a hero?

We Need a Hero

The concept of supererogation, that there are good things that we don't have to do, has been around since the Middle Ages, when it was essential for religious authorities to define what made a person a saint—the idea of a hero is even older. But it really only enters philosophy in the late 1950s, when philosopher James Opie Urmson published an essay called "Saints and Heroes." Urmson argues that saints and heroes—supererogatory figures—pose a problem for traditional moral philosophy. The problem is that moral philosophy has no way of classifying the actions of saints and heroes. Moral philosophers label actions as forbidden, permitted, or required. There are some exceptions, but rarely does an ethical system allow for more than these three types of actions.

What Batman and Superman do isn't forbidden (probably). It's permitted, but that doesn't quite cover it. The choices of a hero don't seem to be on a par with my choice to have a muffin rather than a bagel for breakfast. They're not morally neutral. But these actions can't be required. The other citizens of Gotham aren't wrong for not doing what Batman does. Nothing requires them to risk their lives fighting the Joker or any of the other dangerous maniacs that make up the Caped Crusader's rogues gallery.

This puzzle leads Urmson to call for a shake-up in our moral thinking to make room for supererogation, which he defines broadly as actions which go beyond the call of duty. More specifically and helpfully, Urmson claims that a supererogatory act is one which is praiseworthy but not obligatory. Supererogatory actions, then, are ones which are good to do, but not wrong *not to do*.

But this definition goes much further than the actions of saints and heroes. There are plenty of actions that are good to do, but not required of us. Being a generous tipper or holding the door open for a stranger or sending a friend a "thinking of you" card are also good to do, but not wrong not to do. But those aren't saintly or heroic deeds.

Moral philosophers have fallen into three rough camps in trying to solve the puzzle of supererogation. Some argue that there is no such thing. They usually argue that what we consider to be a supererogatory act is nothing more than the fulfillment of a duty; it's just a duty that most people don't fulfill. On the other side of the debate there are those who follow Urmson in defending supererorgatory acts as deeds that challenge our classification of moral acts. Finally, there are others who fall between these two extremes, who argue that there are supererogatory acts, but that they can be included under one or another of the given categories of moral philosophy, and it is there, in that third middle-ground state, that we realize Batman is a hero but Superman is not.

Why We Should All Be Batman

One of the things we admire about heroes like Batman and Superman is that they don't make excuses. When they make a mistake, they own it. When they cross the line, they don't try to escape responsibility for the act, but instead try to show why it was justified. When it's revealed that Batman has plans for neutralizing his fellow Justice Leaguers or that he created a satellite to monitor metahumans, he simply offers a justification of his actions (*Tower of Babel*). They may sometimes apologize, but they don't excuse themselves.

That makes Superman and Batman exceptional. But it doesn't make them better than they should be—it makes them as good as we should be. The difference between a hero like Superman or Batman and everyone else is that Superman and Batman do what they ought to, while most of us do only what we have to.

There are two approaches that lead to the conclusion that there are no supererogatory acts. One says that we should do what is good; the other says that the good is what we should do. Though they look identical, these are actually opposed approaches to ethics. The first is called utilitarianism, and it holds that we ought to take the actions that lead to the most good. The second is called deontology, and it says that the goodness or worth of an action is based on the duty it fulfills. An action is good if, and only if, it is required by a duty.

Utilitarianism rules out supererogation because to perform a supererogatory act we would have to do more good than we're required to do. But we are required to do as much good as we can. So, to perform a supererogatory act you would have to produce more good than you can produce. So, there aren't any supererogatory acts.

A well-known example of this kind of reasoning comes from Peter Singer. In "Famine, Affluence, and Morality," Singer argues that one action that's usually thought of as supererogatory—the act of charity—is in fact required for most people living in the developed world. Singer's argument begins from the premise that suffering is bad. He then proposes the principle that if we can prevent suffering without sacrificing anything of comparable moral significance, we ought to do so. This seems reasonable, until we play out the implications. If Clark Kent, a citizen of the developed world, can prevent someone's suffering by donating money to charity that he would otherwise use for some luxury, like his costume glasses, then he has a duty to do so. Clark does something wrong when he buys a new pair of pretend glasses instead of donating that money.

On the other hand, the second, deontological, approach rules out supererogatory acts because such acts wouldn't be obligatory. For the deontologist, the moral value of any action lies in its fulfilling a duty. If the duty is fulfilled, then the act is good. To go beyond what is required by duty is, at best, simply a variation on fulfilling one's duty. So, for example, if it's a good thing that Bruce Wayne donates to various charities, that's because giving to charity is one way of fulfilling a broader duty

of caring for others. What good there is in so-called supererogatory acts is based on the fulfillment of the duty. We may praise
them more than others because it may be that this particular
duty is rarely fulfilled—but it's still a duty. Since "duty" means
required, then there are no supererogatory actions—either you
are doing the good you should do, or you aren't. There is no good
action that isn't required by some duty.

Batman's Retirement

In "Moral Saints," Susan Wolf presents a case against this position. Wolf imagines what a person would be like who lived perfectly according to utilitarianism and deontology respectively.
The Loving Saint (utilitarian) and the Rational Saint (deontologist), as she calls them, would be very good at being good.
They wouldn't, however, be very good at being people.

Consider Batman: Bruce Wayne, it has been said many
times, is just a mask. Every action, every thought in his life is
about fulfilling his promise to his parents. This is why many
objected to the ending of Christopher Nolan's *The Dark Knight
Rises* (2012)—it's one thing to say that Bruce Wayne may stop
being Batman, but it's another thing altogether for him to more
or less give up on Gotham, or leave it in the hands of a virtual
stranger. What some saw as Nolan's commitment to realism,
others viewed as a misunderstanding of the character of
Batman. The depictions of Bruce's "retirement" in Frank
Miller's *The Dark Knight Returns*, Mark Waid and Alex Ross's
Kingdom Come, and the DC Animated Universe's *Batman
Beyond* seem more faithful to the character. Physical infirmity
may force him to hang up the cowl, but nothing short of death
(and perhaps not even that—these are comic books, after all)
can make him give up the mission. Devoted and driven, but no
longer physically able to withstand the strain of being Batman,
Bruce ends up a broken, bitter old man, all alone in his cave.

This problem isn't dealt with much in Superman storylines,
but in Kurt Busiek's *Astro City*, Samaritan (who is clearly a
stand-in for Superman) has no kind of life outside of his constant battles and rescues. His job, the carefully crafted persona
of his alter-ego, everything in his life is set up so as not to inter-
fere with his role as the Samaritan. There is too much for him
to do for him to stop and have any sort of a life.

But those who deny that there are supererogatory acts hold that we should all be living lives like Bruce's and Samaritan's, devoted in every waking second to doing the right thing. We should be Loving Saints or Rational Saints. But this asks too much, and does not seem to allow for the kinds of things that make life worth living. Bruce Wayne doesn't have hobbies, or friends, or fun.

Superman, Inc.

To preserve the special status of saints and heroes, we have to defend two claims. First, there are supererogatory acts, which are good but not required. Second, these acts can't be understood in terms of the usual moral categories of the forbidden, the permitted, or the required. By ignoring supererogatory acts we diminish our moral thinking and our view of the world, in several ways.

First, we (non-saints and non-heroes) diminish ourselves. If supererogatory acts are morally required then most people are negligent in fulfilling their duties. The average, decent person is actually a neglectful moral monster. Jimmy Olsen should do much more than simply signal Superman; he should be training and preparing and constantly striving to fulfill his duties. He should be living like Bruce Wayne, only without the fortune or playboy façade. The fact that he doesn't speaks to a weakness of character or negligence in fulfilling his duties, if not outright moral depravity. If supererogatory acts are morally required, then Superman's pal may as well be the Joker.

What's more, when we deny the existence of supererogatory acts we diminish the status of saints and heroes. This might seem a bit backward—since we've lowered ourselves to the status of moral monsters it would seem that there's a corresponding elevation of saints and heroes. But the opposite is actually true: we drag them down with us. If we deny the existence of supererogatory acts then saints and heroes become no more than people who do what they ought to. They are meeting requirements. They are exceptional only because they are surrounded by monsters. It's the difference between being the most moral person in the Justice League and being the most moral person in the Crime Syndicate. The most moral person in the Justice League is an exceptional moral exemplar. The most moral person in the Crime Syndicate isn't really moral—she or he is simply the least evil.

To say that supererogatory acts are morally required is to eliminate something special and important from our moral universe. Part of what's essential about the supererogatory act is that it's optional. What makes saints and heroes praiseworthy is that they don't have to do what they do. They choose to. Nothing requires Bruce Wayne to spend his evenings patrolling the rooftops of Gotham protecting its citizens. Superman's extraordinary abilities are his, and as such, he can do with them as he pleases. When, for instance, the Clark Kent depicted in *Superman, Inc.* uses a fraction of his Kryptonian abilities to become a wealthy celebrity athlete, there's nothing wrong with that. Well, okay, arguably using powers far beyond those of mortals in professional sports is cheating. But imagine Clark had just started a construction/demolition company and had gotten rich doing that. The point is he would do nothing wrong if he used his powers for his own ends, rather than to help others. The fact that Superman dedicates his powers to protecting people is his choice, and seems to be to his credit.

Bruce Wayne's Promise

But, if there are some actions that "go beyond" duty, we need a clear idea of where our duty ends. Sometimes, the distinction between fulfilling a duty and going beyond it is easy to see. But not always. It's easy to say that an average person who rushes in to a burning building to save a child acts heroically. But what about a firefighter who does the same thing? If I interrupt a mugging and chase off the would-be thief, I've gone a bit beyond my duty, but a cop who does the same thing has just done her job.

Take Batman. If we consider Bruce Wayne a random yahoo in a bat costume, then fighting crime goes above and beyond the call of duty. But if we think of him as Bruce Wayne, the man who promised his dead parents that he would dedicate his life to ridding the world of the kind of evil that ended their lives, then he is duty-bound to fight crime (but not to dress up like a bat). You might say that the promise was made when Bruce was just a child and really isn't binding on the adult Wayne. But it's part of what drives him. He may not be obligated to do what he does, but he feels that he is.

Superman is a slightly trickier case, but there are still plenty of actions that the Man of Steel takes that toe the line between fulfilling his duty and going beyond the call. Patrolling the city, looking for people to help certainly seems to go beyond the call of duty. On the other hand, using his powers to help people in immediate danger who are right in front of him would seem required. If you or I saw a person in the street about to be hit by a car, it wouldn't be beyond the call of duty for us to try to warn that person of the danger. Calling out to them would seem to be the least we could do, morally. To shove them out of the way, and place our own lives at risk, might be beyond the call.

Superman, on the other hand, would have a variety of options to save that person's life without unduly risking his own or anyone else's safety: he could simply run, grab the person, and escort them to safety—with his speed, he can easily outrun any car; he could fly the person to safety; he could stop the car; he could lift the car over the pedestrian; or he could use his arctic breath to freeze the whole tableau in place; even a small, generally unnoticeable blast from his lungs could be enough to slow down the car or speed up the pedestrian enough to avoid an accident. But if Superman did nothing, he would be failing in his duty. Even simply shouting out to warn the pedestrian would be a failure on Superman's part, because there is so much more he could easily do to save her life with little to no risk to himself. Superman has a duty to save that pedestrian, so doing it is not optional for him. The fact that, thanks to his super-powered senses, most things are "right in front of him" further complicates the line between duty and heroism.

There are two connected problems here. First we have the original problem that it's difficult to draw the line between what's required or even merely good and what's supererogatory. The second and more troublesome problem is that what actions are and aren't supererogatory seem to be relative to the person. What would be supererogatory for me wouldn't be for Superman—because of his powers—or Batman—because of his promise.

Why Batman Is Better than Superman

This is a problem that neither those who deny the existence of supererogatory acts nor those who defend them outright can deal with easily.

On the one hand, if you say there are no supererogatory acts, then it follows that there should be a hard-and-fast rule about what we should do that we're all held to. I'm just as guilty of not being Batman as Jimmy Olsen. On the other hand, if there are supererogatory acts, then there should be a clear line between doing your duty and going beyond it, and it should apply to everyone.

In light of this problem, I will now offer a suggestion that finds the right position between denying and defending the existence of supererogatory acts. My position is that supererogatory acts would be required in different circumstances, but that the requirement is overridden by some other consideration.

Imagine that you see a small child drowning in a shallow pond. Other things being equal, you have an obligation to try to save the child. Doing so isn't supererogatory. Anyone in your position could, and should, do the same thing.

Now change the scenario slightly. It's still you and a small child, only now the child is in a burning building. You're still required to try to save the child, but because rushing into the building would present a grave risk to you, the action required isn't that direct. You should inform the authorities, help to put out the fire if necessary, and do whatever you can to help the child short of exposing yourself to serious peril. You are under no obligation to rush into the building. To do so would be supererogatory. The obligation to save the child still exists, but it's permissible for you to refrain from rushing into the burning building to do it, because that would put your own life at undue risk.

As Joseph Raz has argued, a supererogatory act is one that we ought to do—we have reason to do it, and that reason is overriding, meaning that it carries more weight than other kinds of reasons. But what makes a required act a supererogatory one is the presence of another reason, one that counters the overriding nature of the reason that requires us to act. This reason cannot just be anything. If I promised to help my friend move, but don't feel like it, that doesn't mean that I'm a hero for helping her move. The reason that counters the requirement must be a similarly moral reason.

This theory explains why one and the same action may be supererogatory for one person but not another—the reason that grants permission not to act may not apply to one person, though it does to another. Giving to charity is a very different action for the Kents and for the Waynes. Both families are required to look after other people. The Waynes, on the one hand, have more than they need or could ever possibly want; as such, they have no reason not to give to charity. The Kents, on the other hand, are not nearly so well-off. To give to charity when they are not sure that they'll have enough themselves is supererogatory.

Now turn to Superman and Batman. Batman has permission to refrain from most of his activities as Batman. They put his life at risk. Although he does many things to minimize that risk, the fact is that he faces death every night. A serious, immediate threat to one's life, in the absence of any other reason to carry out the act, is generally a good reason to refrain from an action. Batman has this reason, and therefore has permission not to act in the ways he does. Batman is a hero.

Superman, on the other hand, generally does not have the same kind of permission. When he faces down a mugger with a gun, Superman is in precisely no danger. This isn't to say that Superman never acts heroically. He certainly does. His courage in the face of the few things that pose any sort of danger to him (kryptonite, magic, Doomsday, and, of course, Batman) is exemplary. But Superman rarely faces anything that poses a serious threat to him, where Batman does so every time he dons the cowl.

Everyday Heroes

But the risks Batman takes, and the fact that he doesn't have to take them, mean that his choice to be a hero is irrational. And, by calling him a hero, we're encouraging people to be irrational. Heroes and saints behave irrationally because the overriding reason for acting is the one which provides the permission.

Say someone offers you a choice: you can go through Door #1 or Door #2. Go through Door #1, and you get a million dollars. Go through Door #2, and you get dropped into a pit filled with scorpions. Knowing this, and not being insane, you're going to choose Door #1. You should choose Door #1. It would be stupid to choose Door #2. Supererogatory acts are the equivalent of choosing Door #2.

Consider the life Bruce Wayne could be leading if he gave up the cowl: a wealthy, charitable business man, possibly still playing the playboy, possibly settling down and raising a family—by any measure, Bruce Wayne's life would be a good one. Instead, he hunts Gotham's rooftops and alleyways as an urban legend, living a life that even he admits he wouldn't wish on anyone (*Superman/Batman* 1). Since Bruce doesn't have to be Batman, it certainly looks like an irrational choice.

But this depiction of my position is unfair. The permission not to perform an act is not the same as a prohibition against performing it. For example, suppose Bruce Wayne is scheduled to attend a fundraising party for a charity. Knowing Bruce's busy schedule, one of the party's organizers calls and tells him that it's okay if he can't make it. Bruce now has permission not to go to the party. But that doesn't mean that he shouldn't go—it just means he doesn't have to.

A better understanding of my position would be to view the permission as leveling the field. Before permission is taken into consideration, the bulk of the reasons to act are on the side of the required act. Other things being equal, Bruce should go to the party. The permission makes refraining from the act an acceptable possibility, not the required course of action. The organizer's call means that Bruce can go or not go. Both choices are equally rational. So, supererogatory actions are optional. Bruce doesn't make an irrational choice by being Batman; he takes one of two equally valid options. The happiness he might achieve if he stopped being Batman is counterbalanced by the good he does as Batman.

This is why Batman is more of a hero than Superman. Because Batman has the permitting reasons, he is making a choice. He's not required to fight crime or risk his life, but chooses to do so. Superman, on the other hand, generally doesn't have the same permitting reasons. He only has the obligations we all have, combined with greater powers to fulfill them. Batman is making a choice to fulfill a duty he doesn't have to; Superman is doing what is morally required of him.

So we aren't encouraging irrational behavior by praising Batman's heroics. Both options, being Batman or not, are equally rational. But, we're committed to a strange proposition—namely, that the reasons for acting and not acting are of equal weight, but those who act are praiseworthy and those who do not are not. It's odd to say that both the person who rescues a child from a burning building and the person who sensibly refrains from putting his own butt in the fire have done the right thing, but only the first one will be in the paper.

Against this criticism, we can offer a couple of possible defenses. First, we can argue that we shouldn't hold supererogatory acts up as examples. Doing so distorts the way we think about morality by presenting the extraordinary as something to be copied, thereby diminishing the value of routine duty fulfillment. In terms of social order and stability, a good cop doing his job faithfully, like Jim Gordon, is a far more valuable example than a hero like Batman. Gordon saves lives, just as Batman does, and he occasionally acts heroically, but for the most part the commissioner is just an honest cop doing his job. Unlike the heroic Batman, Gordon represents a moral standard that anyone can aspire to.

Second, we could argue that the only reason we praise the supererogatory is because it's the exception. "Batman Saves Baby" makes sense as a headline; "Cop Does His Job" doesn't. Batman and Superman may get all the headlines, but their work is only possible because of the everyday, run-of-the-mill duty fulfillment of rank-and-file cops, fire fighters, and EMTs. Being praised and being praiseworthy are distinct things. We praise people like Batman because they stand out, but they stand out because of the praiseworthy but everyday actions of others, the ones who don't get the headlines.

Heroes Aren't Super; Supers Aren't Heroes

There's a moment in Mark Waid and Alex Ross's *Kingdom Come* that always gets me. Superman goes to the Batcave to get Bruce to join him in his efforts to prevent a metahuman war that will probably end the world. After some verbal sparring, Big Blue makes his final pitch. He says that for all their differences, there's one thing they've always agreed on: they don't want to see anyone die. It nicely sums up the odd and often difficult partnership between the brooding and driven Dark Knight and the world's oldest Boy Scout.

But for us, what's more important is what it leaves out. Clark has pinpointed what he and Bruce have in common, but has forgotten all that distinguishes them. And it's in the gulf between them that heroes are born.

The difference between Superman and Batman, at their core, is that Superman has powers and Batman doesn't. Because of his powers, Superman can do the same sorts of things Batman can, but without taking the same sorts of risks that Bruce does. But also because of his powers, these actions aren't optional for Superman; he's morally required to do them. He has no permission not to save the pedestrian or stop the mugger or catch the falling baby. Morally speaking, being Batman is optional; being Superman isn't. So while Batman's a hero, Superman is just a good person with the powers of a living god.

Think about it like this: Bruce is always Batman. There's no vacation, no time off. In or out of costume, Bruce Wayne is always Batman, and he will always do what Batman does, including putting his life on the line to save someone else. Now think about how much time Clark spends as Clark, and not as Superman. He maintains his cover identity, his love life, still manages to visit Ma and Pa, and hang out with Jimmy. Even as Superman, he goes to ceremonies and gets honored and gives press conferences and speaks to world leaders.

Now, I'm not saying that Superman is being lazy; I'm saying he's doing what he has to. Like most other people, he takes time for himself. He maintains relationships and has something like a life outside of his cape. Clark is life-saving Superman as much as he has to be, and maybe a bit more, but there's plenty he could do to help others that he doesn't. Bruce, on the other hand, sacrifices and risks whatever he has to in the name of the mission. Happiness, friendship, love, and all the other things that make up a life only have a place in his life if they serve the mission. Putting his life on the line nearly constantly is what he has chosen to do. The risks he takes and the reasons he takes them make him a hero.

9

Masks, Hearts, and Superheroes

MARVIN LEE DUPREE AND MIRELA FUŠ

Now, we promise you one thing—we will take off our own mask right away. We aim to prove that *Batman is a true superhero, and Superman is not*. We're convinced of this, and if you read further along, I will convince you too.

We all think we know who Batman and Superman are. They are polar opposites who both happen to wear their underwear over spandex pants, or at least they once did. So, for comic purists and fans of the cinematic DC Universe it may seem bold to claim that Batman is a true superhero and that Superman is not a true superhero. As a matter of a fact, we want to claim something even stronger: something we will prove independently, without only comparing them and without having to worry if one comic character happens to depend on the other. We plan to demonstrate that it is not a matter of comparison between Batman and Superman when it comes to the concept: a true superhero. There is something else that is crucial for each comic character that makes one a true superhero, whereas the other is not—and we're am going to reveal what this is exactly.

You can use a method of a comparison and say: *Oh, here is a simple and obvious truth—we look at Batman and Superman as comic and movie characters and simply compare them, and then, on the basis of this meager comparison, we can conclude one is a true superhero and the other is not.* Yet Superman would not be a true superhero even if Batman would never ever have existed. This also means that Batman being a true superhero does not depend on the existence of Superman. Neither of them depends on the existence of the other. What we want to say is that only a man can be a true superhero. And if you stay with us, you will see what role the lives of Bruce Wayne and Clark Kent played in all this.

Obviously, we know that not everyone is going to agree that Batman is a better superhero. In fact, some might even accuse us of being a bit biased. True, we do like Batman better, but that isn't enough. The fact is that Batman is better because he is a *true* superhero. So what do we mean by a *"true superhero?"*

Clark Kent and Bruce Wayne

We will try to dispel the idea that you have to compare Batman and Superman to figure out which one is a true superhero. So, as we said, we intend to use a different standard and independent criteria. It might be useful to begin with the similarities between the two. At first glance it might seem we have two men—namely Bruce Wayne and Clark Kent. Furthermore, we also have two candidates for a true superhero—Batman and Superman.

Now let's take a closer look. The first point we want to stress is that in the end we'll see that we are not dealing with two men, just as we are not dealing with two true superheroes, and being a man or human will, somehow, turn out to be important when judging which of them is a true superhero. Confused? Well, we will demonstrate that only Bruce Wayne fits the first criteria, that he is a true man, whereas Clark Kent is not a true man.

Finally, arriving to the realization that Clark isn't a man reflects our shared values and how we all view heroism. We expect certain kinds of virtues that we desire in a superhero. We also believe there is a simple idea that truly distinguishes one comic or movie character as being a true superhero, and that can also be applied in our Batman and Superman discussion. This idea can also be called a definition of a true superhero and we will now attempt to prove that Clark is not a true superhero.

Now again, we'll start with the things we all agree on, hopefully. We can all accept the following statement: *Bruce Wayne is Batman.* Furthermore, we can also say: *Clark Kent is Superman.* This is pretty much an undeniable reality in the DC comics.

Of course, if you want to nitpick there was brief and regrettable period in the 1990s when Batman wasn't Bruce Wayne, when Jean-Paul Valley took up the bat-mantle and later and Dick Grayson who filled in for Bruce in his "death." Others might mention the controversial comic arc "The Four Supermen" in Superman's case. But let's just say that as a matter of definition, Batman is Bruce Wayne. In fact, we could say Batman = Bruce Wayne.

When we say something like this or like "Superman = Clark Kent" we are making an *identity statement*. This might sound like academic jargon, which is pretty much green kryptonite to good writing, but it is a handy tool to reveal the true nature of how we define a true superhero. So, simply put, identity statements usually consist of two names unified by an expression of identity "is" to identify the same thing. They are composed of two parts, and also presuppose the claim that these two parts are equal and symmetrical. Roughly, in our case we have a first part of statement "Bruce Wayne" that equals to the second part "Batman", and another part "Clark Kent" that equals to the part "Superman."

One further nice virtue of an identity statement such as "Bruce Wayne is Batman" is that all that makes one part it also constitutes the other. So, all the things that make Bruce Wayne Batman are the same things that also make Batman Bruce Wayne—that's why they are equal after all. And the same goes for Superman. All the things that make Clark Kent, Superman also make Superman, Clark Kent. So, Bruce Wayne and Batman are one and the same thing, and Clark Kent and Superman are one and the same thing.

This, we believe, strikes everyone as a true statement. Batman was born on Earth to human parents and is essentially a human being, whereas Superman was born on the planet Krypton and is a demigod due to the yellow sun rays of our Sun. Versions of Superman such as Superman Prime obviously show he is more god than man. So, one is a man, and the other is not. Remember, we said whatever one part *is*, the other part *is* as well. Again, whatever Batman is, Bruce Wayne is as well, and whatever Superman is, Clark Kent is as well. And we all agree that Batman is a man, so Bruce Wayne is a man too. And because Superman is not a man, Clark Kent is not a man too.

A Mask for Someone or Someone in His Heart

Now that we have shown you through identity statements that Batman and Bruce Wayne are one thing and are human by nature, and that Superman and Clark Kent are also a single thing and the same thing, yet not human, we are ready for our next diabolical twist (please try to imagine this last sentence in the voice of William Dozier, the narrator of the 1960s Batman show).

Still with us? Let's move on. But allow us to give you a hint—we're paving the road which leads to our definition of a true superhero.

Okay, so what I want to do next is to introduce the two relations we associate with our two identity statements, namely:

1. Bruce Wayne is Batman. *Relation*: 'being just a mask for someone'

2. Clark Kent is Superman. *Relation*: 'being someone in her/his heart'

The first relation is what we call 'being just a mask for someone' and pair it with the first identity statement: 1. Bruce Wayne is Batman. The second relation we introduce is 'being someone in his or her heart' and we pair it with the second identity statement: 2. Clark Kent is Superman. In other words, we think that each of relations ascribe the core relations within the parts of these statements. More vividly, we want to say that Bruce Wayne is just a mask for Batman, but Clark Kent, in his heart, is truly Superman. So, essentially, Clark Kent, a Midwestern, apple-pie loving boy scout, is in his essence Superman, a non-human. But in Batman's case, Bruce Wayne only conceals Batman, both of them are equally strong and capable and the mask does not take anything away any of his virtues or skill sets. Bruce Wayne remains a martial arts extraordinaire and capable of every single feat Batman can do should he choose so or be forced to. Batman just chooses to be Bruce Wayne for the sake of appearances. However, becoming human would make Superman, on the other hand, only Clark Kent—an ordinary man without any superpowers who would suddenly be forced to achieve feats which are humanly impossible. In fact, when Mr. Mxyzptlk once threatened to turn Superman into a normal human being, Mr. Mxyzptlk did not because he realized that is what Clark truly wanted.

All It Takes to Be a True Superhero

Hey! we're still not done. The most important part is yet to come. But you may wonder how all this nonsense we just wrote matters—how would, after all, being or not being a man or a human matter for being a true superhero? Or why are these silly relations of 'being just a mask for someone' and 'being someone in his heart' of any importance to this matter?

We stated earlier that we want to establish a solid ground for distinguishing a true superhero from a one that is not that, and we do not want to do that by only comparing certain candidates at hand, as we could do with Batman and Superman.

To complete our journey we now need a definition of what it takes for a comic or movie character to be a true superhero. First, our definition of 'being a true superhero' requires that you also be a human as its necessary condition. What we mean here by a necessary condition is that "being a human" is a condition, which necessarily has to be satisfied otherwise you are not a superhero. For you can seem to do the things and actions that are similar to the ones that what we call a true superhero does, but if these deeds are not done by a human being, they have not been done by a true superhero. Only humans, by our definition can be true superheroes since our definition requires you to be a human as a necessary quality. For example, Superman has done many similar things to what Batman did, yet Superman is not a human being, and thus is not a true superhero.

To this we want to add the notion of a true superhero which doesn't rely on given superhuman powers but rather on values and the development of certain skills that a human comic character tends to develop to the extreme heights—which means that the more developed by his own human forces, the more of a true superhero the human character is.

In this way most of us also believe that Batman is a true superhero just like heroes in Western literary history such as Odysseus, and we believe that Batman fits within the virtue ethics theory of Aristotle. In Homeric epics characters often have powerful epithets such as swift-footed Achilles or resourceful or wily Odysseus. This is quite similar to names such as The Caped Crusader or The Man of Steel.

Virtue ethics or, sometimes called *aretaic ethics* (from the Greek word *arete* meaning also a 'moral virtue'), puts stress on the character and the virtues that this character possesses when judging which behavior is considered to be morally good or bad. Aristotle thought that a virtue of character leads one to achieve excellence—and any individual who possesses character excellence does the right thing, at the right time, and in the right manner. Virtue ethics tells us that you should do what an ideally virtuous person would do.

Yes, objections can be raised that this is circular in a sense that what is good is what a virtuous person does and what a virtuous person does is good, which brings us to the second objection, that it gives us no guidance what to do, and this is even more visible when we have more virtues to deal with. Batman tries to balance being just and merciful and we can all see that when he repeatedly does not kill the Joker, even when he can.

When we apply virtue ethics to our definition of a true superhero, we wish to stress the fact that a human comic character must strive to flourish and nourish his capabilities and virtues in order to become a true superhero. So, to be a true superhero, you have to be a human who has mastered certain skills and knowledge. This also ties in nicely with the idea that true superheroes are the ones who have obtained mastery of virtues, so their acts and deeds are not just spontaneous and due to some god-given thing or governed only by sheer luck. This definition of a true superhero fosters something valuable a person should seek in her or his human nature. Becoming a true superhero is hard work for a comic character and a matter of deserved honor. Our definition goes something like this:

> An essentially *human* comic character (such as Batman or Blue Beetle) is somebody who strives and develops powers that go almost beyond the normal or given human capacities, thus this make them a true superhero or a true super-heroine, whereas an essentially *superhuman* comic character (such as Superman) who has their superpowers merely given to them by birth or through some event does not make them a true superhero. The underlying assumption from virtue ethics here is that a true superhero has certain virtues which make them become aware of and work on bettering their

nature to the degree which makes them seem to possess superpowers but those powers are actually a result of their human virtuous strivings.

For example, Professor Zoom and Sinestro possess superpowers but choose not to use them in a virtuous way because they are villains—which shows that only possessing superpowers is not enough to make you a true superhero. It can only make them diverge further from being a true superhero. They lack the aspect of being virtuous—their superpowers are gained rather than being carefully developed.

Kyle Rayner, when he started out as a Green Lantern, was not striving to be a true superhero. Kyle simply gained possession of a super powered ring, but he did not automatically become a true superhero by merely possessing the ring. He flourished and became one. He could have simply possessed immense superpowers all his life, but never been a true superhero had he not had been virtuous. In the same light, pun intended, Guy Gardner who was a Green Lantern—was not always a hero despite having being given tremendous powers via the green power ring.

Actually, these examples are similar to one of philosophy's oldest thought experiments, Gyges's Ring. The idea is roughly this: what if you gained a ring that granted you invisibility? Would you use it for nefarious purposes? Merely possessing superpowers does not make you worthy of earning the title of a superhero, even less a true superhero—a true superhero is the one who develops his or her skills and enhances their powers so they can use them for noble and virtuous purposes. A true superhero should include a human character who utilizes their human powers rather than merely possessing superpowers; showing that a genuine super-heroic individual does more with less.

An Aristotelian Man?

Since their inception, Batman and Superman have always existed in binary relationship, where one represents light and the other dark; and people have also interpreted them as representing different ideologies as well. So many theorists often judge Batman and Superman according to the cycles of popularity and rivalry they have gone through during the history of their comic and cinematographic lives. In addition to that, they sometimes tend to make their interpretations based on what system of values the characters might represent in different eras of human history (such as the Great Depression, the Cold War, or the post-modern-capitalist era). However, we believe that they also shaped their own lives in certain ways, and that is what distinguishes them. We're not denying that Superman lives in Metropolis or Batman in Gotham, or that the way they treated their main opponents Lex Luthor or the Joker, may have influenced their actions. We're merely saying that we have to extract the relevant parts of their virtuous characters in order to find out what makes one, and not the other, a superhero.

Virtue ethics teaches us how to strive towards homeostasis, or the optimal balance, the ideal balance. We often saw how Batman is aware of it, and strives towards it. This struggle for harmony is visible when Batman never kills any villain, no matter their crime—obscure Golden Age era comics don't count! Even though Batman is not being ideal; he fails but he never lets go of the idea of seeking balance.

In *Man of Steel,* Superman kills Zod. Batman always seeks to avoid the taking of life, for example an issue of *Gotham Knights* (#31) highlights this rule to the extreme. Batman knows every single ailment of the people he fights. Batman always plans so far ahead and anticipates everything in order to not kill. Batman is a virtue ethicist, since according to his reasoning, if he were to perpetrate the same kind of violence and mayhem as the Joker, he would become the thing he strives so utterly to destroy.

Virtue ethics does not give ready solutions; it embraces the complexity of life and demands that we think and act to develop our virtues. There might be a clash of virtues and then we have to decide. As Aristotle pointed out, acting with no regard for our own wellbeing would be foolhardy, whereas never placing our wellbeing at risk would be cowardly.

An example of someone who sees the world in black and white would be the DC comics character Rorschach from *Watchmen* whose sense of morality is pretty much as black and white as the color template of his mask. When he considers good and evil, he cannot perceive the world's shades of gray. Batman, on the other hand, lives in the shades and gets to know them better than anyone else. He takes actions that tend to be in accordance with what a virtuous person would do.

In *Batman Begins,* Bruce did harbor fantasies of killing the murderer of his parents. Yet, instead, he turned into Batman. In doing so he follows the Aristotelian middle road which he follows as a superhero. On the other hand in stories such as *The Dark Knight Strikes Again*, we see how Superman's god-like powers can make him more subservient to human laws yet according to a deontological ethicist, Superman should have intervened earlier, which Batman certainly does. This idea is also toyed with in *Red Son*, where Superman has become a tyrant certain in his own ideological beliefs, aided by his god-like power. Obviously, because of his powers Superman often fails to find this golden middle way, also because he is either considered a great threat or a god.

Virtue ethics is an Aristotelian idea, and might sound as if it is tailored only for someone who is financially secure like Bruce Wayne who nothing better to do with his time, and therefore fills his idle existence with vigilante justice.

To the contrary, we believe that striving to be a virtuous man is not being self-indulgent. We're convinced that what Batman does can be applied to everyday people. Even if he were poor, he would be a true superhero who is also just an everyday man, because he is Bruce Wayne in his heart. But Superman is not a man, much less an everyday man, and cannot count as an Aristotelian hero.

Becoming a True Superhero

We can now proudly claim that Batman is the *true superhero*, whereas Superman is not. Bruce Wayne is only a mask for Batman, and Clark Kent is Superman in his heart. Our definition of a true superhero requires for them to be an Aristotelian virtuous human—a condition which Batman fully satisfies. You do not need to be an alien or have a freak accident occur in a lab. Everyone can pursue the values that make for a true superhero.

We don't need gods to intervene on our behalf or to gift us with superpowers. Batman shows us how to become a super-hero—by striving for the Aristotelian virtues.

10
Gods Are Overrated

NICOLAS MICHAUD

Superman is a god. Not necessarily *the* God, but a god nonetheless. If we mean by "god" something that is super-powerful, immortal, and far beyond our capacities, then he is a god. For heaven's sake he is basically omnipresent. Superman can move so fast that he can pretty much be everywhere at once.

Sure, Superman isn't as awesome as an absolutely perfect God who has no flaws whatsoever, but Superman is so powerful, so *nearly* perfect, that he would at least fit amongst the pantheon of Greek Gods. What could Zeus do? Throw lightning bolts? Supes can shoot lasers from his eyes! The problem is that if this is true, if Superman is God-like, then all of the philosophical questions that can be applied to God can be applied to Superman too, and he has some explaining to do . . .

I Don't Believe in Superman

So there is at least one obvious reason why Superman fails when compared to Batman. Batman is just one more human. True, a very smart, very rich, very dedicated human, but a human nonetheless. Superman, on the other hand is invulnerable to almost everything, to the few things he is vulnerable to he still heals from super-quickly, not only can he move super-fast, he can *think* super-fast and therefore is capable of reading *everything* on the planet, and thus at least has the potential to be super smart. Basically, Superman is super-powerful, if not all-powerful, super-intelligent, if not all-knowing, and, as he constantly reminds us, he is *good*. Or at least he is supposed to be good.

Here's the problem then. David Hume (1711–1776) pointed out that there is a serious puzzle about those three qualities, omnipotence, omniscience, and omnibenevolence (being all-powerful, all-knowing, and all-good) existing together in a world with so much suffering and evil in it. In Hume's case, his concern was for a God who supposedly has a plan for the world. It's pretty common to think of God as that being who has created a universe according to a plan. We usually call this idea, "intelligent design." We tend to believe that the world demonstrates purpose and complexity, so there must be someone who designed it—after all, how could such a complex and intricate universe just *appear*? But, if God designed the world, why design one with so much evil and suffering in it?

It seems easy to ignore that problem. But to put it really simply . . . God is all-knowing, all-powerful, and all-good. This means that God loves good, and doesn't want people to suffer, God knows that people are suffering, and God can stop that suffering, so why let it continue? The same thought applies to evil. If God can stop evil, knows it exists, and doesn't like it, why let it exist? We call this the "Problem of Evil."

Pretty quickly we reply with something like, "Well there is a plan." But that doesn't fix anything. We say that because we don't understand "all-powerful." If God is all-powerful, then God can make the plan happen *without* evil and *without* suffering. We can't say that God *must* allow evil for the plan, because if God is all powerful the word "must" doesn't apply. Simply, God could just make the plan happen without the evil. If we say God can't do that, it sounds like God isn't all-powerful. The same problem applies to Superman. If Supes is supposedly so good, then why does so much evil still occur in the world?

Another answer to the Problem of Evil is "free will." We like to think that since we have free will that we are the cause of evil in the world and God must allow it if he is going to play by the rules. So it isn't God's fault that evil exists, it's ours. But that argument doesn't work because there are all kinds of evil that have nothing to do with humans. In other words there are all kinds of terrible tragedies out there that have no human cause like tsunamis and earthquakes. In these events many children who have done no harm to anyone die.

Think of all of the events that don't even involve humans at all. Imagine a situation in a desert with no humans at all where an animal dies of thirst, slowly and painfully without any other animals around to even eat the body. It just suffers and then dies. What purpose might that suffering serve? In Superman's world this kind of stuff happens all the time. Superman could run around forests and deserts at light speed saving suffering animals that die for no reason. If he doesn't, he allows suffering to happen because he's too lazy to stop it.

We might answer this whole thing by saying something like, "No! Free will means that we are the original cause of sin and evil in the world. All that suffering, even the suffering that has nothing to do with humans is the result of human beings choosing sin in the Garden of Eden." But again this doesn't really work. It's only human arrogance that makes us think that we are the original cause of evil. If the Garden of Eden story is true, then evil was already in the world before humans chose to commit any sin. Evil existed in the form of the serpent. So we can't be said to be the first. Sure, we might be pretty evil, and clearly we choose it a lot, but that only makes God, and Superman, more culpable for not stopping us. Any time Superman allows an evil event or allows suffering to occur, he isn't being all that super is he?

Well, perhaps God doesn't have to answer to the above problem. We can just give up and say, "It isn't up to us to know the mind of God" and choose to believe anyway. Superman, however, does not get that kind of easy escape from the problem. Since Superman isn't the all-knowing creator of the universe, he doesn't get to say, "Oh well I made everything so you just have to take it on faith that I did everything right and shame on you for even asking or thinking about the problem, and if you try to think about this problem I'll send you to Hell."

Okay, fair enough, so we stop asking questions about God for fear of eternal damnation at the hands of an all-loving being who sends people to Hell for doubting or asking questions. Superman, though, is just being lazy. Superman doesn't really get tired, and could literally patrol the Earth 24/7 to stop as much suffering as possible, which, at the speeds he can move is *a lot* of suffering.

The fact is that every time Superman is out on a date with Lois as "Clark Kent" he is letting someone else out there suffer and die. I guess we could argue that since Superman moves so fast that time basically comes to a standstill over short distances and so when he and Lois are having a picnic Superman can continue patrolling while also talking with her. I imagine that in the fractions of a second between each word he says to her he could zip off, save someone and zip back, but at least as far as the comic universe is concerned that isn't a regular thing he does. So the greater likelihood is that Supes takes time off, but when he does that, people die.

How can Superman claim to be good when he chooses a hot date over saving a life? It stands to reason that how good Superman is, is directly correlated to how much he is willing to sacrifice to stop evil and stop suffering. The reason we think Superman is so good is because he's willing to sacrifice his own life to save others, as he does with Doomsday. If Superman is willing to take time off, even just a moment now and then that could be used to stop a crime, save a child, or do general good he isn't as good as he *could be*. If that choice not to save a life comes at the cost of Superman sitting down for a movie with his girlfriend, then comparatively he is letting someone die so he can watch the newest Avengers film, which really seems not a very Superhero thing to do. Batman, on the other hand, pretty much has given up his entire life to do good. Given that fact, despite the fact that Batman can't do as much good, he is still the hero who, himself, is *more* good.

The Best Laid Plans of Supermen

Another major problem that gods have, particularly all power-ful gods who have a plan for the universe is that we all know that we are part of some great plan. Therefore, everything that happens, even if it's pretty bad, isn't really that bad because it's part of the plan. Kids starving in Africa, homelessness in the US while the rich throw away good food, mass genocide in Rwanda . . . don't worry, it's all part of a plan. We don't have to concern ourselves with it, because if it should be stopped, God would stop it.

So, two major concerns come to mind when we think about gods and their plans: One problem is the issue that we don't have to worry too much about the evil that we do. It doesn't require much of a search through the comics to find moments where the Joker and Lex Luthor remind their respective neme-ses that heroes *need* villains. How bad can Lex feel knowing that on some level Superman needs him? To quote the Joker to Batman . . . "You complete me." How guilty can Luthor really be if somehow Superman's existence justifies the existence of a mass-murdering supervillain?

What if Superman's prohibition against killing provides further evidence of this kind of crazy thinking? Lex knows that Superman *could* kill him. But obviously Lex hasn't been bad enough . . . yet. So Superman acts as a kind of evil litmus test for Luthor. If Luthor does something *truly* evil, Superman will tear his heart out of his chest, but till then, it really isn't that bad! It isn't that hard to think that same way about God. After all, if it is all part of the plan, any evil we do is part of a plan. Soooooo, if I want to burn down an orphanage, then the best way to find out if it is part of God's plan is to *try*. If I fail, then I know God doesn't want it. If I succeed *well then it was all part of the plan.*

Which leads us to one of the biggest problems with having gods flying about: We don't have to feel that responsible for evil at all. Not only do we not have to feel bad about the evil we do, but all the suffering that happens in the world *could be stopped by someone more capable.* We can just leave the suffering of others in "God's hands." I could try saving that kid from the burning building, but why would I when Superman could do it? And, if he doesn't, how bad can I be? After all, I'm just a man. Superman is almost a god, so if he chooses not to, or he can't, how bad can I feel? In other words, if God doesn't stop genocide in Rwanda, why should I? God's far more powerful than I, and if it was really that bad, wouldn't God stop it? What can a pitiful human do to in the face of such evil in comparison with an all-powerful entity?

What if Superman . . . what if gods . . . create an excuse for us to sit on our asses while assuming that someone more capable will take care of doing right? And if bad things happen, then it's part of the plan, and if Superman can't, or won't, stop it, how could I be expected to do so? So Superman is our great excuse. Let the Justice League handle the justice, I should focus on the things I can do something about. I guess this would explain why so many of us will take the time to protest movies like *The Da Vinci Code* or fight gay marriage, but we just can't seem to find the time to stop homelessness in the US or feed all of the starving children around the world. What's funny is, we could do it. We have the means: we have the food. We have the ability, but we choose not to save them. We act almost as if those who are suffering must deserve it, otherwise God would do something about it.

True, there are some who try to do something, but if we were to compare the number of people who will vote for religious candidates who share their values for political office with the number of people willing to go to another country to feed starving children, it's a bit uneven. I can't help but wonder how many of us wear our blood-diamond engagement rings into church when we get married and swear to do God's work. Somehow, we can't find the time to stop suffering, but we are willing to buy diamonds that look pretty and cost hundreds of children's lives and wear them into the space we believe is dedicated to doing good and self-sacrifice for that good. Maybe we do these things because we believe there is someone stronger, better, and more capable of stopping evil than us, so we might as well chill in the meantime.

Where Have All the Supermen Gone? ...To Hell

Gods do us one more harm: They make us think we have forever. It's nice to believe in a God that won't let us die. That belief is so important to us that we will kill for it. If someone challenges our belief that we get to live forever in heaven, or wherever, or if their version of heaven differs from our version we occasionally go to war in one way or another. We seem quite confident despite the belief in thousands of different kinds of heaven and God that we will in fact live forever in one form or another. That belief is a bit like having Superman always watching over you. Having Superman in your city must be like having a nice warm safety blanket to cuddle with whenever you are cold that can also rip out the spine of a burglar through his eye sockets.

Lois knows that Superman is always around to save her. Would she take the same risks if her omnipotent boyfriend wasn't around to pull her ass out of danger every week?

If we know that God is always going to be there for us, as long as we follow the rules or believe the right beliefs, how seriously do we have to take our lives and the lives of others? It's odd to realize that a holy war literally absolves one of murder by virtue of doing away with the possibility of killing others. To kill someone in the name of God is technically not to kill them because no one really dies, everyone goes to heaven or hell, so really we are just hurrying them on their journey to the next plane of existence. So not only do we know that we are killing people who've chosen the wrong god, but we also know they aren't really dead anyway and if they were good people we are just sending them to a better place.

There is this prevailing assumption that atheists are less likely to take life seriously and more likely commit heinous crimes. I'm not convinced. Certainly, given the number of people who kill and die in the name of one god or another, there isn't a lot of reason to believe that the belief in God prevents murder and causes one to treat life as precious. In fact, what if our belief in the afterlife makes it possible for us to not worry so much about death? In fact, that seems kind of the point, doesn't it? That we get to not feel too sad when we lose a loved one, and don't need to panic over our own looming deaths, because we get to go somewhere better?

How many of us would call our mothers more often if we *really* believe that this life *might* be it? I'm not even saying that we need to be atheists to ask that question. What if we just thought there was a small chance that we are wrong about living forever. Granted, that is a dangerous belief since any doubt is reason to believe one goes to Hell, but even so, how would we act if we thought we only had one life to live? Might we do more with it? Might we try to be more super? Might we make sure to tell Mom we love her? Would we try to live life to the fullest? I'm not convinced we would all run around murdering each other, as having only one life usually means you don't want to spend it in prison. In fact, consider how many prisoners find God in prison. Might they do so because the thought that their one life might be wasted in prison is just too heartbreaking to bear? So they *need* belief that there will be more time after they die to make their burden tolerable?

I wonder if we would take not just our lives but the lives of others more seriously if we didn't believe that God was going to save us after death. How would we treat the lives of those we love? How often do we hurry loved ones off the phone, yell at a good friend, or ignore a spouse because we assume we have more time? But we all know what it is like to realize we don't have more time. We have all gotten that phone call that someone we love has died. In fact, it's entirely possible that we'll get that phone call today. Do we rush Dad through the same meandering story so we can play video games because we know we will see him later? But maybe we don't see him later. Maybe we'll never see him again. How would we treat our loved ones if we believe this might be the last time we have with them?

Superman Is Dead

Friedrich Nietzsche infamously wrote that "God is Dead." Really, we don't think that he meant it literally. He didn't think there was a God at all. He thought, instead, that God was no longer the best explanation for the world. Explaining how the world works, and how the world came into being no longer required God. So, at least as far as science and philosophy were concerned, to him, God was dead. But let's be real, God isn't dead. Because God doesn't exist for us to explain the world anymore. In fact it's been a long time since we used God to explain the world. We use God for a purpose far dearer to our hearts . . . to make us special.

That desire to be special is why no matter how much evidence there could ever be for God, we would never give up the idea. Just a bit of reflection causes us to recognize that regardless of if God exists, most of us don't believe for any divine reason. We believe because we're scared. We're scared of facing an infinite night. We're scared that we don't have a purpose. We're scared that we're not special.

That is the real tragedy of gods and supermen. We could believe in God because it gives us a reason to be better, kinder, and more loving. We could use it as inspiration to feed the world, to change it, to make it as heavenly as possible. But we don't. Like Luthor and the Joker, we use our superheroes to serve our own ends. We pray to our gods to save us. To help us find better parking spaces . . . to help our team win the big game . . . to take us to heaven. Each of us could be a superhero in the eyes of someone who needs food, water, shelter, or love. But while God is alive, we apparently see no reason to be more than what we are. We let the gods be the heroes and beg them to save us.

Maybe it really would be better of God were actually dead to us. Maybe it would be better if we didn't believe in that version of Superman. We would have to be scared then. We would have to be terrified. It would be up to *us* to stop the Luthors of the world. We couldn't wait. We couldn't depend on anyone else to save the day. We would have to make meaning out of our lives before we disappeared into the dark depths of death. And maybe we would view each life as small, but precious—limited, finite, and irreplaceable. What would we be if we refused to believe in Supermen who would save us—that this time is all we get?

Superman does us a disservice. He makes us think we're less mortal than we are. We know that somehow he will save us . . . like believing in God. And because of that, we believe that mortality isn't quite as terrible, not quite as immediate. But the fact is there is no Superman. We may not be saved. Superman does the humans of Metropolis a terrible harm. He makes them feel safer than they are. He gives them reason to take their time and relax. How might those people act if they didn't think he would be there to save them? What would they try to achieve? Might they be a bit more like Batman and try to better themselves?

Maybe we should all be a bit more like Batman and instead of counting on someone else to save us, spend a bit more time trying to save someone else.

The Best Man for Tomorrow

11
Of Bats and Supermen

BEN SPRINGETT

A few miles north of New York City, the sky is cloudless and blue. The air is cool and you can finally do it—you can actually fly. Unaided by any of the usual vehicles that allow humans to move above the ground, like planes or helicopters, you're a thousand feet above the sidewalks, gliding through the surrounding atmosphere. Enthralled by the wonderful feeling of lightness, you find your way around the tallest skyscrapers and look down to see the glistening streets and the miniature people on the sidewalks below.

The pleasure of flying around is suddenly interrupted by bright green laser beams coming from outer space and hitting the buildings below, setting streets on fire. People are now running around frantically and more beams are being shot from above you by a host of noisy spaceships, their engines screaming in a pulsing high-pitched whine: the sound of incoming intergalactic war is being declared on Earth. It falls upon you to take care of this situation and to take action immediately. You fly upwards and collide with one of the spaceships, sending it hurtling back into space.

But wait! One of the spaceships sounds suspiciously like your alarm clock. Your superhuman capabilities suddenly evaporate. You have no such responsibilities and it was all just a dream. Your name is Bruce Wayne and you're about to get up and exercise. Even Batman can only dream of flying like Superman and having the responsibility of looking after the wellbeing of all of humanity. A thousand push-ups should help bring your focus back down to Earth.

Superman is a far superior superhero to Batman. Superman, and not Batman, is exactly the kind of superhero that we'd like humanity to evolve into in the future. If we could direct the course of human evolution, Superman would be a far better goal than the Earth-bound Bat!

The Dream of Transhumanism

Popular fascination with superheroes suggests that we want to improve ourselves and live like our favorite superheroes do. Transhumanism is the cultural movement which aims to make super-human life possible. Were they to meet us, we'd seem like superhumans to the people of the medieval period, whose mortality rate was much lower and who could only communicate about as far as they could shout loud. The point is that we're going to stand in a similar position to the people of the distant future, unable to quite comprehend what humanity will be capable of. One day, humanity might be altogether transcended.

We're starting to see sure transhumanist changes: biotechnology, genetic engineering (designer babies), and enhancement drugs in sports. But would we ultimately rather aim to be like Batman or like Superman? No doubt, we're closer to being like Batman, but Superman represents the more ideal mode of living even if it might seem near-impossible now. Batman is clearly a passable stage, whereas Superman is less so—he looks like the pinnacle of the transhumanist movement.

The aim of the transhumanist movement is to transcend the human condition. Clearly Batman hasn't quite achieved this. He has limitations in what he can do with his body and has to continually work for his abilities (just look at his training regime). Batman may be more hard-working and dedicated than Superman, but transhumanists want to reach a point where we no longer need any further improvements. Superman is certainly one realization of that perfection. Batman's always trying to improve himself so he's basically working toward becoming something like Superman, even if he doesn't realize it. In one respect it may seem as though Superman is less transhuman than Batman because Superman doesn't do anything to improve himself whereas Batman does daily. Batman is in many ways a transhumanist, from the way he exercises to his use of technology he changes himself to become more efficient, effective and powerful. But Superman has already transcended the human race—being unhindered by any of our limitations— whereas Batman hasn't. So the goal of transhumanism doesn't necessarily have to be that we always try to transcend our every condition, only that we fully overcome our condition enough. Superman is a preferable goal for finally transcending the human condition.

There's a crucial aspect of transhumanism in which we want to improve the efficiency and aesthetics of our lives. We want more things quicker and easier to obtain, want to get to destinations quicker, want to be happier, healthier and have more pleasure in our lives, more often. We spend a lot of the time just thinking about how our individual lives might be improved. At some point everybody is asked, "What superpower would you have?" People usually answer super-strength or invisibility or flight . . . My favorite answer I've heard so far has been the ability to boil water for a good cup of tea and not have to wait for the kettle. That makes for a much more efficient beverage in our day-to-day lives. This superpower has become redundant since the advent of instant hot water dispensers. Life not only gets easier for everyone as transhumanism progresses, but we could realize our every dream! We could relentlessly improve every aspect of body and mind and edge closer to having all of those superpowers we've always wanted. Superman seems an ideal goal for transhumanism and more preferable to Batman.

The Nightmare of Eugenics

But maybe we should play it safe. The route to Superman might require millennia of genetic engineering. To become Batman we'd need a nice blue and grey costume and some rope to swing from one building to another. There's a danger that as we proceed with our transhumanist future, toward being Superman, we're running the same risk of eugenics. Eugenics is not to be confused with the 1980s pop band Eurythmics. Eugenics is about improving the genetic quality of the human race through higher reproduction of those with desired traits and reduced reproduction of those with undesired traits. This sounds like Social Darwinism: the view that the fitter should survive. One result of this is that at the level of human behavior, the stronger should see their wealth and power increase and the weaker should be further diminished. Social Darwinism and Eugenics have a bad reputation and rightfully so. Both resulted in the Nazi movement of forwarding the "Aryan" race and the attempted elimination of Jewish people. One worry is that transhumanism is not all that different from eugenics—it seeks to fill the world with apparently fitter individuals who look and can behave a specific way.

With this risk that transhumanism looks like eugenics, should we try and put an end to transhumanism? As we proceed with transhumanism, what's to stop individuals becoming totally self-absorbed and selfish? Won't we end up with a world of self-interested DC supervillains? No. Transhumanism is different from eugenics because it doesn't focus on any alleged sub-group of people. It's focused on the whole of humanity and improving conditions for everyone. Part of the transhumanist movement can work on improving our moral traits. We'll select genes for good behavior, for example. We'll focus on creating and being individuals who want to do good.

Superman should be evidence for Social Darwinism since he has so much more fitness than everyone else. But he isn't, because he acts against such an idea by constantly saving the less fit. Superman is a counterexample to Social Darwinism. It's our fixation on superheroes that shows that we're interested in a transhumanist future without any eugenics or Social Darwinist element to it. We can proceed to improve body and mind.

Embodied Minds

We often hear, even from neuroscience, that there's a brain and there's a body. One, the brain, does the thinking, and the other, the body, just does physical stuff. There's good reason to believe, though, that as our brain is *physical*, it's a *body part* and so we think with our bodies. Not only do we think with the brain-part of our bodies, but we think with the whole body! This way of looking at things is known as the *embodied cognition thesis*, which maintains that individuals *think with their bodies*. Cognition means the ability to think and process experiences. Embodied means that our conscious experience is contained within our whole body and shaped by our environment, not just contained within the brain. The thesis is a general one and applies to anybody with a mind and a body—animals and ordinary humans.

Let's look at two everyday examples of embodied cognition:

1. Lois Lane has an impending deadline on an article at the *Daily Planet*. Thinking about this workload makes her feel slightly nauseous, with the feeling located as a churning in her stomach. As she starts to resume work on the article, the feeling begins to alleviate. Notice how her thought process didn't include just thoughts in the brain—her stomach and nervous system played a role in helping her think about an issue and act on that issue.

2. Alfred Pennyworth is running an errand for Bruce Wayne. Having entered one of the many rooms in Wayne manor, Alfred finds that he has completely forgotten what he went in there for. He physically goes back to the room he was in previously to help jog the recall—a common experience we're all familiar with. Alfred goes a little further and when he returns to the original room he specifically adopts the bodily posture he was in to help with the recall. He was looking out of a window at the grounds of Wayne Manor with his hands on his hips. And there it is! He needs to call Lucius Fox about a delivery of new vehicles to go on the drive.

Exactly how far does our embodiment affect our thinking? In some areas of our lives, the human body may seem totally irrelevant. It might seem that aspects of our identity and our idea of right and wrong don't have anything to do with our body and that what's really important is just the conscious choice that we make. It doesn't seem like our toes have anything to do with our moral principles. But all aspects of the mind are shaped by the body. Maurice Merleau-Ponty (1908–1961) was a French philosopher who claimed that the body is really important to the way we think and affects every aspect of what we think. He believed that rational thinking, including *moral reasoning*, is grounded by our perceptual experience and the situations we experience with our bodies in the world.

Our bodies affect our thinking. Our toes, for example, may not produce "thoughts" but they are part of the whole experience that generates our thoughts and feelings. And if you've just stubbed your toe, you might care less about swearing in public. The study of body language shows that the way you feel and think is heavily influenced just by the positioning of your body. Popular body-language manuals will advise you stand straight with your fists on your hips as this causes you to feel more confident. Feeling more confident will also cause you to reason about yourself differently. You might further conclude that you can carry out certain tasks that you otherwise wouldn't have.

There are examples where people's bodies tell them what to do in moral dilemmas. After the event, the hero can't really rationalize what they did, for example, in the case of Lenny Skutnik. In 1982, the Air Flight Florida 90 had crashed into the Potomac River and, without a second thought, Skutnik dived into the icy water to save a woman he didn't know. An individual's sense of right and wrong is expressed as a feeling in their body that causes them to want to act in certain ways.

Another case is that of Wesley Autrey in 2007. Waiting at a train station, a student had suffered a seizure and fallen onto the railway tracks. Autrey jumped on the tracks and held the student still as a train went over both their heads, saving the student's life. Afterward, Autrey said: "I just saw someone who needed help. I did what I thought was right". Though Autrey says "thought," it's clear he didn't have time to really think it through. His moral actions were expressed through his body, a feeling, and action. Seeing an individual in need, he made a judgment about his bodily capability in relation to the time of the incoming train, the available space and the individual in need of help. The media called Autrey "the Subway Superman" because of his actions.

Autrey and Skutnik carried out good deeds based on instinctive and gut reactions, which is just as much the body as the mind. The more an individual carries out good deeds in day-to-day life, even small ones, the more likely they are to also do so in more serious situations because their actions have become habit. Habits may initially start as conscious actions, but eventually they are done without any thought at all, as the body takes over. We can infer that Autrey and Skutnik have carried out good deeds on a smaller scale in their day-to-day lives, given that their actions in the extreme moral dilemmas were carried out without much conscious thought at all. Batman is an example of someone who's constantly making himself stronger with the aim of protecting others, of altering his body and making it a matter of habit that criminals are crushed and good people saved.

I Fly Therefore I Am

Having thought about the importance of the body of ordinary citizens, how does having a super-body in Superman's case, or an enhanced body in Batman's case (via technology), affect every aspect of the way they experience and think about themselves and the world they live in? If I witness an explosion in the distance, I am a helpless observer. If I can fly and have super-human strength, or have easy access to a Batcopter, then I would see the event very differently. My relation to the situation would change depending on my capabilities.

Merleau-Ponty thought that we discover ourselves in the world, as part of the world. If I find myself assisting someone in need in a situation, I might realize that I want to do good in the world. I might realize this during the act in which I help others. Bruce Wayne is constantly learning about himself in the situations he places himself in. Clark Kent, a domesticated alien, struggled with his powers in his upbringing, and Bruce Wayne, being brought up in Gotham, a city of moral vice, decided to enhance his bodily capabilities as a result.

The bodily capabilities of Batman and Superman transcend those of ordinary people but what does it say about their minds? In changing his body, might Batman be changing his mind? We assume that the two aren't connected, that even if Batman decided to have new cybernetic night vision eyes installed in his head, and super-hearing implants in his ears, that he's only different physically. But that isn't true. He has transformed his relation to the world that he experiences and the way he thinks.

Superman has capabilities that surely shape the way he experiences the world. He's much more self-contained and independent than Batman. Superman doesn't depend or rely on how the environment is or behaves. If a building collapses,

Superman has to do nothing but Batman has to use rope to escape and always be ready for many different possible outcomes. Superman isn't as subject to sudden changes in the environment as Batman is. Their differing capabilities and limitations run deep into the way they think and plan all their actions and the way they continually perceive the world. Their relation to other people is also altered with enhanced capabilities in terms of what they can do to help others.

Being able to fly unaided, and at greater speed, Superman gets involved in more moral situations and bigger ones at that—on a global scale. Moral situations impress themselves on an individual, as they did on the Subway Superman who instantly saw a problem and knew he was capable of solving it. Similarly, world events continually impress themselves on Superman. His history of living on Earth contributes to his reaction to world events now. He grew up with a loving family that invested in him and selected nurturing environments for him. Being able to fly at super-speed makes him feel physically involved in these world events and moral dilemmas.

Batman is able to fly with the help of technology and he actively involves himself in the world. His earlier life experiences imprinted on him and he acknowledges this as a motive for increasing and maintaining his enhanced abilities. He's worked on his ability to fly so that he can get involved in local moral dilemmas. Superman can fly without the need for technology. Batman can only ever fly using special equipment. Either way, being able to fly alters our relation with other people—we might be asked to give people a lift more often, for example. The difference between our two superheroes is that being able to fly without reliance on other objects allows an individual to broaden their horizons. Superman is an individual who sees a lot more of the world than Batman. These experiences really make up exactly who Superman is. He can't fly to a tsunami around the world and not be affected by it. Similarly, his ability to fly allows him to see more of the good in the world—never-ending sunsets over vast oceans. To be able to fly unhindered—we want this capability, which is much preferable to Batman's version of flight which relies on rope, gliders, or planes. With a time-span of ten thousand years into the future, we'd do better to aim our transhumanist goal at flying like Superman. There's both an aesthetic dimension as well as one of effectiveness in being able to fly as if in a dream and so to make Superman our transhumanist target.

Can Superheroes Understand Us?

Part of the risk of the transhumanist route is that by changing our embodiment, we'll be changing our very thought process: our reasoning and morality. So we can't be sure what the transhumanist future has in store for us.

Superheroes represent the first glimpse of our transhumanist future. There's actually little reason to believe that a Batman or a Superman would act as heroically as they do given their embodiments. There's little reason to believe that anybody with such embodiments would act in such helpful manners to other people or bother wasting their time with other humans—they might develop into different beings with their own sense of priorities that frankly don't concern humans. Superman seems to be moral enough in the comics, but would we be so if we were to actually become Superman in the future?

As we evolve we leave ourselves behind. In a sense we want to, because it's a sign we've moved on and transcended humanity; do we care about the single-celled organisms we evolved from? Can we care? Though the implication is that if we transcend our species *Homo sapiens sapiens* we'd be similarly justified in not caring about our current selves, this seems wrong. It seems like we should care even though we've moved on.

Batman shows his waning ability to care through his inability to understand others. Given the specific nature of Batman's embodiment (that he continually works at), it's hard for him to understand or empathize with normal individuals! He's good at everything so he can't think like a lazy person! On Marxist readings of Batman, he's upholding class divisions. It's not hard to find pictures of Batman really violently beating up criminals. He apprehends everyday criminals because he doesn't understand nor sympathize with their experiences—that they live in conditions which don't help them to realize their full potential in life and that the actions of criminals are the result of their embodiments just as much as Batman's are.

Batman's embodiment allows him to do whatever he wants. He has the finances to develop weaponry to increase the strength of his embodiment. His lack of capacity for self-doubt that most ordinary people have leaves him without many restraints on his actions. With extraordinary strength of will, he's unlike most other humans. His different embodiment allows him to forge and feel a different set of morals to others, which causes conflict with the local police, best seen in Nolan's *Dark Knight* Trilogy.

We might actually expect this lack of understanding from superheroes, given their altered embodiments. It seems like the more transhuman Batman becomes through his efforts of increasing his embodied capabilities, the less he understands ordinary humans.

But Superman does appear to understand us to some extent, as evidenced by his behavior. He's open to our value system. We might think that the difference in Superman's body would result in him not understanding us at all—because of the close relationship of mind and body and his embodiment being so different. He's able to think and read with super-speed, able to fly over us, looking down at us like ants. How could this not affect the way he perceives us? But he does appear to at least try to understand . . .

The authors of comics assume that superheroes would act like us—good and bad people, selfish and selfless. It may be another character from the DC Universe, Doctor Manhattan (of *Watchmen*) who's a more accurate representation. He's a character who suffers the usual radiation accident but comes out with qualities only seen in quantum mechanics (amongst other abilities, he's able to be in two or three places at once). By the end of the movie (spoiler alert) Doctor Manhattan becomes completely uninterested in the human race. He doesn't hurt humans but he's completely indifferent and unmotivated to understand them! This is a result of his embodiment. He's able to see many more world affairs and human actions than most other superheroes and his own bodily capabilities start to move him away from caring about the human race. Might a godlike figure such as this simply realize that humans don't matter? In a sense, this may be desirable—transhumanism, by its very definition, wants us to transcend the human race.

Superman does save us, despite his radically different embodiment in terms of his capabilities. So assuming that superheroes do help others, as the comics suggest they do, that draws transhumanism and Social Darwinism apart, making transhumanism a potentially good project. You can get to a super-fit stage and still want to help others. Superman may not fully understand us but he seems to be sympathetic to the human race. As far as we can tell now, this is a trait that we want to keep into our transhumanist future!

The Problem of Superhero Minds

Is it superheroes (like Batman and maybe Superman to some extent) who can't or don't want to understand us, because of the difference in embodiment, or is it we who can't understand superheroes?

Is it impossible to understand what it's like to undergo the experiences of Superman? The usual way of reading Superman is as though he's just like a human with advanced powers. But sometimes his actions may remind us of the possibility that nobody has any idea how he thinks at all. He's an alien, after all. This may make it as difficult to imagine his experiences as that of any animal.

In a very famous philosophical paper, Thomas Nagel asked "What Is It Like to Be a Bat?" Nagel's idea is that, because of the different body shape and abilities of the bat, we're even more incapable of imagining what it might be like to be a bat than imagining what it's like to be the human seated next to us. I'm asking: what is it like to be Superman? He has the superficial shape of a human, but since he can do much more, how can we be sure what it's like to be Superman?

A traditional problem of philosophy is the problem of other minds. The person sitting next to us may have all of the behavior of someone with a mind, but how can we really know for sure that they do have a mind—that they have any conscious experience *at all*? The problem of *superhero* minds is similar to the problem of other minds with an added complexity of working out what the reasoning process of superheroes is. Unlike the problem of knowing what it's like to be a bat, we share with superheroes an ability to use language and reason about our actions. But if their reasoning process is embodied and their bodies are radically different, how could we know how superheroes think any more than we could know how bats think? Superheroes appear to do morally good actions—but how can we know why they do what they do? Superheroes could tell us what they're thinking, but how could we be sure we're even talking the same language? These are crucial questions to ask because superheroes represent our future!

Since Superman has such a different embodiment, we understand him less than we understand Batman, who's just a more efficient human. It turns out we don't understand superheroes as well as we thought we did! The only way we can come to understand what it's like to be a superhero is to become one ourselves. We will do this via transhumanism. There's a risk that we'll no longer understand human beings, but that may just be part of the process of moving on and evolving, in the same way that we can't relate to the single-celled ameba we evolved from.

The truth is that we don't really know for sure what we'll behave like or exactly how we'll think when we have superpowers. Given the close relation between mind and body, we should expect the way we think to be as different as our bodily capabilities are different. Transhumanism seeks to alter our embodiments. Superman, not Batman, is the goal of transhumanism. It's not so much that Superman doesn't understand us, but we who don't yet understand what it is to be in the position of having transcended humanity. Traveling on the transhumanist road won't be an easy one, but we're already on it and Batman is no place to stop.[1]

---

[1] My two chapters have undergone their own transformations. I was helped to move them along by these people: Nicolas Michaud, Ryan Beeston, Roger Sabin, Faith Springett :-), the Gould families (including Bob), the Bootle family, Carmino D'Agostino, Kim Smith, (A)Lex Bethell, the audience at a conference in Windsor and Victoria Ross, my Lois Lane.

12
Vigilante Wanted

CHRISTOPHER KETCHAM

It's our third and final round of seasons of dust storms in this old Kansas town. Final, well we don't know the dust that began to blow ten years ago is going to end at the end of this year 1940, but it is our end, my end. Me and my family are in our car, waiting and watching as the bulldozers of foreclosure knock down our home and barn. We done sold the livestock, what was left of it, last week for next to nothin'. We ain't got more than a few dollars of gas. We ain't goin' far, not like those who went to California and worked the orange groves for nothin'. No, we're to my gram's place in town. It's gonna be crowded there in that little house and she's just barely holding on too because the general store she took over the runnin' of after my grandfather died is just barely holding on in the little town.

My daddy says it don't pay to get angry no more. But I'm angry, angry at the bank that foreclosed on the farm. Dunno what they're going to do with this dust-bitten wasteland but we still called it home. Sister coughs a lot 'cause of the dust, and that gets me angry too. We lost the baby a few years ago to the cough in the second round of storms; sis's sounding the same. Won't be any better in town.

The preacher at the church—he's new 'cause the other died last year; he was old. The new one's young and he preaches forgiveness. He says the dust's God's will but we can't blame God. I think that's just garbage. Then he says it ain't just God, it's us! The people out here let the dirt get kicked up by the wind that came 'cause they didn't know what they was doin'. I say that's garbage too, but I'm just a kid. I seen how hard they all worked. If you work hard, the preacher says, that's good and you get God's love 'cause of that. They all who been repossessed and my family and me, we all worked hard. Now it's gone. "Whaddya got to say to that?" I say in my head to the preacher.

I keep thinkin' I wanna hire a vigilante who'll come to town and burn down that bank which is the biggest cause of our troubles after the dust. Can't do nothin' about the dust, but the bank's another matter. In the picture shows we used to go on Saturday afternoons in town at the Bijou across from the bank, sometimes there's a vigilante who rides into town and saves the damsel in distress or kills all the outlaws who have taken over the town. Sometimes it's an evil sheriff who needs taking down. Always the bad guy's somebody who thinks he's got the right to boss everyone else around or take their stuff. Until the vigilante comes, nobody has any peace and the town or the ranch just seem to founder. It's like that here in our little town. Even the Bijou is closing. We and the owners want it to stay open, but there ain't enough townsfolk to keep it goin'. They're sayin' they'll open back up when there'll be good economic times again which is when we will be in the war in Europe against the Nazis. I doubt it.

See, even though I can't do much about it as a kid, I think it's time that someone did something about that bank. It closed once when the there was a run on it, or so daddy said, in 1930. But then folks from back East who had cousins in town opened it back up when the laws again got favorable. As I see it, it has been their one aim to take all the lands of the county for themselves. For what, dunno, but there is the principle of the thing that's got my feathers up. You just don't go about stealin' another fellow's land, or so they say in the movies. Even the preacher says that the Bible says, "Thou shalt not steal." I agree, it ain't fair. Ain't fair and I wanna figure out how to get it stopped. I figure if the bank building is blowed up or burns down the eastern banker folks'll move back and leave us alone.

You Got to Choose, Boy

The movies we seen every week didn't get the folks' backs up on all this foreclosin'. Most just moved out. What's left in towns or on the farms is just hanging on to what they got. Everyone's kind of mopin' around, stooped over, even when there's no wind or dust. It's all kind of gray now too.

When we got to cleaning out the house for the move, Momma said I could take one box and one box only from the closet full of comics I send away for that comes in the mail. I earnt every one myself by doin' extra work on the farm and for others that wasn't my chores. So I sat down and spread all them comics out. Seems like they's the only color left in the county. Mostly Batman and Superman. Some others, but the others went in the pile to burn with other stuff we didn't want the bank to bulldoze away. We got our pride still.

I decided, because I just did, that I was gonna keep only the one superhero who could become the vigilante I needed to blow up the bank. A kid can dream, can't he? You hear stories all the time in the dime novels and stuff Dad reads now and again in the paper about the person who wishes hard enough and gets it. Well, I'm wishing hard enough. So you got to understand how I figured out who was gonna be my vigilante.

Sure I thought a bit about what the preacher said about forgiving the other who done you wrong. But I seen the bank president when he handed Pa the papers. He just shrugged his head and said, "It's the law." Do you give a guy like that forgiveness? So I'm done with the whole forgiving thing, for now. So here's how I done it—how I decided whether I would take Batman or Superman with me.

What about Superman?

What's really good about Superman is he's one of us, well sort of. Clark Kent grew up in Smallville, Kansas. I got to thinkin' that it just may have been our town, but I never knowed anyone named Kent who lived here. Maybe it was a long time ago—a long time before the dust got here. You see, he knows what's what with livin' in a small town and on the farm and stuff. Yeah, he can fill the barn with hay faster than any of us could, but he got grit in his teeth. That's before he moved to Metropolis to work for the big-city paper. That's a mark against him, you know, as a vigilante that is.

I can see Clark Kent in the place back East where the bankers come from and him listening to them tell him how wonderful they are. "Nope, we ain't taking nothin' from the little guy that ain't rightfully ours," I can hear them bankers saying, "but these farmers got to be running a business like the rest of us. You just can't take loan monies and not pay 'em back." And there's Clark Kent in his black suit and skinny tie scribbling away on his notepad even though he's got a mind that remembers everythin', though he's forgotten everythin' about how hard it was for his parents back on the farm in Kansas. So, I put all the Superman comics in a box and stare at the box a bit. It's like I'm seein' a seesaw, Clark Kent on one side, and the man of steel in the blue and red suit and cape with the huge S in front on the other. As they balance, my mind sees one then the other inch closer to the ground. I can't make up my mind thinkin' just about Superman.

So I go to my Batman pile and begin thumbing through the issues, one at a time from the beginning, his beginning as a kid who becomes an orphan. Well, so was Superman, an orphan. See, I keep going back and forth trying to unbalance the see-saw. Well, I got two seesaws going now. One with Clark Kent and Superman and another with Bruce Wayne and Batman.

So What about Batman?

So, I went to sleep. You see we had about a week before the bulldozers would come, so I had plenty of time to think my thoughts and make my decision. That week I keep having this dream, a nightmare of me as little Bruce Wayne watching his parents die in a darkened alley, shot down by a crazy robber who disappears into the darkness, leaving me an orphan. But he ain't like the orphans of the Charles Dickens novel I read in fifth grade. No, this kid, me in the dream, is the richest kid on the planet. But then I realize after I wake up that these riches aren't helping him sleep neither, 'cause the evil and the horror stays with him, smoldering like the stump Daddy burned last fall that smoked clear through the winter. Batman come a year after Superman so I ain't had him in my head as long as Superman, but I get what he's about. So I'm thinking about it hard and it comes to me.

Superman may have drifted. Maybe he's listened to the bankers out East too much, but Bruce, on the other hand, Wayne's the real deal. He's everything I've come to hate. He's rich like the bankers, he's babied—let's face it he's got more than you and I'll never dream to have—more than any one person deserves to have. But he hates the killer of his parents as much as I hate the rich bankers from out East. Like me, he hates evil and wants revenge.

Then I am thinking real hard about Wayne and Batman on the seesaw. I hate what Wayne is whether he was born into his riches or not. Sure he hates evil. But let's face it, his evil is a crazed bandit who killed his parents. But he can't find this bandit. Wayne and Batman ain't fighting bankers or dust storms like me. No. Batman's fighting carnival sideshow freaks and other creatures that we could only come up with in a bad dream. Think about it: the Joker, the Riddler, and the Penguin? We got far more real evil-doers to deal with than these creatures. Then it come to me that Batman's revenge is directed at clowns, evil clowns. How can I ever respect that? Who would ever want a person who fights clowns to be a vigilante for him?

I'll Be Aroun' in the Dark

Daddy bought John Steinbeck's *The Grapes of Wrath* last year cause everyone said you got to read it. When he got done with it he lent it to me. Wow. There's my vigilante. I'm keeping this book 'cause I can.

See we have Tom Joad. He's no superhero, just a regular guy you'd find just about on every farm in our county. Tom's lost his home like us but in the dustbowl down in Oklahoma and has gone to California to the orchards with his big family to work for wages that don't feed nobody. Then he rebels. He's out to get the camp bosses and their goons. And he works behind the scenes and one night he comes home and says to his ma, "Then it don' matter. Then I'll be all aroun' in the dark. I'll be ever'where—wherever you look. Wherever they's a fight so hungry people can eat, I'll be there. Wherever they's a cop beatin' up a guy, I'll be there. If Casy knowed, why, I'll be in the way guys yell when they're mad an'—I'll be in the way kids laugh when they're hungry an' they know supper's ready. An' when our folks eat the stuff they raise an' live in the houses they build—why, I'll be there. See?"

That's my superhero, for sure. He's got everybody who needs somethin' in him and he's the vigilante I could surely use right now.

I Need to Look Different at It

So I am thinkin' back to last year in class where we read Shakespeare. I liked Hamlet, could relate to him. He couldn't make a decision neither, but he was tryin' to figure out how he was goin' to take down his evil stepfather who kilt Hamlet's father and married his mother. But in the end Hamlet was kind of a goof. He kilt the wrong guy and eventually got kilt himself. That's not how I want to see this go. I'd rather have a Henry the Fifth, you know the king who invades France and yells, "Once more into the breach" as he begs his tired soldiers to once again get it together and defeat the French for the glory of England. The odds were against Henry at Agincourt, and we knows that Henry didn't altogether defeat the French at Agincourt but they give him the crown anyway. I want a vigilante like that!

Sure Batman is a quiet stalker and he has all sorts of contraptions to foul up the French lines. But do I have any guarantees? And have you ever seen Batman against more than just a few people? This is the whole French Army! I'm thinkin' that Batman hasn't got much of a chance here.

I turn to Superman. Hell, he can blow the entire French line off a cliff with one breath. There's no other choice. It must be Superman. So then I say to myself, go ahead, ask him. I'm hesitatin'. I'm kinda stumped. Superman's got to have a very good reason why he should blow the French off the cliff. Superman ain't gonna drop everything to fight a battle he don't understand. And that's the problem with all of this, ain't it? My vigilante has to be just as angry as me or at least have a very good reason why he's gonna take down the bad guys. So you see, whether it's blowin' the French off the cliff at Agincourt or blowin up the bank, Superman's got to have a pretty good reason. No, it can't be just that we got repossessed and our house bulldozed by the bank that everyone, even Daddy, says has the legal right to knock it down. I'm beginnin' to feel like Hamlet. Every time I come up with a contest to find out whether Batman or Superman'll win, I don't get no answers. I go back to thinking about the bank job again. Well, it's all I got, really.

So it's back to Batman. I figure that as the bank is burning down I can take the money from inside and give it to Batman. Then I realize he has lots of money, doesn't need it, can't be bribed. He'll see right through me.

Like Hamlet, again, I'm stuck, so I'll sleep on it for a few days. I ain't got a few days. Tomorrow's the last day when I need to decide—which box do I keep, Batman or Superman?

What about Lex Luthor?

Both superheroes got the same arch-villain, Lex Luthor, and he come into my dreams that last night. He's evil to both of my superheroes. He's evil like the bank president who rode behind the bulldozers in his fancy sedan after he give us the papers to say that he could take down our home.

Luthor, like the bank president, is a coward, slinging his technology around while he hides out in his city suspended from a dirigible. Well, not the bank president, he ain't got a dirigible that I know of. But I'm thinkin' if we could put up a picture of the bank president next to one of Lex Luthor, I'm sure Superman would see that this bank president is as evil as Luthor.

I'm kidding myself, so I tell myself. I got to decide now. Dad has started the bonfire and Momma's yelling for me to bring down junk to burn. Soon she'll be up when I don't come down. I'm panicking or at least my heart's pounding now.

I want justice just like in the movies; I want revenge just like Hamlet. But I would just really like our home and farm back. I want to tear down the bank president's building as ours is about to be torn down. Is that justice? I think so, just as much as Henry V wanted justice for all the wrongs the French had done to England over the course of their hundred years' war. It seems like we've been battling dust and bankers for what seems like a hundred years, or at least as long as I can remember. But I'm just a kid still.

So I do what they do in the movies and what momma's been doing with us every night and that is to pray to God for rain and a good crop and that if we get it all we won't ask for nothin' from you ever again. Amen.

So I promise. I promise that my revenge will be fulfilled when I see the flames of the bank glow in the night. My days of searching for a vigilante will be over. Justice will be done.

I hear Mom's footsteps on the stairs. My mind races. I could, of course, ask Luthor to help. He just might help me but at what cost? I'll be ever in his debt, and he'll have me do things

I'll really regret and get me caught and thrown into jail or worse yet, hanged. Then like the preacher in Sunday School said, I'll escape one pact with the Devil . . . well Luthor, but the preacher don't talk about Luthor. But the preacher says that if we done wrong to someone and kept up the anger and revenge, we'd have to cover up the crime we made in our anger by doing another crime and this will go on and on until we are goin' to burn in Hell for sure.

So I think I'll write to DC Comics to get Superman and Batman both at the same time to go after and take down Luthor—after, of course, he burns down the bank. But there just too many risks involved. Besides Superman and Batman need an enemy and the writers aren't going to kill off Luthor because a kid wants him gone.

My mind's racin' as I hear mother clear the landing. The bank's made of stone. Batman, for sure, would have something to blow it up but he might leave bat-bomb residue behind, some evidence that would get back to me. Superman only needs to fly low over the bank building and knock the thing over with one swish of his cape. Nobody would ever know what that streak was in the sky. Probably nobody'll get a picture of him doin it. Besides he'd use his x-ray vision to make the picture go black. Nobody would suspect Superman . . .

Superman's the better vigilante, ain't he? But he's so damned good and honest I don't know how I'm gonna get him to help me. But he's all I got.

Mom appeared at my door. "Ready," she asked? I shoved my Batman box and the comics I was already gonna burn over to the side. "These can be burned," I said bravely.

After the Burning

So, now it's done. Batman got burned. I'm kind of sad because he didn't do nothin' to hurt me. He just wasn't what I needed at the time. So I just let him go. I keep wondering whether superheroes can forgive. Do they need to forgive? I can't see Wayne forgiving the guy who killed his mom and dad. Maybe that's why I let him go get burned up. Maybe I was getting' tired of all that anger and hate against the bank and their meanness to us and to all the others. Maybe it's time I move on from this and give up the hate. Maybe that's what I done when I give up Batman and Wayne. I dunno.

It's crowded at Grandma's. It's starting up again, you know, the blowing, and Momma is putting the wet towels in the window cracks. Dinner will be gritty and sis will cough and cough. Maybe I kept Superman not 'cause he's a better vigilante but 'cause he got me to thinking about holding back my anger like the preacher said. Maybe he's the kind of strong the preacher says we should be even when the bad is so bad you can't stand it. Yeah, I'm done with Wayne and Batman. But Superman's no longer the same for me. I'm thinkin' his thinkin's too much like mine. Maybe I need to move on from him too.

I can see the bank from my window. It's gray like everything else is with window bars and a painted sign, weathered from the dust that has blasted most paint away. It don't look all that big and bad any more. In fact it looks poorly like the rest of the town. It's funny how that goes. You get all angry and want to act right away against the guy that hurts you and then the hurt kinda fades away.

So I guess I'll forget about the vigilante stuff for now. But I don't know whether I want to go back to readin' Superman any more. He, like that sign on the bank has kind of faded too. Why? I guess cause he's a me that was, like the farm, like the old house and our barn, and Batman who probably's just dust in that wind that's howlin' down the street.

13
Time to Choose

NATHANIEL GOLDBERG AND CHRIS GAVALER

Imagine that Lex Luthor and the Joker have teamed up to rob a bank. After emptying the vault, they rig two bombs, each ready to kill hundreds of innocent people. Superman and Batman arrive just in time—or *almost* so. Each superhero has to choose: either catch a villain or defuse a bomb. Luther is headed for his rooftop helicopter, the Joker for his basement escape tunnel. Their bombs are ticking at opposite ends of the lobby. What do Superman and Batman do?

Tick

The answer to that question reveals fundamental differences in their moral codes. Though Superman and Batman both fight crime, they do so for different reasons. Superman decided from an early age that "he must turn his titanic strength into channels that would benefit mankind" (*Superman Chronicles* 4). This is a future-focused mission. For Superman, the right thing to do is to bring about the greatest good for the greatest number of people. And, because he's superhuman, he can bring about those consequences better than just about anyone else.

Batman, on the other hand, decided to become a superhero at an even earlier age: "I swear by the spirits of my parents to avenge their deaths by spending the rest of my life warring on all criminals" (*Batman Chronicles* 63). This is past-focused. For Batman, the right thing to do is to fulfill his duty and uphold that oath. Moreover, because that duty involves vengeance, Batman's mission is punishing to others and arguably even to himself.

Superman and Batman are two of the oldest superheroes in comics, and their philosophies have been at odds since their earliest adventures. Each has evolved through the pages of comic books and novels, in episodes of radio and television shows, in video games, and on the big screen. But to get at what's most foundational about their characters, you only have to look at their founding stories. For Superman, that's *Action Comics* #1 (June 1938) to *Superman* #1 (July 1939) anthologized in *The Superman Chronicles* Vol. 1, and for Batman, *Detective Comics* #27 (May 1939) to *Batman* #1 (Spring 1940) anthologized in *The Batman Chronicles* Vol. 1. Those first, defining stories are the best way to see whether Superman or Batman has the better moral code.

Superman the Super Consequentialist

Superman's future-focused, greater-good mission makes him a *consequentialist*. The most famous real-world consequentialist is the British philosopher John Stuart Mill (1806–1873). In *Utilitarianism*, Mill argues that the only thing that makes an action moral is if it brings about the greatest good for the greatest number of people. Mill—and Superman—aren't the only consequentialists of course, and the view as stated is pretty vague. Mill himself winds up understanding good as the presence of pleasure and absence of pain. An action is then morally right if it brings about the greatest amount of pleasure, and least amount of pain, for the greatest number of people. That kind of consequentialism is known as utilitarianism.

Though Superman is a consequentialist, he's not necessarily Mill's utilitarian kind. Superman aims for outcomes like safety, peace, and justice. While these might lead to pleasure and the avoidance of pain, that's not Superman's concern. Regardless, like all consequentialists, Superman thinks that morality has everything to do with positive results, however understood. He wants to "champion the oppressed" (p. 4) to better their lives.

As a consequentialist, Superman is therefore focused not on punishing past wrongs but on creating future rights. When Superman captures criminals, he wants to prevent them from harming anyone else. Sometimes that means incarceration. But mostly Superman prefers reformation, because that can lead to the greater good—for both victims and perpetrators.

In his third adventure, Superman traps the owner of the Blakely Mine in a cave-in so he's forced to endure the dangers of his employees' working conditions. Afterwards, the owner promises that "my mine will be the safest in the country, and my workers the best treated. My experience in the mine brought their problems closer to my understanding" (p. 44). When Superman gives a munitions dealer a taste of his own medicine, the dealer declares: "When it's your own life that's at stake, your viewpoint changes!" (p. 23). This sentiment is later echoed by a once lackadaisical mayor: "You've shown me a viewpoint I never saw before! I swear I'll do all in my power to see that traffic rules are rigidly enforced by the police!" (p. 166). In each case, Superman reforms the wrong-doers, which results in their betterment as well as the betterment of those around them. In all these instances, he's motivated by concern for future well-being.

Superman even devotes himself to aiding others when it doesn't involve battling wrong-doers. He donates his services to a circus to prevent the owner from going bankrupt (p. 88). He knocks down a slum to prevent its "poor living conditions" from causing more juvenile delinquents (p. 108). He cleans out his own savings to purchase worthless stock from people who had been swindled (p. 142). In a special *New York World's Fair* comic, Superman completes the "infantile paralysis exhibit," so the display will raise contributions for those children (p. 172). When destroying the cars of traffic violators, Superman does say: "I think I'm going to enjoy this little war!" (p. 156). That sounds like Batman's "warring on all criminals." But Superman remains results-driven. His "little war" is only a means to the end of improving public safety.

The unimportance of "warring" is also apparent in many of the battles that Superman fights. Unlike Batman's, Superman's battles are often anticlimactic because the criminals are easily defeated. His very first adversary, a nightclub singer who framed another woman for murder, is unable to fire her gun before Superman grabs it from her and forces her to write her confession, saving the innocent woman from execution (p. 199). Likewise, the wife beater he faces next faints before Superman can make good on his promise: "And now you're going to get a lesson you'll never forget!" (p. 9). Though the criminal goes unpunished, the lesson is still learned. And

that lesson—because of the positive outcome it will produce—
is what matters to Superman.

Batman the Dark Deontologist

Batman's past-focused, duty-driven mission makes him a *deontologist* and so a partial follower of the German philosopher
Immanuel Kant (1724–1804). In *Groundwork of the Metaphysics
of Morals* (1785), Kant argues that the only thing that makes an
action moral is if it's done from duty. We have to intend to act in
a way that follows from our obligations. Pleasure, safety, peace,
justice, other sorts of benefits that might result as a consequence
from the action—for Kant, these are all morally irrelevant.

The only thing that matters is intending to act consistently
with what Kant calls the "categorical imperative." In its clear-
est form, Kant's categorical imperative maintains that we must
intend never to use someone as a mere means to some other
end. Our intentions must always respect human beings as ends
in themselves. While Kant doesn't want our actions to make
the world less pleasurable or safe, whether or not they do does-
n't matter morally. It's the intention—and only the intention—
that counts.

To understand what Kant is getting at, we need only consider Batman and his trusty batarang. When Batman throws
his batarang at the villainous Carl Kruger, it's deflected by an
invisible sheet of glass (p. 67). According to Kant, Batman is no
less moral for failing to stop Kruger. You can't blame Batman.
He was just unlucky. In another incident, Batman does have
luck on his side. When fighting the Joker, "Batman side steps.
The killer-clown stumbles forward into the building driving the
knife into his own chest!" (p. 189). Here, according to Kant,
Batman is no *more* moral for succeeding in stopping the Joker.
The two scenes result in opposite outcomes, but Batman's
morality is the same. Good luck, bad luck—these might affect
consequences, but for the deontologist they don't affect morality.

That's because deontologists, from Kant onward, don't
believe in moral "luck." Invisible glass and fumbling forward
can't make someone or thing moral or immoral. Morality does-
n't depend on chance. Because consequences, however, do,
deontologists claim that moral evaluation should itself depend
only on factors within our control. And the only thing that we

have real control over, on Kant's and many of their views, are our intentions. So they're the only things that count in their moral codes.

Nonetheless, what makes our intentions moral, and so gives us a duty to follow them, differs for Batman and Kant. While they're both deontologists, Kant's moral code is based on reason. It's rational, Kant argues, never to intend to treat people as mere tools. By contrast, Batman's deontology is darker. As established by the vow that he makes in his origin story, Batman's code is grounded on vengeance. When Batman swears to avenge the deaths of his parents, his intention is retribution. For the rest of his life, Batman abides by that intention—always (dutifully) aiming to fulfill his oath.

As a dark deontologist, Batman is therefore morally bound to war on criminals, "preying upon the criminal parasite, like the winged creature whose name he has adopted" (p. 99). Like any deontologist, morality for Batman doesn't concern consequences. He's not even motivated to help innocent victims, though that tends to happen anyway. Batman is so focused on his duty that, like Kant, he takes the consequences of his actions to be morally irrelevant. After the Joker murders his first victim, "Henry Claridge, the millionaire," Robin asks: "But Bruce, why don't we take a shot at this Joker guy?" (p. 141). Batman responds: "Not yet, Dick. The time isn't ripe" (p. 142). Nor does Batman do anything as the Joker claims his second victim, Jay Wilde, stealing the "Ronkers Ruby" in the process (p. 143). For Batman, the right time to strike is independent of any good that may result.

In fact, Batman is so focused on his war that he appears almost pleased when the Joker escapes: "It seems I've at last met a foe that can give me a good fight!" (p. 147). Yet Batman's failure to capture the Joker leads to the death of a third victim, Judge Drake. Batman doesn't attempt to save the judge either. He patrols outside Drake's house in the hopes of apprehending the killer after the murder, which he eventually does. Similarly, when the Joker returns in a later episode, Batman waits until two more victims are dead, including the police chief, before acting. Batman does prevent the Joker from murdering his next target, Otto Drexel. Nevertheless, according to Batman's moral code, failing to save innocents is not failing to be moral. Consequences are inconsequential.

Because Batman is focused on vengeance, he needs criminals to show their hand before acting against them. That might seem to explain why he lets the Joker continue killing—so that there's no mistake that Batman is after the right bad guy. Nonetheless, Batman knows from the Joker's first murder that he's a villain. Batman's motivation can't be to wait for the Joker to show his hand. He simply has a blatant disregard for consequences.

In Batman's first year, only one adventure is consequentialist. When Carl Kruger attacks Manhattan in his Dirigible of Doom, "buildings explode, hurling their wreckage upon the crowded streets below" (p. 64). A child shouts: "Help! Mamma, save me! Help!!" After the dirigible leaves, the rescue work begins. "Bruce Wayne helps," lifting a steel girder trapping an "old man." The situation is more typical of a scene from a Superman comic, but note that it's "Bruce Wayne" not "Batman" helping others. Bruce's consequentially motivated aid is not part of his Batman mission. As long as Bruce is helping the needy in the streets, Batman is not pursuing his deontological duty. When Bruce pursues and battles Kruger as Batman, however, his dark deontologist self returns.

Round One: A Philosophical Tie

In some ways then, Superman and Batman are opposites. Superman strives for the greatest good for the greatest number of people. Along the way, past wrongs might be righted. In that sense, Superman might be thought of as avenging the innocent. But that's beside the point. Superman has instead devoted "his existence to helping those in need!" (p. 196).

Batman, by contrast, is duty-bound to vengeance, consequences be damned. Even if Gotham eventually became irredeemable and all its citizens criminals, Batman would still continue his war, even though no one would benefit. He's duty-bound to his oath. That innocent people often do benefit from Batman's actions is for him beside the point.

Admittedly, as members of the Justice League, Superman and Batman eventually team up. Though they subscribe to different moral codes, their differences don't get in the way. They just fight crime for different reasons. Regardless, Superman and Batman *do* have different codes. In fact, "super" consequentialism and "dark" deontology disagree on too much for both to be correct. Which moral code, and corresponding crime fighter, is superior?

Each theory has something going for it. Deontology's main advantage is that, to do the right thing, Batman doesn't need to depend on anything beyond his rational control. As often as fortune smiles on us, misfortunate frowns, and Batman's theory can accommodate that. Moreover, that appears to be the right attitude for Batman to take. While being lucky or unlucky is one thing, being moral or immoral does seems like something altogether different. While Superman needs to keep in mind how others will act and what affects his actions will have on them, Batman's deontological reasoning focuses only on him.

Meanwhile, consequentialism's main advantage is its future orientation. Regardless of Superman's intentions, his action is moral so long as it makes the world a better place. Consequentialism isn't held hostage by past oaths or anything else. Every day can be a new day for Superman. Batman, conversely, is imprisoned by his past. And whether it's based on vengeance or, in Kant's case, reason, once a duty is established, it's supposed to guide action—not for the future's sake but for duty's own sake.

Though consequentialism does have the benefit of its future orientation, it nevertheless faces the problem of moral luck, which deontology avoids. Remember Batman and his batarang. Deontology says that whether or not glass blocks his batarang is morally irrelevant. It's Batman's intention that counts. As a consequentialist, by contrast, Superman must recognize that luck can come into moral play. In fact, when a villain dies in a Superman story, the outcome is presented as morally appropriate. When Superman is leaping with a mobster in his arms, the mobster attempts to stab him. As a result, "Superman smashes against a nearby building, instead of alighting on it as he had intended," and the mobster falls to his death. Superman explains: "If he hadn't tried to stab me, he'd be alive now. —But the fate received was exactly what he deserved!" (p. 185). The outcome is what mattered, even though it was accidental.

Likewise, sometimes Superman succeeds through lucky timing, as when he leaps atop a passing train for no apparent reason and then just happens to overhear an important conversation. Superman thinks aloud: "A crooked coach hiring professional thugs to play football! —Sounds like just the sort of set-up I like to tear down!" (p. 48). And so he does tear it down. Superman the consequentialist thinks that he does the right thing, even if what he accomplishes is helped by chance.

When it comes to moral luck, many philosophers side with Batman. They have difficulty understanding how something outside our control can make us moral. Deontology seems to have the upper hand simply by responding that it can't. While Batman has his share of good and bad luck too, none of it matters morally. Doing the right the thing just means fighting the good fight, regardless of whether you win or lose or good or bad luck intercedes.

The possibility of moral luck seems to be a problem for consequentialism. And it would be a problem for Superman, were it not for one thing. Superman is no mere consequentialist. He's a *super* consequentialist. Superman is so powerful that he can limit the effects of fortune—or misfortune—on his actions. He's is still vulnerable to luck, but his superpowers go a long way to smoothing it over.

It's bad luck when Superman "braces himself against the rail—and in that second it gives way! He is flung twisting and turning, into the ocean!" (p. 21). The thugs think he's drowned, but of course he's back in action and out-swimming the ship. When it docks, "Superman subjects the toughs to the severest thrashing of their lives!" (p. 22). A moment's bad luck makes no difference to the final outcome. Nor should it, given Superman's "super" consequentialism. While there is something fishy about moral luck, Superman's superpowers allow him to control for a lot of it. He's less subject to fortune or misfortune than the rest of us.

Nevertheless, if you apply consequentialism to Batman, he also turns out to be pretty darn "super." Although he can't deflect bullets the way that Superman can, Batman "trains his body to physical perfection" and his intellect to the level of a "master scientist" (p. 63). Add in his seemingly unlimited financial resources, and Batman can counter bad luck almost as well as Superman. True, Batman does suffer more bullet wounds and knock-out blows to the back of the head during his first year than Superman does in his, but all of their adventures end essentially the same: with the superhero victorious. Batman doesn't care about moral luck, because, as a deontologist, he doesn't believe in it. Nonetheless, he's nearly as immune to luck generally as Superman is. So Superman's superpowers aren't what separate him morally from Batman.

Round Two: Super Knock-Out!

There's one area where Superman clearly does beat Batman. Consequentialism casts a broad net over who's morally relevant. Namely, everyone is. Aiming to get the greatest good for the greatest number of people, Superman is out to benefit all humankind. His super consequentialism makes it more likely that he actually can.

By contrast, Batman's dark variety of deontology casts so narrow a net that it really only includes himself. That's why victims play such a small role in his early stories. Otherwise readers might notice Batman's indifference to their existence. When Batman battles a gang of jewel thieves, their intended targets are named—"the Vandersmiths," "the Norton home" (14)—but the individuals are never shown. Also, they're only threatened with the loss of property. Were Batman concerned with the greatest good for the greatest number of people, stopping thieves from robbing millionaires would be low on his list.

In fact, Batman is failing the greater good every time he selects an adversary who poses a lesser threat. Consider Professor Strange, "the greatest organizer of crime in the world," who targets faceless companies: "The Case National Bank reports a loss of $250,000, and the Bond Exchange Bank $100,000" (p. 102). Strange's thugs don't even harm the night guard. As it turns out, that guard is Batman, who disguised himself because he needs to fulfill his oath to fight criminals, no matter the level of threat or amount of good that each battle might bring about.

In Batman's world, victims sometimes aren't even victims. After Batman rescues "Joey" from a gang of thugs torturing him, he knocks Batman out and guns down the thugs himself, because they had found out he was double-crossing their mobster employer. While Superman might have tried to reform Joey, Batman doesn't even attempt to save him when the boss later stabs him to death (p. 118). Batman has a self-centered duty to fulfill his oath, and the well-being of others just doesn't matter.

Admittedly, Batman is a *dark* deontologist. Other deontologists can cast broader nets if they'd like. Kant himself claims that we have a duty never to intend to use people as mere means. But even that duty is a duty about what *not* to do. Kant can't generate from his system the duty to *help* all humankind, even if he tried. Other deontologists are likely as restricted. So, not only does Batman himself cast the narrowest of nets. Odds are that, even appealing to other deontological resources, Batman could never cast a net as broad as Superman's.

But should superheroes cast broad nets? We non-superheroes can't always be looking out for all humankind. And even Superman needs to sleep. Nevertheless, the thing that morally separates superheroes from the rest of us isn't their powers or utility belts. It's what we've come to expect from them: always having the welfare of others in mind above all else. Batman does achieve a lot of good for other people. But it's a side effect, not his core mission. Despite how much good we see Batman do, his moral code is itself the problem. Regardless of how many people either of them can save, Batman's philosophy is inferior because it allows for situations in which he'll let others die.

Tock

Let's return to the example we started with. After robbing a bank together, Lex Luthor and the Joker placed two ticking bombs, each set to kill hundreds of innocent bystanders. Superman and Batman each have to choose whether to catch a villain or to defuse a bomb. Based on his stated mission to "benefit mankind," and his subsequent actions during his first year in *Action Comics*, Superman wouldn't think twice: he'd defuse Lex Luthor's bomb, allowing Luthor to escape in the process. But Batman, based on his mission-defining vow of "warring on all criminals," and his adventures in his first year in *Detective Comics*, would make the opposite call. Batman's deontological job isn't to help people but to catch villains. Though it would mean letting hundreds of people die, he's duty-bound to chase the Joker.

So forget dark deontology. Superman is superior to Batman because he strives directly for outcomes that benefit people in need. Only super consequentialism can bring about a brighter tomorrow.

14

Who Watches the Justice League?

JACOB THOMAS MAY

The sky over Gotham is dark, much darker than the usual smog-ridden skyscape that normally clings to the overhang of the city. Batman stands atop the Wayne tower, looking for the telltale glimmer of red he knows is his opponent. *He has changed,* thinks Bruce. *What could have happened? I need to end this quickly and quietly before he causes damage on a massive scale . . . but how?* There, he sees the shimmer of red and blue that used to be as close to a friend as Bruce would ever admit that he had. He flicks a switch on his power armor, opening the hidden lead compartment in his Batsuit. The pulsating glow of the radioactive rock known as Kryptonite bathes his suit in an eerie, iridescent green as he powers up the small engines in his armor and rockets toward the Big Blue Boy Scout. "Why?!?!" he screams toward the heavens as the rain begins to pour. "Just tell me why, Clark! Don't make me do this!"

How does one determine who would ultimately "win" in this fight between heroes? Would the decision be based on strength? Perhaps it would be based on will, or cunning, pure intellect, or toughness. —Or maybe the test of who is greater between Batman and Superman is the one's willingness to do whatever it takes to create a world where justice reigns unchallenged. Both Superman and Batman have killed quite a few people, and both have been beaten to the point of near-death. Both titans are brilliant and have access to technologies that can change the world. They are the heroes, the ones who stop the villains and make the world safer for everyone.

What if . . . ?

But what if they weren't? Imagine a rampaging Superman hell-bent on destruction. Or a Superman who just wanted to rule a slave society. It's also not that far-fetched to wonder what Gotham would be like with a Batman who decided he just wanted to kill every criminal. Or a Batman who used his power, influence, and money to become an all-powerful over-lord. Who would be responsible for stopping either Clark or Bruce then? And if there were someone with that responsibility, would they be capable and willing to meet it?

There are times, as in *Injustice*, when Superman has been envisioned an evil entity; one who was pushed too far by events and could not stay the big, blue Boy Scout we all know and love. This Superman does not care about the lives of others and even goes so far as to punch all the way through the Joker's chest in retribution for causing him to lose Lois and their unborn child (Injustice issue #1 and *Injustice Gods Among Us*).

And what about Batman? There are stories where the caped crusader could have the given the Joker a run for his money when it came to body-count. In those, he was more than happy to go on rampages against the villains of Gotham with guns blazing and casualties mounting. This Batman had no qualms about torturing and killing, going so far with one denizen of Gotham as to hang them up from the Batplane by a noose and proclaim that they were "better off this way" . . . dead (*Batman* issue #1, 1940).

So, although there have been numerous times when these "heroes" of our imaginative world have saved us from impending peril, there have also been times when they were the villains. And while we're more than happy to keep on reading month after month and rooting for them when all hope seems lost, what do we do when they turn their fantastic powers on the very people they have sworn to protect? And what should *they* do if the other goes evil? Should they live in blissful ignorance of the possibility that one day their friends could turn on them, or should they prepare for the day that they hope never comes by preparing weapons of their teammates' destruction?

Both Batman and Superman have contemplated this same conundrum, albeit from differing perspectives. This very question has been brought forth numerous times and in varying formats, most notably in regards to Vandal Savage ("Justice League: Doom") and Ra's Al Ghul ("Tower of Babel"). In essence, we're looking for the "best hero." The better hero is the one who will plan ahead; the one who contemplates every possible scenario that could come about and effectively creates the best "on-call" action plan to combat those scenarios. This hero needs to try and plan for the unplannable; they need to even be prepared should they or their friend decide to turn around and fight against them. We all like to think that Batman is the Great Detective, the man who plans for everything; but when we delve into the darkest corners of the Batcave and the iciest reaches of the Fortress of Solitude, we see that it is actually Superman who is the most prepared (Big Blue Boy Scout, anyone?) There are philosophers who believe that being ethical means thinking about future consequences. We call this worry about future goods and bads (especially those concerning suffering) consequentialism.

How to Become the Hero We Need (Not the One We Want)

Tried and true heroes need to think about the future. They need to plan ahead and try to analyze scenarios they have the abilities to either stop or help stop. They can reduce the number of people who suffer in any given situation—since they have a plan for it ahead of time and can put that plan into action extremely quickly as they are already prepared for it.

According to consequentialism, truly ethical heroes would be the ones who think ahead and try to evaluate most if not all of the what-if scenarios and set out plans for them. In this, they would be acting to reduce the number of people who suffer from any situation and the total overall suffering any specific event will cost the total population. And if they did their job ethically in this respect, then they will come out on top and be the best hero imaginable.

One form of consequentialism is utilitarianism—the belief that we should maximize happiness and minimize pain. Another kind of consequentialism is negative consequentialism. While utilitarianism focuses on how to bring about the most happiness for the most people, negative consequential-ism focuses, instead, on how to reduce the most suffering overall, especially in regards to the future possibilities that may arise. While they may sound like the same thing, there is an important difference between utilitarianism and nega-tive consequentialism: utilitarianism focuses on the happi-ness aspect, while negative consequentialism focuses on the suffering.

Negative consequentialism, then, helps us in trying to pre-pare for and prevent the most possible suffering should one or more of the Justice League members decide to go bad. We've seen that the hero who prepares ahead and has a possible plan also has the potential to put that plan into action more quickly. The faster a hero could respond to this what-if scenario, the less suffering the world would endure; effectively making that hero the best negative consequentialist. Both of our potential heroes seem to follow this code of ethics; they don't try to pro-mote the most happiness, rather they both prevent suffering. They are superheroes after all; they are the ones who save us on a regular basis. So the question then becomes . . .Who's bet-ter at it?

People try to plan for potential outcomes of human behavior all the time. For example, it isn't very difficult to imagine how much suffering could be caused by specific members of the League—especially one as powerful as The Man of Tomorrow—should they ever turn their sights on us. If he ever decided that he was simply done with Earth, Clark could literally just push the Earth into the sun. He has moved bigger objects before (*Worlds Finest*, issue #208, 1941). Seven billion lives . . . gone in the less-than-ten-minute span it would take Superman to fly us into a giant nuclear reactor.

So, how does one plan for the outcome that one day our heroes may turn against humanity and all that they have sworn to uphold and protect? How far are our heroes willing to go to ensure that should they ever turn evil, humanity would still be safe, especially from them? The answers vary, and while both Batman and Superman have valid plans for protecting the world against the other, only Superman is will-ing to go the distance in ensuring that we're truly safe . . . from himself.

Is the Last Son of Krypton a Self-preservationist? (Or Does He Just Want Us to Think He Is?)

We all like to think of the Man of Tomorrow as an infallible beacon of Truth, Justice, and the American way; but what about when he's forced to take a life? In several instances he has been known to cross that line and kill in order to save the civilians who trust him to act for them. The great eighteenth-century philosopher David Hume would look at Superman as being a slave to his emotional state at any given time. Clark is completely controlled by his own emotional state when it comes to making tough decisions; his rationality is simply subservient to his feelings.

We see this very early on in *Man of Steel* when Clark trashes the rig of the guy who tossed beer on him in the bar. His own emotions ruled him in the heat of that moment, so why should we assume he does not have the capacity to turn cape and become a force of evil? Hume would look at Superman's "decision" to kill General Zod as one of necessity and, in the heat of the moment, as completely morally sound. The untested Man of Steel had no recourse but to snap Zod's neck as Zod bore down on a family cowering in fear for their lives. But what kind of impact would killing someone have on an all-powerful being like Clark?

We've seen the outcome of such events in the comics. When Superman banished Mr. Mxyzptlk to the space between dimensions, essentially killing him, he was so distraught that he walked into the secret gold kryptonite room in the Fortress of Solitude, effectively killing himself in the process (*What Happened to the Man of Tomorrow?*). This raises a whole slew of questions: Why would Superman end his own life, knowing we would likely need him in the future? Why would he have been so distraught over killing an evil being? And why did he have all that lethal gold Kryptonite stored in his fortress, anyway?

Hume's own arguments about rationality and passion would have us believe that Superman would be right in killing himself at the realization of what he had done. It could also be argued that Superman would have had no choice in the matter.

In knowing that he had killed, and with the forethought and understanding that he could do it again, Clark acknowledges that the moral line that once guided him was broken. Not trusting anyone else to be able to take him down, Clark chooses to instead take his own life because preventing is the core of what Superman does; *he prevents harm*. Even if this means preventing harm that he himself might do (on quite a massive scale, in fact) it would be the correct choice.

Superman doesn't just stop harm, he has to try and predict future suffering and prevent it. When Superman saw Doomsday marching toward Metropolis leaving devastation its wake, Superman *predicted* that Doomsday would do the same in Metropolis (*The Death of Superman*). Clark didn't know for sure. Perhaps Doomsday just wanted to get an autograph from worldly famous Lois Lane or watch the Metropolis Sharks play football. Heroes do this all the time. You stop a mugger assuming that they will not, immediately after taking the money, confess that they only took it because the money was actually radioactive and they were trying to save lives. So Superman takes his best guess when he sees Lex Luthor, General Zod, or Brainiac, and tries to stop them *before* they do harm. Shouldn't he hold himself to the same standards? We're reminded that heroism, rather than promoting happiness, has us choosing the paths which avoid the most possible suffering. Philosophers such as David Hume and Karl Popper, who both wrote about the virtues of negative consequentialism, would believe that preventing the possible suffering of all the lives Superman could choose to end by, instead, ending his own life was the correct course, even at the expense of all the lives he could have made better by living. This offers up an explanation as to why Clark would store a personally volatile and lethal substance in his own home.

In the recent comic-event-turned-video-game, *Injustice*, the Superman of alternate Earth did much of the same thing. Clark gave the other members of the Justice League the means by which to incapacitate him should he ever turn his glowing red sights on the citizens of Earth. And although the other members of the League were part of the plan, he entrusted the care and housing of the device to Batman alone, keeping the device in Bruce's Batcave. This definitely correlates with Hume's and Popper's ideals that preventing the most suffering is paramount in living a moral life. Superman was committed to giving the other members of the League (people he shares victories, defeats, holidays, sorrows and good times with), and even more so Batman himself (safeguarding the device underneath the lead floor of the Batcave) the means to his defeat. Superman is willing to stand for his own set of negative consequentialist ideals.

Can Batman Trust Anyone? (Or Could That Be His Killing-Joke?)

Many people like to think about the Batman as no more than a rich playboy who puts on heavy armor and beats up the bad guys when they need it. We like to imagine him sitting around in his enhanced vehicles, listening to the police scanner and waiting for things to happen so that he can head out and take action against these criminals. We all forget that Bruce started out as a detective—nay, *the* Detective—and that his powers of deduction are the primary component that makes him such a formidable opponent and worthwhile member of the JLA. Batman made his debut in Detective Comics issue #17 and then became the primary character in the series before becoming a star of his own series. He continued to (and still does in the reboot universe) star as primary lead in the Detective Comics series, lending credence (at first) and then becoming one of the reasons for the backing of his story about being an extremely proficient detective.

In almost every Justice League story—comic, cartoon, or movie—Bruce finds out the identities of the other members of the JLA on his own. This leads him to better know his fellow Leaguers (as well as more *about* them, even if they themselves are unwilling to give up that information), but that doesn't mean he trusts them.

Hume would argue that Bruce's compulsion to investigate crime and potential dangers is necessary in order to obtain a world that is free of suffering and pain. This compulsion is the negative consequentialist ideal that defines Batman to the core. Bruce feels compelled to investigate because he is convinced that it is necessary to determine methods of crushing his enemies—but also his "friends," should they ever need to be taken down. In this, Hume and Popper would stand by Bruce, both cheering him on.

In *Justice League: Doom*, the animated film, and the *Tower of Babel* comic arc, Bruce does prepare to defeat his teammates: he creates counter-measures for each member of the JLA and has them ready should they ever need to be implemented. As Bruce puts it, he only conceived of and created "measures to incapacitate, not kill" the other members of the JLA. This is in standing with modern incarnations of a character who is unwilling (anymore at least) to go the distance and permanently eliminate his enemies. The only problem with his pre-emptive plans is his own arrogance.

Bruce creates plans for Martian Manhunter, Superman, Wonder Woman, the Flash and the Green Lantern; however, nowhere in his reflections and preparations does he create a failsafe for his own persona, the Batman. Is this because he believes himself to be immune to corruption, or does he think that he needs no failsafe because the other members have one for him? In both the movie and in the comic arc, Superman confronts Bruce about this very issue, to which the Prince of Gotham simply replies, "My failsafe is the Justice League."

This—Bruce's complacency or his arrogance demonstrated in failing to create a failsafe for Batman—presents problems, especially when we go back and consider Hume's argument for necessity and negative consequentialism. Hume would suggest that necessity demands that we explore every option for failsafes in regards to the JLA (as Superman did when he enacted his own suicide), but Bruce just falls back on his JLA excuse, hiding behind the other members' capes as a way to ensure his own actions are stopped should he ever turn sides. This is either a display of arrogance or of an oversight that Bruce should have attended to in his plans.

When we look at Bruce's reasons for creating the failsafes (pre-emptive planning to be able to immediately respond to his League members turning evil—a definite example of negative consequentialism), we should note that Bruce suggests his plans were necessary, "should one or all of the members of the Justice League simultaneously become threats." What if they did? If *all* members of the JLA became affected at the same time, that means that he—the Dark Knight, himself—has also become a threat. But in this scenario, how could Bruce rely on the JLA to stop him? He simply couldn't. This reflects poor planning on Bruce's part and ultimately doesn't lend any help to Batman if being a hero means being willing to prevent any possible harm, even harm caused by oneself.

Un-Trusting League (The Heroes We Want?)

So in a battle between Batman and Superman, who wins? At least in this philosophical battle of willingness to make prepare for the future, it is Superman who ends up the victor. Following the ideals of negative consequentialism, Clark is the more ethical superhero. Not only is the Last Son of Krypton willing to go the distance (taking his own life, on multiple occasions), but he's willing to give the power of taking it to others. This shows a notable level of trust: both Batman and Superman, on a regular basis, have to entrust their lives—and those of their loved ones, as they know each other's identities—to each other and other members of the League. The fact that Bruce is either unwilling or unable to entrust his own downfall or demise to his closest friends is something which is kind of arrogantly dictatorial. Superman gives the other members the tools, and in the event that those tools fail, has his own way to ensure his own demise. Batman cannot claim to have such forethought or follow-through in planning; and if he really were the "World's Greatest Detective," you would think he would have at least considered it.

15
Infinite Environmental Crisis

CRAIG VAN PELT

LOIS LANE: Batman, . . . how do you feel about being ranked the number three environmental villain in the world?

BATMAN: What are you talking about?

LOIS LANE: Your use of technology results in constant environmental damage.

BATMAN: What I do is often misunderstood by people.

LOIS LANE: I don't think you're misunderstood. People understand the crisis. People want and need Superman. And people are not willing to settle for your way of doing things.

BATMAN: Miss Lane, you are fishing for your next story. But there is no story here.

LOIS LANE: Are you really going to hop into your Batmobile and drive off like none of this is your fault? The poll ranked you as more dangerous than the Joker . . .

BATMAN: I fight to protect Gotham City. I fight to protect Metropolis. I put myself in harm's way every day to protect the people of this world.

LOIS LANE: Batman, . . . the planet is dying because of overuse and overproduction. You're fighting to protect our way of life . . . but our way of life is killing everything. Don't you see that?

BATMAN: I save lives.

LOIS LANE: You're no better than Lex Luthor. Our skies and rivers are polluted. Our oceans are a disaster zone. Batman, you're stuck in an infinite loop. The more you build . . . the more you take from the Earth. And the more waste you return to the Earth. Why can't you see the real problem? What's the point of saving human lives if we kill the planet?

Batman: Public Enemy

Batman has the best toys when it comes to crime fighting. When Batman needs to battle the Joker, he fires up the Batcycle. But when it comes to Bane, or some of the other nasties in Batman's gallery of rogues, Batman upgrades to the Batmobile or the Batwing. Batman is always upgrading to something better when it comes to crime-fighting gadgets.

But maintaining and upgrading his crime-fighting gear is not cheap for the environment. Think of all the years that Batman spent flying around in Batwings, or speeding through the streets in the Batmobile. Sure, one man does not have that big of an impact on the environment. But *one man* typically doesn't use a military plane to help him extract another man from a skyscraper in China, and then return to the United States.

Much of this has to do with a fundamental flaw in how Batman views nature. Batman views nature as something to serve the needs of humans, but not as a mutual relationship. Batman takes minerals and nutrients from the environment and returns those minerals as waste faster than the planet can naturally process them. This is a disruption in the human-nature relationship called *the metabolic rift*.

Dr. John Bellamy Foster used the work of Karl Marx to discuss the 'metabolic rift' through agriculture. England was taking more nutrients from fields than they were returning through agriculture. The excess nutrients were accumulating in the cities as waste. This metabolic rift left the fields starving for nutrients, and left large amounts of waste in the cities at a rate faster than the cities could safely process it.

To fix the nutrient starved fields, instead of adjusting the agriculture, England created a new metabolic rift by importing guano (bat poop) from Peru as fertilizer. This helped the nutrient-exhausted fields in England, but caused a problem in Peru because nutrients were not being returned to Peru's ecosystem.

The problem with metabolic rifts in the environment is that they're often not driven by human needs, but instead by profit-seeking industries such as agriculture. This process creates an infinite environmental crisis, in which there are more and more metabolic rifts generated through the broken human-nature relationship.

Batman's Infinite Crisis

LOIS LANE: You are blind.

BATMAN: I see clearly enough.

LOIS LANE: You take material from the Earth . . . you transform it into a new Batmobile, or a Batcopter . . . or a new Batsuit . . . and then when it's broken or outdated . . . you return it to the Earth in a form the Earth cannot process . . . so it becomes waste. You take from the Earth faster than it can naturally replenish . . . and you return your broken equipment in a form the Earth cannot process as quickly as it is returned. There is no way to build your way out of this. You have to fundamentally change how you do everything, including how you fight crime.

BATMAN: What do you want me to do? Should I hit Doomsday with flowers? Do you want me to catch the Joker with a pile of mulch? Miss Lane, I live in the real world.

While Batman's exploits help save Gotham City and the world, they do not come without environmental cost. In the graphic novel *Kingdom Come,* a much older Batman, who must use an exoskeleton to help him walk. In addition, he has a fully-armed battle suit that allows him to fly, along with an army of Batdrones that help patrol Gotham City. In the movie *The Dark Knight Rises*, we see Batman gets a bionic metal brace that adds strength to his leg. Batman relentlessly consumes from the environment to continue fighting crime.

Lucky for Batman he is his own benefactor, Bruce Wayne. Through Wayne Enterprises, billionaire Bruce Wayne finances his crime-fighting alter ego Batman. Wayne Enterprises is a multinational corporation that operates in a wide range of industries such as media, food, technology, medicine, and military weapons. If it exists, Wayne Enterprises most likely has a corporate hand in it. But this is what makes corporations like Wayne Enterprises so harmful to the environment, because they do not view their interaction with the environment as a relationship. Corporations often view the environment as a source of profit instead of a relationship. A balanced relationship with nature means taking only what is needed to survive, and returning nutrients and minerals to the environment in a form that can be processed.

Infinite consumption cannot be supported by finite resources. Currently, "infinite" consumption is supported by creating more and more metabolic rifts. Most people do not see the environmental or social impacts of their consumer lifestyle. Through globalization, many parts of a piece of technology can be made in separate locations, shipped to a plant where they are assembled into a product, and then redistributed to sales markets around the world. How much fuel and electricity was spent producing and shipping Batman's crime fighting gear across the world? That's a big carbon footprint . . . especially when the equipment needs repaired on a regular basis.

Superman has a gentle relationship with the environment. Superman's power comes from the solar energy of our yellow sun. In *Kingdom Come*, we learn that Superman has been on the Earth so long that kryptonite no longer hurts him! Wow. That is truly a win-win for Superman's relationship with the environment.

When it comes to the environment and the debate of Batman versus Superman, Superman wins. Argument over, right? Not so fast.

We Are Bruce Wayne

LOIS LANE: Batman, are you familiar with Wayne Enterprises?

BATMAN: I've heard of it, yes.

LOIS LANE: When Bruce Wayne shows up at a charitable event to support environmental protection, do you think he ever feels like a hypocrite?

BATMAN: Why would Bruce Wayne feel like a hypocrite?

LOIS LANE: He profits from the destruction of the environment. He makes money by taking resources from the Earth and returns those resources as waste. The packaging for Wayne Enterprise products, the shipping costs, the production facilities, . . . all of it hurts the environment. He gives an amount of money to protect the environment. But Wayne Enterprises makes phones and cars and other junk so Wayne Enterprises can make money.

BATMAN: That doesn't make Bruce Wayne a bad person. Wayne didn't create this problem . . .

LOIS LANE: And that's the crisis. Haven't you ever read Naomi Klein? What about Carolyn Merchant? McKibben? Pollan? You're trying to save people . . . you're trying to save the world . . . by protecting the problem. The lifestyles you're protecting are an infinite environmental crisis of infinite consumption and waste.

BATMAN: Every day I fight evil. I put my life on the line every minute I wear this suit so that I can stop criminals.

LOIS LANE: You don't get it. I wish you could be more like Superman.

BATMAN: No, Miss Lane, . . . you don't get it. I *am* Bruce Wayne. You *are* Bruce Wayne. We are *all* Bruce Wayne.

Superman is, after all, an alien from the planet Krypton. This means Superman operates outside our current understanding of physics, chemistry, and physiology. When it comes to humanity—when it comes to discussing every woman, man and child on earth, we are not Superman. Look in the mirror. Who do you see? Look closely. Do you see a Kryptonian? No. You see a human—you see Bruce Wayne. When it comes to the environment, the bottom line is that humans are *all* exactly like Bruce Wayne. We are human, and therefore we must interact with the environment to meet our needs.

We are all Bruce Wayne. Awesome! Wait, what? Holy Crap Batman! If only we could be more like Superman! But humans are limited to human capabilities. Humans do not have Kryptonian physiology. Humans cannot transform solar energy into unassisted flight, the speed to dodge bullets, or the strength to body slam an aircraft carrier.

Just like Bruce Wayne, humans are dependent on taking minerals and nutrients from the environment, and giving minerals and nutrients back. But how we interact determines our environmental impact. In a balanced relationship, we take *only* the nutrients and materials we need for survival from our local environment. In a balanced relationship, humans return those nutrients to the same land we took them from. But human society is wildly out of balance with nature.

Human cities, like Gotham City and Metropolis, put a tremendous strain on the environment. Food is normally shipped to cities because of where food is often grown. Fresh water must be pumped to cities because there are so many people living there. Energy is consumed in mass quantities by cities to power light poles, traffic lights, billboards, parking garages, and strip malls. Cities require air conditioning to counteract living in concrete jungles. Because many people work in cities, but live in the suburbs, cities require some form of transportation to get people to work every day, which normally involves cars that burn fossil fuels. Cities disrupt the human-nature relationship because people are removed from the sources of their food, clothing, water, and energy. This means large concentrations of waste begin to accumulate in cities. Nature is not separate from human society. Human society is, and always has been, part of nature. The idea that a person can leave the city to reconnect with nature is a myth, because even our cities are part of nature.

And like Batman, many people in rich Western countries relentlessly upgrade their technology. If a human lives to the age of seventy-seven, and gets a new smartphone every four years starting at age thirteen, that is sixteen smartphones that person uses in a lifetime. Add to that consumption laptops, tablets, clothing, food . . . toss in a car every ten years. The Westernized ideal of infinite consumption is high impact for the environment. On a more basic level, whether it is food, clothing, or shelter: we all interact with the environment on a daily basis.

One of the most basic things we take from the environment is water. Corporations and industrial farms are incredibly violent to the planet because of how they use fresh water. These industrial giants need to take enough water from the environment not only to survive, *but to profit.* Fresh water provides streams for fish, life for plants, animals, and humans. Fresh water is also a key component for manufacturing many of the products sold by corporations such as Wayne Enterprises. Manufacturers have a long track record of taking fresh water from the environment, but returning waste and dangerous chemicals. Farmers have a long track record of taking fresh water, but returning pesticide runoff into rivers.

But fresh water is a finite resource. In the future, paying $500 for a glass of nontoxic fresh water will not be an issue for Lex Luthor or Bruce Wayne. But what about the rest of us? Will wars be fought over fresh water in the future?

Who Wins, Who Loses

BATMAN: Lady—

LOIS LANE: My name is Lois.

BATMAN: Miss Lane, . . . I'm tired of this nonsense. Superman is clearly the biggest environmental threat to planet Earth. Not me.

LOIS LANE: Really? *Really?* How is Superman the biggest threat to our environment when all he does is feed off the sun?

BATMAN: Well, he is a Kryptonian. *News Flash*: Krypton no longer exists! His planet was destroyed which is why he is living here. It's our sun that gives him his power. *Super*-man would be only a man if he was living on his planet. But he can't live on Krypton because Superman's planet is a dead. The Kryptonian lifestyle, the Kryptonian technology, none of it could save them. We can't learn anything from his people because they failed to protect their environment. Superman is not an environmental hero . . . he's an environmental refugee.

LOIS LANE: I think we will just need to agree to *disagree* on this one. But at least . . . you know . . . even on your worst day of environmental violence, you are nothing like Bruce Wayne. That's something, right?

BATMAN: What . . .

LOIS LANE: Bruce Wayne is ranked the number one environmental villain. Wayne Enterprises is so big that even with its environmental-friendly push, the corporation still takes from the environment at an alarming rate. As the main stakeholder of Wayne Enterprises, Bruce Wayne is clearly the biggest villain to the environment.

BATMAN: Soooo, . . . let me get this straight. Your environmental threat poll ranks me, *Batman* . . . as the third biggest environmental villain. And this other guy . . . Bruce Wayne . . . uh, Bruce Wayne is ranked the number one environmental villain?

Lᴏɪs Lᴀɴᴇ: That's correct.

In *Batman v Superman*, because Superman is a solar-powered weapon, well, Superman clearly wins the award for minimal environmental impact. Yes, if Superman were to punch someone as hard as he could, it would be like several nuclear bombs simultaneously exploding. But this argument is not about who "could" cause the most damage in a fight. This argument is about whose lifestyle, whose source of crime-fighting power, does the most damage to the environment. Superman doesn't even need money to maintain or upgrade his crime fighting weapons. In this environmental showdown: Superman is the clear winner.

But Batman's loss to Superman is a more personal one. Look in the mirror. Remember? We are all like Bruce Wayne because we are human. The planet cannot infinitely support infinite consumption. At some point, infinite consumption of resources such as fresh water will reach their maximum possible usage. Something needs to change about the human relationship with nature. We all make choices about how we interact with the environment. It is not human society *and* nature. Human society and nature are all on the same planet in one giant ecosystem.

16
You Made Me First

Nicolas Michaud

Let's be honest, the reason why Batman is so damnably popular is because he's so *dark*. These days, we really aren't dying to see a guy in blue and grey spandex tightrope walking around Gotham city rooftops. For whatever reason, the old Batman, the cheerier Batman of the 1960s, is just obnoxious to us today. For most Batman fans that old BAM!, BIFF!, POW! TV show is like the drunk uncle we try to keep away from the family reunion. And any reminder, like Joel Schumacher's *Batman and Robin*, makes Batman fans cringe.

Then came Frank Miller and Tim Burton. These two, one a writer, the other a director, brought into the 1980s and 1990s a vision of Batman that fit a grittier, more moody modern era. If you were alive in the 1980s you probably remember that crime was a major concern and that metal bars on doors and windows were becoming more and more common. I remember the old joke that we were locking the innocent in prison to protect them from the criminals. And by the 1990s we were just *emo*.

So what we were given to match the times was a gothy Batman dressed in all black who no longer reminded kids to do their homework and choke down their Wheaties. Instead, Batman became a man who didn't want to talk to anyone. He was broody, he was bad, and he needed to be Baker Acted. (Holy-men-in-white-coats, Batman!)

The point is just this, Batman became a more realistic (if that word can be used when talking about superheroes) product of his youth. Simply, it was hard to believe that a boy who watched the brutal and senseless murder of his mother for a string of pearls could become a pretty cheerful fellow with a family of Bat-colleagues. Heck, when I was a kid I remember the thing I hated the most about *Batman and Robin* was the "family Bat" aspect. It was like the Partridge Family in anatomically correct black tights decided to fight crime. Batman's origin story is just too screwed up for him to be so, well, *adjusted*. We all knew, somewhere in the back of our heads, that in the less LSD-induced delusional world in which we now lived in that someone who went through the traumas that Bruce did as a child would be all kinds of screwed up.

That's really the issue here: Batman can't escape his past, which, in the end is a brutal, death-centered one. Superman, on the other hand, in all his insanely obnoxious bright red and blue glory, emerges from *hope*. Yes, his family dies tragically too. But he doesn't get to stand there and *watch*. Instead, in a last act of lovey-dovey, sweet as saccharine, make me want to throw up effort of love, Kal-El's parents send him out into the universe to make a positive difference and then he is raised *by the nicest most wholesome people on the whole *$#&ing planet!* So if where we come from has anything to do with who we are, Superman wins out, because he emerges from *hope* while Batman emerges from fear, and death, and tragedy, and loss, and abandonment, and violence . . .

Just Throw Him off the Cathedral Already

There's a great scene in Tim Burton's *Batman* where Bats and the Joker are arguing, albeit a bit pettily, about who is responsible for the carnage that the Joker causes. Joker, who just isn't able to keep up with Batman in a fight (an aging Jack Nicholson can only be asked to do so much) tries to appeal to the Dark Knight's lighter side by pointing out, "You made me." To wit, I guess he expected Batman to put down his fists and apologize when Bruce realizes that all the crap that's been going down is actually his fault for dropping a homicidal maniac in a vat of green goo. But things do not go down that way: Batman's response is pretty reasonable, as he is looking at the man who gunned down his parents, "You made me first."

Joker, having realized he has brought up a sore subject, resorts to putting on a pair of spectacles, "You wouldn't hit a guy with glasses on, would ya?" In that moment, Batman proves that the old happy 1960s perspective on the Dark Detective is gone. Adam West's cheery Batman would have hesitated . . . Michael Keaton punches him full in the face, knocking the joker off of the cathedral roof, and the spectacles are left broken like the dreams of free love and mini-skirts.

So why reminisce on this moment? Because it reminds us how important origin stories really are. In that movie some license is taken with Bruce's parent's killer. Normally, it's a random(ish) robbery, and it's Joe Chill who's the robber. Burton's *Batman* tries to tie Joker and Bats together in their dark origins, and in doing that Burton gives us even more reason to reconceptualize Batman as a truly dark force. It isn't some random robber who makes Batman—it's the Joker himself. And somehow, that origin infects Batman's character. It makes him a bit darker; we are more wary of him, and we understand why he is a bit screwed in the head. It is like finding out that some young serial killer's parent was Charles Manson. You just go "Ohhhhhhhhhhhhh. Well *that* explains *a lot.*"

This is just all to say that we can't ignore origins. In the US we tend to be a bit inconsistent about origins. We believe everything we do is totally a free choice. But we like to know that some nut job who likes to slice the skin off of live puppies and wear them on his head while disco dancing does it because he was beaten with a rubber hose every day as a kid. Otherwise, if he was just born that way we want to know it is because he is some sort of genetic wrong direction. If on the other hand our puppy-killing, Bee-Gees-dancing psycho had a great childhood and there is no chemical imbalance that makes him do what he does, we get uncomfortable. For my part, I think we get uncomfortable because we realize *"Oh shit, if he wasn't made into that, and he isn't a hormonally imbalanced freak, then I could end up just like him!"* In other words, what's to stop you and me from being murderous super-villains who like to drink the blood of kittens if neither our biology nor our environment makes us who we are?

That's where we can get a bit inconsistent. We also like to believe that we have free will. If anyone walks up to us and says, "You don't have free will, your fate is predictable, and you just do what you do because the past has determined your future," we would dangle them from the rooftops until they cry and apologize. So on the one hand, we want to believe that we would never be evil like the Joker, because we didn't have some totally messed-up childhood and we don't have whatever chemical imbalance gives him such a charming smile. But, think about it, if our idea of free will is true, then it might well be that the Joker had an awesome childhood with plenty of chocolate milk, he has no "psychopath" gene, and the chemicals that gave his skin that lovely pale hue never got into his brain at all. He just woke up and decided one day to have some *fun*. And let's be honest, that would be the *best* origin story for the Joker, because it would be so damned scary. Why does he do it? No reason. Just funzies.

I Was Rooting for Doomsday

I'm old enough to remember when Superman died. *It was awesome*. Back then Superman comics were going the way of the Dodo, and DC was desperate to do something to make some money off the big blue bastard before doing away with the comics altogether. So they came up with the idea of killing him. And holy-cash-register Batman, did they make money! The death issue of Superman became a ridiculously expensive collector's item that everyone wanted. It was so popular that now it's practically worthless because everyone has the damn thing (I think I have three. When I get depressed I read one of them and chuckle). Anyway, the point is this. Superman just wasn't what we wanted anymore. We wanted Batman. Superman was all happy and nice. Batman on the other hand had issues, like we do.

Superman's death, though, reminded everyone how much they really liked the asshat. It was truly tragic, and, to be honest, I don't think we would have had the same response to Batman's death. In fact, I *know* we wouldn't because every time they kill Batman in DC *no one cares*. Sure, part of that is because we all know that they'll bring him back, likely in a darker shade of black and a few more psychological scars to keep it interesting, but man, when Supes died, people were actually *sad*. Sure, a few of us held up drinks to toast a world without blue-yellow-and-red spandex, but while the Super-Haters were patting each other on the back celebrating a Superman-free world, the Justice League and everyone in the our real US was lamenting the loss. People did newscasts about it. The damned event really was mimicked effectively by the comics. In the comics there's a massive funeral, a big-ass statue, and everyone is generally saddened at the loss, and truth be told so were we in the real world.

Why were we sad that Superman died when we don't care what happens to Bats? I think it has something to do with the fact that Superman . . . *Clark* is actually a nice guy. Worse yet, he is a nice guy who can and does bring hope to the world, both in the comics and in ours. His origin, unlike Batman's doesn't assume a tragic end. Given the way Bruce's life started, if he does die happy, of old age, with a nineteen-year-old supermodel on his lap, we would be *disappointed.* His origin is so tragic that we can't help but feel that his end should match it. It only makes sense that Bruce's life should follow the trajectory set out from the beginning. But Clark, on the other hand, he had real promise, both for himself and for the world. Without him, the world doesn't lose something dark—it loses the *light.*

Kal-El is sent to Earth precisely for that reason, to bring Earth a new opportunity. He is almost literally born from his parents' willingness to hope even in the most extreme circumstances. Their act isn't just one of love, it's one that holds the flickering candle of *belief* up in the darkest winds of tragedy. They know that the chances that their child will live, nonetheless become the near-God who will save a world rather than savage it, must be unlikely. They are *scientists,* for crying out loud. But something gives them reason to believe that their little boy, despite all odds, will not only live, but become a truly good man despite the fact that *no one can make stop him from doing evil.* That is an impressive hope. It is the kind of hope that is necessary for success.

Their actions bring to mind something pointed out by William James (1842–1910). James pointed out that some things are only possible if you have faith, if you have the kind of hope that's so strong that you truly believe that the extremely unlikely is something you can do. It's like jumping over a chasm. Let's say you have to jump across a chasm, and if you don't you'll die. If you run up to it thinking, "I can't do it. I can't do it. I can't do it." You probably won't. You'll be held back by your own lack of belief. But, on the other hand, if you *really* believe it's possible, you just might. It isn't a guarantee, but that faith is *necessary* for the possibility of success. It is like Bruce escaping from prison in *The Dark Knight Rises*; the rope that he wore was holding him back. He had to *believe* that he could make it, leave himself no other option, and *jump*. And that is exactly what Clark's parents do. They are left with no other option, so they give the universe a son born purely out of hope.

The True Tragedy of the Batman

So what it really all comes down to is the sad realization that Batman really is a bit inferior to Superman. And I say it is sad for a pretty good reason. . . . *We can't be Superman*. Batman, though unlikely, is kind of possible. At the very least, it's possible to be someone who busts his ass to become awesome. We can work out, we can train, we can *learn*. But we can't move at the speed of light, we can't pummel planets into dust with our fists, and we grow old. I *want* Batman to be better because he, at least, is a faintly attainable goal. While Superman is something none of us will ever be.

I'm sure you're thinking, "Screw you, old man, I can be what I want." And that's when we realize how insane we are. We truly believe that we're so free that even the laws of physics can be bent to our will. But we aren't free. We never really had free will, and we really can't escape our origin stories. Like Batman, we're trapped in a tragic story that will eventually come to a tragic end, every human story . . . every. single. one.

Why do I say we don't have free will? Why am I saying that we can't escape the fate that is destined for us? Simple. The kind of free will that most people talk about when they say, "free will" is just kind of silly. When I ask people, "What do you mean when you say you have free will?" They reply, "It means I can do whatever I want." But we know that can't be true. We can't do whatever we want. We've never been able to do whatever we want. I mean, don't get me wrong, we can do lots of things, and some of those things are pretty awesome (like parkour. Holy-broken-ankle, Batman, I wish I could do that!) But there are a lot of things we can't do, no matter how much we want to do them. We can't read minds, we can't create energy from nothing, and we can't flap our arms and fly. Now, before you get cute and say, "Well maybe science someday . . ." Yes. I know science will someday make us all invincible, immortal semi-gods who can fire green lasers from our nostrils, but until then I, *and you*, are pretty restricted by the laws of physics. If you don't believe me, then try it. I dare you. Take this book, put it on the ground and move it with your mind alone. No *cheating*. Just, you know, Green Lantern-style, use that "free will" we all have to make the magic happen.

Okay, if we're being honest with ourselves, we know there are lots of things we're prevented from doing. Sadly, no matter hard I try, and I really do try often, I can't move stuff with my mind. Not even light switches, or pennies, nothing. It's a constant reminder of how limited I am. For that matter, I remain bad at Calculus. Seriously. The fact is that I can't just hold up a Calc textbook to my head and learn it. I have to actually read the damn thing, and study, and practice . . . *because I am limited.*

I realize the fact that I'm limited in what I can do basically goes against everything we have been taught to believe. It seems that pretty much all of us were raised to believe we could be whatever we want, president, astronaut, even Superman. *But not all of us can.* The fact is that even with science, at my height, with my eyesight, and well, my phobia of flying, being an *astronaut* was never really in my future, and I'm not so sure that I should be ashamed to admit it. So on one hand Superman, and his origin story, is a reminder of the power of hope. But on the other hand, he's a constant reminder of the things that, despite my free will, I can never be.

Up, Up, and Away

Generally, when philosophers talk about free will they have come to accept that definition, "I can do whatever I want" doesn't work so well. So if we want to believe we have free will, we need a different definition. The fact is there have been a few; generally, the most popular is "The ability to do otherwise." Which, honestly, sounds pretty blasé. It isn't a half-bad definition though, as far as philosophical definitions go. It basically just means that in *some* circumstances we can do one thing or the other. I can choose to fight crime or not. I can choose to eat chocolate or vanilla ice cream. I can wear black tights or blue. There are a lot of philosophers who believe we have that kind of free will. They believe that maybe we can't do *whatever* we want, but we do have the ability to make a choice, and had we not made that choice, we would have been able to do something else.

I'm not all that convinced, because I recognize the power of origin stories. If I'm honest with myself I recognize that in a lot of ways I am a product of my environment and my genetics. Sure, maybe I could have been an astronaut, but I would have to change the past to make that happen. In a world in which we could go into the past and change how my parents raised me and changed my genetics so that flying doesn't make me hurl, sure, I could be an astronaut too. *But we can't.* We can't change the past, and the *past causes the future.* So why are we so sure that we can change the future and that we really have free choices?

Think about it like this . . . It's true that Bruce could have chosen *not* to become Batman. He might have decided to become a doctor instead. What would we have to change to make that happen, though? First, we would likely have to prevent his dad from being shot. So we would have to go back into the past and prevent that event. If his dad doesn't die brutally in front of him, Bruce doesn't have whatever schizoid break that causes him to be Batman. Instead, he is raised in a loving environment around his doctor-role model dad and becomes a doctor instead. We might argue that he would become Batman anyway, but that is a bit hard to make sense of. If his parents aren't killed *why* would he become Batman? At that point we start looking for answers in genetics, "Maybe he is just nuts."

Genetics might explain the whole *Red Son* concept as well. In that graphic novel Kal-El lands in Soviet Russia instead of the US. Raised by the Soviets, their version of Superman becomes an enforcer of dictatorship. The end result, though, is that he still ends up being a good guy in the end. Why? Well my only guess would be genetics. Clark is just genetically predisposed to being a nice guy, so even when raised by jackasses, he still just doesn't feel great about doing mean stuff. This makes a lot of sense. Some kids, who have great families, still just like to pull wings off of flies, and throw kittens in rivers. Other kids cry if they think their teddy bear has experienced even some small psychological trauma. Heck sometimes those two kids are in the same family! (Which usually results in the one torturing the Hell out of the other).

If that's true, then how free are we? *Really.* Maybe we really can do one thing or another, but does it really mean that much? Arthur Schopenhauer (1788–1860) famously said, "We can do what we will, but we can't will what we will." Okay, maybe we do what we want, but the fact that we want it is the result of our biology and our upbringing, neither of which we have any control over. We can't go into the past and stop the murder of Bruce's parents *so he wants vengeance.* He can't stop wanting to stop crime. And even if after a lot of therapy it were possible for Bruce to stop wanting to stop evil, *he doesn't want to.* And that fact is something he has no control over. He can't make himself be someone who wants to seek therapy to change his wants, even if it is possible to do so. So Bruce is trapped by his origin story, and so is Clark.

This all means that Superman's origin story is one that wins out in the end. As far as superheroes go, Bruce will always be far more restricted by his. Bruce's origin denies him hope. Unless something biological triggers in him to make him a more cheerful dude, Bruce will never believe that human beings are truly capable of leaving evil behind. Heck, that's why we need him, because we know that we probably won't leave evil behind. But Superman, that fool's lot in life is to believe that we can overcome our crap. He makes us believe that we can do amazing things. He inspires us not just to be super, but to be good. His origin story allows him to have hope, to believe that the least likely of possibilities are still *possibilities*, and that is why humanity shouldn't be wiped from the face of the Earth, because even if it's unlikely, we might choose to believe in ourselves, leave behind the selfish evil we do, and *fly*.

It's Always Darkest Before the Knight

17
Batman's Mask in Aristotle's Drama

RAY BOSSERT

With his mask, the troubled aristocrat, orphaned in an act of violence, becomes the sleuth, the detective, the last hope of a dying city. With his mask, he gains the strength, the quickness of wit, and the wisdom to deduce what ails his people. With his mask, he can root out the plague of evil and restore justice to the citizens of . . . Thebes. Or, at least, the actor playing King Oedipus might seem like such a hero whenever he put on the *prosopon*—the ancient Greek stage mask. Anyone can become a figure of myth and legend if they put on the right mask—and the ability to pass a mask from one actor to the next creates a kind of immortality that even a superman cannot achieve.

What really separates Batman from Superman is that Batman wears a mask and Superman doesn't. Now, this might seem a minor point considering the age-old debate regarding whether Batman is really a superhero in the same way that Superman is. That is, can Batman really be a superhero if he has no powers? Batman is basically a walking Sharper Image catalog, whereas Superman has seemingly limitless cosmic powers built into his DNA. But these kinds of abilities tend to be mere plot conventions. Batman can build or purchase any kind of technological enhancement to close the gap between himself and Superman, and whether it is a comic, cartoon, or LEGO video-game, Batman usually keeps some kryptonite handy just in case he needs to even the odds. The physical differences between the characters are actually less significant than their costumes, especially for characters who appear in predominantly visual media.

The mask of Batman has a special property. It isn't simply the black mask of a Zorro or a Lone Ranger. It is a mask that imitates a living creature: the bat. This idea of imitation makes Batman stand out among most of the well-known DC heroes. Wonder Woman, Superman, the Green Lantern, the Flash, Aquaman—all of these characters wear costumes as uniforms or as disguises. Yet their superhero identities don't really imitate anything in particular (although some versions of the Green Arrow do like to cosplay as Robin Hood). They aren't trying to be anything other than themselves. Batman's decision to imitate the bat, however, often confuses the citizens of Gotham. Is he a man? A super-human? A supernatural monster? Batman's bat-mask invites us to consider him through the lens of *mimesis*—defined by Aristotle as the act of imitation. Put more simply, Batman is a theatrical performance; it's an act.

Thus, Batman needs to be a superior actor to Superman because Batman must use his theatrical talents to misdirect opponents (including Superman). Since Batman's approach to heroism is imitative, it can be reproduced in any number of other non-superpowered people. Therefore, Batman is both more indestructible than Superman and a more powerful force of change in his fictional world.

Action Comics versus Acting Comics

As the heroic alter-ego of playboy millionaire Bruce Wayne, Batman is a fiction even in his own world: he's a role played by a citizen of Gotham City. And Bruce Wayne's repertoire of staged characters is not limited to the Caped Crusader, either. He repeatedly disguises himself as other characters: whether they are homeless women, police officers, or even Superman.

Bruce Wayne wears many masks—literally and figuratively. However handy Batman's utility belt is for escaping traps, repelling sharks, or taking down alien super-beings, it's the mask that grants Bruce Wayne the freedom to act as a vigilante. At the very least, his disguises keep him from being arrested for countless legal violations, but the Batman mask also gives him an even more significant advantage: a psychological influence over other character's minds and even the minds of the real world audience. His mask plays upon our fears and transforms a mortal man into something more frightening.

Superman, on the other hand, does not need a mask to feel free. Even if the police could track him to his home, they wouldn't be able to arrest him. His unstoppable powers allow him to dispense with disguises. But there's another reason that might account for Superman's uncovered face: he's pretty darned scary *without* a mask.

People fear Superman because they know he has the ability to tyrannize the Earth—that we are at his whim. Superman needs to dress in a way that makes him less frightening to the mere humans he wants to help. His costume does not evoke the dangerous mystery or threatening uncertainty that come with Batman's cowl. Batman wants to scare people; Superman wants to put them at ease. The mask—or choice not to wear a mask—represents how these characters think about their own natures and how they attempt to interact with the world around them. Whereas Superman wants to share himself with the world, Batman almost always interacts with others through a false persona, even when he is Bruce Wayne.

Bruce Wayne isn't really the playboy millionaire that everyone perceives him to be. The millionaire part is completely real, but Bruce Wayne's public personality is often as much of a performance as Batman. Bruce Wayne is virtually always "in character," as they say in theater. Again, Superman is almost the complete inverse: although he knows he is a Kryptonian named Kal-El, he continues to identify with Clark Kent. After all, the lifetime he spent as the son of Ma and Pa Kent back in Smallville was real. True, the Clark Kent of Metropolis perpetually "performs" acts of clumsiness. Sometimes this clumsiness is purely to throw people of his trail. Sometimes it cleverly conceals a random act of heroism that only the audience observes (what we call "dramatic irony"). Sometimes Superman really is just too big to fit comfortably in an office bullpen. However, Superman doesn't think of Clark Kent as an act or as inauthentic to who he is.

Despite the performances he gives as a mild-mannered reporter, Superman typically embraces his Clark Kent identity as his real self (or, at least, as no less real than his identity as Superman). Grant Morrison (writer) and Frank Quietly (artist) portray this version of the character in their *All-Star Superman* comic. Their Superman tries to prove the authenticity of Clark Kent by using the "Mirror of Truth" which has the power to reflect things as they really are. Standing in front of the mirror, Superman puts on glasses and adopts the slouched posture of Clark Kent. The image in the mirror, however, is the typical, dashing Superman with a puffed-out barrel chest. There's not a trace of Clark Kent in the reflection—not even the glasses. Superman *wants* the mirror to tell him he is really Clark Kent and that he is not acting a part.

Whereas Superman believes or wants to believe he's always his true self, Batman is almost always acting. Philosophically speaking, then, a main difference between Batman and Superman is mimesis—artistic imitation. Mimesis is the essence of drama, as Aristotle defines it in his *Poetics*. Drama distinguishes itself from other art because it uses real actions to imitate the actions of human beings. Acting requires actual people telling a story directly through the physical actions of their bodies as opposed to retelling stories with words or painted images. For Aristotle, mimesis is artificial in nature; it expects the actor to use conventions of the stage to make people believe in what they see. Sometimes, a fictional depiction of an action is more believable than what people do in real life. Moreover, Aristotle believes drama, as a poetic art form, imitates things as they *should* be rather than as they actually are (the latter being the job of historians not playwrights).

Although Aristotle wrote at length on the value of dramatic mimesis, his predecessor Plato (circa 428–347 B.C.E.) was more skeptical. According to scholars, Plato feared instruction through mimesis because it meant that audiences would learn through something that was, by nature, not real. Something imitated is not the thing itself, and therefore it might give false representation. In this sense, Batman is the more Aristotelian, and Superman the more Platonic. Batman wants to mislead people; his operations depend on believing falsehood. In *The Dark Knight Rises*, Batman lets Gotham City believe that he murdered Dent, even though Dent falls to his death in a fight with Batman after attempting to kill Gordon and his son. Batman would rather Dent be remembered as a hero than as a deranged monster—and having himself thought of as a potential murderer makes Batman a more terrifying force on the streets.

Batman's willingness to lie seems directly opposed to Superman's quest to defend truth, and it would certainly ruffle a news reporter whose job it is to ferret out what's real and dispel misinformation. But Batman, like Aristotle, acknowledges that emotional appeals can be more persuasive than cold, hard facts.

For Aristotle, the goal of all this theatrical make-believe is to achieve tragic *catharsis*—the audience's experience of pity and fear. Pity and fear are two emotions that come readily to a discussion of Batman, much more so than Superman. As scholars suggest, Aristotle believes these emotions are most effectively created through generating suspense in an audience—and that suspense is manifested when the consequences of actions are uncertain and yet still logically predictable.

At a basic level, suspense is built when audiences wonder whether or not the hero will fulfill his desires, accomplish the mission, or otherwise win against the bad guys. On the one hand, it's hard to create this kind of suspense for Superman (which is one of the reasons why DC is always tinkering with the extent of Superman's powers). It's hard to fear becoming Superman when we all fantasize about having his powers. It's hard to really pity him, too, since whatever difficulties he faces seem more than compensated by having those powers.

On the other hand, Batman's limitations generally allow for more suspenseful plots. On a basic level, Batman's lack of powers make his successes more difficult to achieve, and therefore less certain. On a deeper, more complicated level, suspense can be built when we ask what our heroes are willing to do—or what they are willing to sacrifice—in order to save the day. Batman stories often excel at this kind of suspense because we are always uncertain if Batman will finally cross the line and become the monster that he pretends to be. With less immediate powers at his disposal, a Batman is more tempted to cut corners with moral codes than a Superman. Each time Batman throws a punch, we have to wonder if this will be the time he uses lethal force. We can feel both pity and fear for Batman— he's a tortured hero constantly being stretched to his psychological limits.

With Superman, you pretty much always know where you stand. He's the model superhero: forthright, just, honest, and moral. The guy doesn't really have anything to hide, and the reader always knows Superman will win and do the right thing in the end. DC comics occasionally try to create suspense with sensational plotlines: killing off Superman, making him go momentarily insane, or depriving him of his powers. Even so, he always comes back as good as new. This certainty of Superman's goodness and triumph exists not just for the reader, but for characters within Superman's world as well. Indeed, Superman's inevitable successfulness and his boy-scout morality drive his arch-nemesis Lex Luthor to villainy.

In most iterations the Caped Crusader is a far more morally-confusing figure. Some trust him, like Commissioner Gordon, but others are skeptical of his vigilantism. The Joker seems to believe that Batman is just one more dead sidekick away from snapping. Much of this uncertainty comes from the costume. Superman's lack of a mask means he has nothing to hide, which makes him seem like an inherently trustworthy guy. But Batman doesn't want you to know who he is. He doesn't want you to know what he wants, what he's capable of doing, or what he believes.

The audience knows that contemporary Batman has a code: he never uses guns and he never kills. Crooks in Gotham, how-ever, don't seem so sure of this, and even if they have caught on that Batman uses non-lethal force, there's quite a bit of dam-age he can do to you that won't kill you. Whereas the lack of a mask makes Superman's philosophy transparent to other char-acters, Batman's mask makes his philosophy opaque. Since Batman's intentions are concealed, criminals (and ultimately audiences) have to fill in the blanks—they have to imagine what they can't actually see or know.

Making People Think You're Worse than You Are

One of my favorite Batman sequences deals with precisely this issue of deducing Batman's intentions. It occurs in the *Batman: The Animated Series* two-part series "Feat of Clay"—which is, coincidentally, about an out of work actor who becomes the vil-lain Clayface. (Actors, right?)

Batman corners a goon in a hospital storage closet and needs to get him to spill the beans. The detective notices that the criminal is germophobic, so Batman plays upon his fears in order to extract information. Claiming that a jar above the goon is filled with fatal crimson fever, Batman punches a wall, which makes the jar shimmy to the edge of the shelf. The criminal is so riddled with terror that the jar will fall, break, and contaminate him that he tells Batman everything he knows. When the scene closes, the jar turns out to be filled with "Seawater for analysis." Batman tricked the goon into thinking his life was in more danger than it actually was, and thinking that Batman is some kind of violent, sadistic lunatic (and maybe he is).

This example reveals how far Batman's "I'm your worst nightmare" is from Superman's "I'm here to help." Batman wants people to think he will do worse than he intends. He has to imitate a villain in order to convince villains he is as dangerous—or more dangerous—than they are. In this way, the bat is an effective creature to imitate. In general, people are terrified of the little flying mammals, partly because we are biased against their appearances and partly because of folkloric myths and associations of vampires. Yet most urban-dwelling bats are both harmless and useful predators (unless they have rabies). Imitating or pretending to be a bat means that other people do most of the work for you to create fear. For Batman, bat-mimesis brings tactical advantages.

Batman's performances are designed to activate criminals' imaginations: to make them imagine what his next action will be. This relates to the narrative concept of "closure"—the imaginative act on the part of the reader to fill-in the actions, objects, and gaps of time. Writers and artists can exploit closure by misdirecting us to assume one thing is happening, and then take us in another direction. The effectiveness of Batman's performance frequently relies on precisely this use of closure. First, Batman's mask and costume obstruct our view of him: criminals don't know who is in there or what he is capable of, so they must imagine what kind of person he is for themselves (and they typically don't imagine him to be a very nice man). This closure is a form of projection. Because Batman is typically dealing with not-very-nice people, it's only natural that their projections onto Batman are less-than-benevolent. If criminals imagine Batman doing to them what they themselves would do in his position of power, then no wonder they are so easily terrified.

Batman's Mask Is Superman's Real Kryptonite

Artists and writers frequently link Batman directly with theater. For instance, Wayne Manor's secret entrance to the Batcave appears by pressing a button in a bust of William Shakespeare—as in the Adam West television series and *The Brave and the Bold* cartoon.

Theater, in this case, becomes a literal entry-way to super-heroism. Perhaps less kitschy, Bruce Wayne is often tragically orphaned after his family exits a theater. In Frank Miller's *The Dark Knight Returns*, the family attended a screening of *Zorro*—a movie that later triggers Wayne's compulsive desire to put on his own mask and fight injustice.

One of Batman's most theatrical performances coincides with one of the most famous showdowns between the Dark Knight and the Man of Steel, again in Miller's graphic novel. The two heroes come to blows after federal legislation outlaws costumed vigilantes (although Superman continues to don his cape as an agent of the United States government, weaponized by a cartoon Ronald Reagan in a shadow war with the Soviet Union). When an aged, retired Batman resumes his illegal watch over Gotham, Superman arrives to end it. The outcome of the final battle depends greatly on dramatic performance.

For the most part, the fight is real. Superman really intends to stop Batman, and Batman shows up in power armor. When the Green Arrow intervenes to strike Superman with a dose of kryptonite, Batman pummels Superman and then begins to choke him. Once again, Batman acts as though he is willing to kill his enemy . . . but stops short. The internal narration lets the reader slip behind the mask:

> I want you to remember, Clark, in all the years to come . . . in your most private moments . . . I want you to remember my hand . . . at your throat . . . I want you to remember . . . the one man who beat you.

Batman wouldn't be thinking about what Superman will remember in the future if he wanted him dead. Rather, Batman wants Superman to contemplate Batman's dominance over him. Still, these are Batman's private thoughts; and it's unlikely that Superman can deduce Batman's motives while being asphyxiated. From Superman's perspective, Batman stops not because of his code of non-lethal violence but because he has a sudden heart-attack, the weakness of age catching up with him. And Batman falls dead during his triumph over Superman.

As it appears on the page, this sequence seems to contradict my argument about the value of masks. The moment when Batman conquers Superman (or, rather, conquers "Clark" according to the thought caption), Batman is not wearing a mask: he appears to have abandoned mimesis, and perhaps even the Batman identity. This is not so much Superman versus Batman as Clark Kent versus Bruce Wayne.

Except, Miller has stolen a page from Shakespeare: like the Bard's Juliet, Batman had previously ingested a drug that temporarily stops his heart during the battle. This way, he only *appears* to die. Superman believes what he sees, and even attends Bruce Wayne's funeral. However, his super-senses eventually betray the ruse at the interment. Clark Kent uncovers the truth, as he always does. He hears Bruce Wayne's heart begin to beat again, but his wink to the new Robin implies that he will conceal the truth this time. Batman was performing during their battle, and Superman fell for it. In this case, Superman is beaten by Batman's fists and thespianism.

Superman Saves the World while Batman Tries to Change It

In literary scholarship, mimesis has a slightly different definition. Basically, "mimetic criticism" is the literary study of how "realistic" a work is (we call this realism "verisimilitude"). In this approach to mimesis, Batman still has the upper hand. Because Batman is ultimately just a human being with the resources to invest in extreme personal training and very expensive gadgetry, Batman narratives lend themselves to a higher degree of verisimilitude. Take, for instance, the recent *Dark Knight* trilogy by Christopher Nolan, which attempted to imagine a Batman as he might exist in a real world. Although the events in this movie are often highly improbable, they do not come off as entirely impossible.

Superman, by his very nature, eludes mimetic critics like a speeding bullet. The second you have an alien who gains super-powers from Earth's yellow sun—a humanoid that can shoot heat beams out of his eyes and fly under his own power— pretty much everything you know about reality is subject to question. At its most mimetic, a Superman story might exist in what literary scholars call "magic realism," a genre of literature often attributed to South American authors. Magic realism typically imagines a familiarly realistic world with one unusual exception. The recent *Man of Steel* movie seems to have attempted this kind of approach to Superman, at least until Earth suddenly falls under an invasion of equally superpowered aliens. Once Superman steps onto the scene, other fantastical elements aren't far behind.

Despite the vast destruction in the *Man of Steel's* climax, everyone seems pretty much the same as they ever were when Clark Kent arrives at the *Daily Planet* at the end of the movie. The introduction of Superman hasn't really changed the world. This kind of ending is predicted in an essay called "The Myth of Superman" by Umberto Eco (author of *The Name of the Rose*). Eco argues that classic Superman, despite his tremendous powers, does very little to alter the world around him. For Eco, Superman's laxness is owing mostly to commercial market demands on comic books to have formulaic plots. One aspect of this formula demands a world that the reader can recognize. To oversimplify Eco: if Superman used his powers to change the world once and for all, then Superman's world would no longer be recognizable to the reader. If the nature of Superman stories change, the profitable formula would be lost for DC.

Of course, Superman comics have changed quite a bit since Eco's essay. In Grant Morrison's *All-Star Superman*, we see that Professor Quintum has been actively experimenting on Superman and drastically changing his world with super-hero derived technology. Whereas classic Superman famously protects "Truth, Justice, and the American Way"—all of which Superman usually assumes already exist—modern versions of Superman are often quick to assert that they are citizens of an internationalized planet Earth. DC's marketing department assumes that this makes the character more palatable to its global media markets, and commercialism still reigns supreme in geeky franchises. Still, even modern Superman does not have much of an agenda or imagination for directly changing the world. He is less interested in making a new world than preserving the current one. And while Eco's argument about formulaic writing might equally apply to classic Batman (there's an endless supply of criminals in Gotham City), Batman has always had a more subversive agenda than Superman.

Before Batman first dons his cowl, Batman stories usually depict crime lords overrunning Gotham City with anarchy and lawlessness. As a victim of this world, Bruce Wayne imagines a better place—and he begins to take action to change it. Batman actively attempts to make his surroundings other than they are. He might always turn criminals over to the legitimate authorities, but he recognizes that the status quo is insufficient for maintaining law and order. Although Batman usually changes his world by solving one crime at a time, he has another tactic at his disposal: training disciples to imitate him and adopt the philosophy of the Batman.

Batman Wins Because He Is a Philosophy

Because Batman's effectiveness relies on mimesis as imitation, Batman himself can be more readily imitated than Superman. This ultimately gives Batman the final advantage over Superman because it means that Batman is a role that can be passed from person to person—infinitely reproduced without end. Superman is too rooted to his origins: the alien refugee Kal-El. He can't teach Earthlings how to fly or see through walls. Anyone, however, can become Batman.

Indeed, imitating Batman is almost too tempting. The opening of *The Dark Knight Rises* suggests that copycat Batmen are plaguing Gotham. Likewise, the *Batman: Imposters* story arc explores the possibility of less-than-heroic figures trying to steal Batman's thunder. *The Dark Knight Returns* also features episodes of copycat Batmen, and it concludes with Batman preparing to train a whole Batcave of successors. Recently, DC experimented with *Batman Inc.* in which Batman set up regional franchises of Batpersons. Substitute Batmen are constantly filling in whenever Bruce Wayne is severely injured or killed. The animated series *The Brave and the Bold* tackled the succession of the cowl to Bruce Wayne's son, Damien Wayne, after Dick Greyson (formerly Nightwing, formerly Robin) performed the role of Batman. During a climactic confrontation with an aging Joker, Dick Greyson claims "Batman is an idea; you can't kill an idea." (This appears to paraphrase a quote by the Civil Rights activist Medgar Evers: "You can kill a man, but you can't kill an idea.")

Superman is not so readily emulated; to behave like Superman requires Superman's abilities. If a citizen of Metropolis tried to impersonate Superman, he'd be hospitalized after his first attempt at flight. He would also need plastic surgery (the lack of a mask makes identity-theft far more difficult). This irreproducibility is a problem in *All-Star Superman* (although Lex Luthor does comment on men styling their hair with the Superman "swoosh"). When Superman's cells begin to self-destruct, Dr. Quintum frets over what will happen to the world after the hero's demise. His attempts to clone the Man of Steel are unsuccessful. Indeed, almost all "Superman"-derivative characters in the DC Universe are either native Kryptonians, clones, trans-dimensional beings, or time-travelling progeny. Not just anyone can imitate Superman.

But being Batman is not really dependent on gadgets or even physical powers. During the climactic anarchy that breaks out in the *Dark Knight Returns*, Miller strips Batman of almost all of his attributes: he is not as fast or as strong as he once was, and all of his hardware has been immobilized in an EMP blast. Without a single operational bat-vehicle, Batman rides into Gotham City on a horse. All that is left is his costume and his ability to act. To bring order to the city, he assembles former gang members who call themselves "The Sons of Batman." They don't quite understand Batman's methods yet, and plan on killing anyone who is breaking the law. They have made a mistake with closure: like the criminals they once were, they still project malevolence to the mind behind the mask. They still imagine him to be worse than he is. So Batman stops them, breaks one of their rifles (he calls them "the weapons of the enemy") and makes an offer: "Our weapons are quiet—precise. In time, I will teach them to you. Tonight, you will rely on your fists—and your brains." He offers them the promise of being trained by him, to become him, in return for restoring Gotham. The idea of becoming Batman is enough to convert them. The hero who imitates is now being imitated.

It might not be a superpower, but mimesis proves Batman's most powerful crime-fighting tool. As the new Robin in Miller's comic contemplates what strange influence Batman exerts over these former hoodlums, she realizes that it is "Just his voice. Just him." By equating "his voice" to "just him," Batman is reduced to a spoken-word performance delivered in an animal mask.

At his most essential, Batman is a performance that can achieve something greater than leaping a tall building in a single bound, something more powerful than stopping a locomotive: the performance of Batman can change hearts and minds.[1]

---

[1] Special thanks to Dabney Rice for sharing her expertise and enthusiasm for all things bat-related.

18
Superman the Super Dick

Noah Levin

Superman could kick Batman's butt in a fight. Without kryptonite up his sleeve or on a batarang (or anywhere else), Batman—or pretty much anyone—will get a royal Kryptonian ass-whipping at the hands, eyes, toes, nose, and hair of Superman should he engage in fisticuffs with the Man of Steel. Let's just briefly break down the traits of these two heroes:

> **BATMAN:** The Dark Knight (or Dork Knight, according to The Joker), The Caped Crusader, or sometimes just Bat. A mortal man with no real superpowers, unless being a billionaire genius that is extremely skilled in acrobatics and martial arts combine to give a superpower. I don't think they do, so he's just more of badass "hero" than a "superhero."

> **SUPERMAN:** The Last Son of Krypton, The Man of Tomorrow, The Man of Steel, or sometimes just Supes. Full of superpowers: faster than a speeding bullet, stronger than a locomotive, and invincible to virtually everything but the very rare kryptonite (which seems to be abundant and easy to come by if you hate Superman). Of course, there's also the laser vision, x-ray vision, super breath, super speed, and pretty much everything awesome someone could do. Superman is the example of a "superhero."

Clearly Superman is better. It's even in the name—sure, they both have "man" in their names, but one starts with "Super" and the other starts with "Bat." No contest, right?

But does might make right? Is Superman *better than* Batman? Absolutely not. Superman is a Super Dick because every instant he's not saving someone, he could be, and he could do so at little to no cost to himself. Batman, on the other hand, risks his mortal life on a daily basis to stop any bad guys he encounters. When comparing the two, Superman is clearly a worse hero because he does the *unheroic* thing of willfully not doing as much as he could, which makes him a real dick.

> **It's a bird . . . It's a plane . . . It's . . . Superman! . . . and he's just flying? Can't he fly faster? Shouldn't he be saving someone? Is he just out for a leisurely fly? Seriously, why is he going so slowly I can see him when he could be out saving someone right now?!**

Here's a scenario that has happened more than once: Superman hears an old woman getting beaten and mugged, yet he continues on his way without getting involved. Then he sees a man beating a puppy for fun—and carries on his merry way, yet again. He knows where bad things happen, yet he chooses not go there, lest he has to do something. No, he sticks to what he knows and loves, and lays low most of the time, ensuring that he can live a mild-mannered life as Clark Kent. Perhaps he's at his regular job while these events are taking place, or maybe grabbing some lunch. Perhaps he's just brushing his teeth (if he even needs to do that). At any given moment, he knows that bad things are happening, and knows for certain he can help. He just chooses not to, perhaps because it's too bothersome, he's worried someone might recognize him while dressed as his alter-ego, or because his Lois Lane needs his help because she has a knack for being in the wrong place at the wrong time *a lot.*

Certainly no "superhero" would allow such bad things to happen when he can stop them! Superman should stop every crime that he can, right? Yet, this is how Superman lives his life, doing nothing when people need his help, *all the time.* Of course, Superman could do something —he's *Superman*, not *Mediocreman.* What can't he do? Yet, he chooses to do nothing. What a dick.

My calling Superman a dick requires further explanation. Why choose the word "dick"? Why not just "jerk"? Or "not-as-good-as-I-had-hoped"? Harry Frankfurt, the Princeton philosopher, has paved the way for philosophers to analyze colloquial terms such as these. Dr. Frankfurt gave us an excellent understanding of the word "bullshit" by defining it as a statement that is said *without* regard to the truth. A "bullshitter" just says things without even caring if it's true or not, whereas liars say things that they know to be false. Thus, I would like to define what a "dick" is.

dick (dik) *n. Slang*
a person who willfully and/or knowingly disregards the comfort, desires, and/or needs of others, especially those in close proximity to oneself.
'*That guy just cut me off because he didn't even see me coming! What a dick!*'
'*That woman just cut in front of that pregnant lady to take the last donut! What a dick!*'
'*Did you see that kid with headphones walk right by that old lady who fell? What a dick!*'
'*She said she totally looked ugly in that dress and thought that being brutally honest was the right thing to do. What a dick!*'
'*He kept spitting the sunflower seeds on the floor of the bus. What a dick!*'

Certainly other adjectives can apply as well to dicks, including those in the examples, but the unifying element that makes you a dick is a complete lack of caring about the impact of your actions on others around you. None of these actions are necessarily morally wrong or even malicious. The dickery might not even be intentional, but the willfulness of the offending actions, whether malicious or not, are what makes you a dick.

There's a fine line between ignorance and dickery. For example, a person caught up in his thoughts blocking a shopping aisle in the supermarket, who promptly apologizes and moves out of the way when realizing what is happening, is not a dick. Someone who has the attitude everyone can go around him and blocks the aisles regardless of what is going on around him *is* a dick. Refusing to move when asked would also make said person a jerk—moving when asked, however, does not stop them from being a dick, as the offending actions still qualify as evidence toward dickery. The former individual who was merely ignorant of the actions is not necessarily a dick, as there was no willingness or knowledge of the offending actions as being such. The person was just absent-minded. In the latter case, the dick purposefully chose not to care about others. Superman chooses to disregard the needs and comfort of others in ways that is unacceptable given his abilities. I'm not a dick for not flying across town to stop a car from hitting a pedestrian since I'm not willfully ignoring it, I'm just completely unaware of it. Superman is choosing to be unaware of it, and, even worse, failing to act on it despite that fact that it would be really, really easy for him to do so.

Superman does do a lot of good and save people. I'm not going to call the guy a total douchebag, since he certainly doesn't do bad things. I'll give credit where credit is due: he really probably has done, and will do, much more than Batman ever can or will. This is why I won't label him a bad person or, similarly to e.e. cummings calling us man(un)kind, a super(un)hero. But I will call him a dick.

Superman is a dick because he has the ability to do much more with his power. If he concentrates, he can use his super-hearing to hear many crimes going on at once. Sure, it takes some concentration and takes a toll on him emotionally to listen to all these bad things at once, but he can do it. He can then use his super-speed to stop all those crimes in almost the same instant. His multiple races with The Flash have shown that they are of comparable speed, so he could rescue everyone from everything (except maybe a laser beam once it's been fired, since he can only travel *as fast* as light, and not faster). It might be taxing to figure out the optimal route, but he could do it. He might get tired, but he could just recharge with a super-nap or something. Even if he doesn't stop *all* of the crimes in, say, just Metropolis, he could certainly stop more than he does while he wastes his time working at the *Daily Planet*.

If you had to choose between working at a newspaper or saving the world, which one would you pick? If you said the former, then I'm going to have to call you a dick. The only reason Superman keeps his Clark Kent alter-ego is for himself, as anything Clark could do, Supes could do better. If every criminal knew that Superman could, and would, show up at any moment during any crime, they would think twice and cower in fear when they actually chose to defy the law and test the Man of Steel. Thankfully, Superman would rather actually work at the *Daily Planet* instead of just eavesdrop and use them for intel. I'd much rather be a criminal in Metropolis where I know that the Superhero isn't lurking in the shadows waiting for me like that scary dude over in Gotham is.

Who's Afraid of the Big Black Bat?

Everyone is afraid of Batman. Even if you're a good, upstanding citizen of Gotham, you're afraid of the big black bat. Why? Because he's scary. Batman doesn't show up to wish a kid happy birthday. No; when you see Batman, you know something's going to happen. Who's afraid of Superman? A lot of criminals would rather not meet him, but they're not really scared of him. You know who should be scared of him? Everyone. Because he can know where you are at all times and what you're doing if he just decided to spend an instant of his time looking at you. Good thing for criminals Superman is too lazy and self-centered to care enough to keep tabs on them when they commit <insert heinous criminal act here>.

Supes, when compared to Bats, just simply doesn't get dirty enough to be feared by criminals. That's because Batman always shows up when they least expect it and stops anything and everything he comes by—and he does his best to find everything that he can stop. Superman, however, lets crime happen. Batman would never let a crime occur that he knows is happening, but Superman does. What makes Batman even scarier is that he's just a man. He's risking his life every time he enters a dangerous situation and still beats the baddies. He fears nothing. That makes him a badass, and to top it off, he tries his hardest every moment. Doing this, and not willfully looking the other way, makes Batman definitely not a dick. But what would happen if Batman were more powerful, like as powerful as Superman?

SuperBat versus ManMan

In the comics *Superman/Batman* #53–56 we get a wonderful story: apparently Batman's deepest desire is to have Superman's powers because he gets them when Banshee unleashes the power of the Brooch of Cawdor that grants those desires (at a price, of course). Batman gets Superman's powers and becomes "SuperBat" while Superman gets Batman's "powers" and becomes a normal mortal, whom we will have to call "ManMan" to maintain balance. The way the two react to their new characteristics is enlightening, and shows just how much more awesome The Dark Knight is than the Man of Tomorrow.

Batman, being a mortal man, gets severely hurt in the encounter with Banshee. While being operated on by Alfred, he suddenly gets completely healed and is on his way to being SuperBat. Meanwhile, in Metropolis, Superman starts his slow decline of losing powers and turning into ManMan. After realizing what happened, ManMan trains SuperBat in the ways of Kryptonian awesomeness. While hunting for Banshee to find a way to reverse the spell, ManMan enjoys the life of actually being boring, mild-mannered Clark Kent and the calmness it brings. Of course, he tries to stop a mugging, apparently having forgotten that he is no longer the Man of Steel, and just a Man of Meat, and gets shot. Meanwhile, SuperBat ditches Robin for holding him back so that he can clean up Gotham in a night. And he pretty much does that, even flying to the Caribbean hideout of Bane to stop the manufacture and distribution of a drug at its source. He uses harsher (but not inappropriate) techniques than he normally might, and he gets the job super-done super-fast.

ManMan is trying to heal up and gets some help from friends at the Justice League who are a little disturbed at how far Batman has gone in his crime fighting, especially when he hurts his friends that try to stop him from going "overboard." Apparently going hard on murderous criminals and stopping all of them is a bit much for The Justice League, though I'm not exactly sure why. SuperBat follows the night cleaning up every city as darkness descends upon it. In one long night he stops every single crime that he can, and that's a lot of crime that puts a lot of baddies in jail.

A few thoughts enter SuperBat's mind while he's getting "drunk" on his superpowers: Why is Superman such a whiner about his powers and the responsibility that comes with them? Why doesn't he stop more crimes than he does? SuperBat finally has the power to do everything he always wanted to do and finally put an end to all crime. The responsibility is great and madness can come to someone with such abilities, but a little bit of focus and training can mean a whole lot of good can be accomplished. And SuperBat does accomplish a lot of good. So why hasn't Superman done more to clean up the world? Why doesn't he do so on a regular basis? Notwithstanding his few moments of glory to try to get world peace—like *Superman IV: The Quest for Peace* (1987)—Superman really does seem capable of doing more than he does. A whole lot more, especially if he's let so much crime go on under his nose that SuperBat fills all the jails everywhere he goes in only a few hours, and that's when he's just getting started.

SuperBat goes nuts and captures all of the bad guys (and girls) he can *because* he can. He no longer has to sleep or even eat—or ask Robin for help. He can do anything and everything to catch every human smuggler in at least a five-mile radius of where he is at any given time. SuperBat goes on an endless crime-fighting spree because that is what heroes do: heroic things, like stopping baddies and saving innocent people. To be able to stop crimes but refraining from doing so is unconscionable for SuperBat. He's the opposite of a dick (except for maybe the fact that he is not the most personable hero, but that just makes him a jerk, not a dick). The story arc ends with, predictably, Superman getting his powers back and Batman returning to his normal self. So why doesn't Superman do more with his powers and save more people? Should he even be saving more people? Or can he just continue to save people when he feels like it and it appears to be convenient?

Saving People Is Super-Necessary, not Supererogatory, Superman

Supererogatory is a very fun word that ethicists use. To call an action "supererogatory" is to say that it is an action that is good for people to take but lies beyond their moral obligations. For example, we are morally obligated to not shoot human children for fun. Most people are not morally obligated to stop and check on the people involved in a car accident that occurs just in front of them while driving on a busy freeway, at the very least because doing so could be dangerous. Those trained or working as emergency personnel, however, ought to. If you think that a regular person should stop and provide aid, then doing so should be supererogatory. Helping would be going above and beyond what you need to do and into the realm of nice to do. Someone gives you a delicious box of Belgian chocolates made only a day ago in a wonderful chocolate shop in Brussels. Do you *have* to share it with your chocolate-loving friends? Probably not. Would it be nice of you? Definitely. Sharing is usually supererogatory, at least that's how I'm teaching it to my five-year-old daughter so she doesn't expect everyone to always share with her. So, is saving people obligatory or supererogatory for Superman?

My argument that Superman is a dick rests on the answer to one important question: Can Superman save more people than he currently does at little or no cost to himself? If he can, then he's a not a superhero, and barely even a hero. On top of that, if he willingly chooses not to save those people, he's also a dick. Let's examine a situation that may very well happen to Clark Kent: While sitting at his desk at the *Daily Planet*, Clark Kent gets the urge to enjoy a delicious chocolate treat. He opens up his desk drawers, fumbles around, and finds eighty-five cents, in the form of eight dimes and a nickel. This is just enough to buy his favorite baked chocolate good from the vending machine, so he is quite happy. Finding the change took him exactly forty-seven seconds. He then walks over to the vending machine, puts in the coins, and pushes E-1. Nothing happens. He tries it two more times, and then looks at the screen: it only registered that seventy-five cents was inserted. This whole process has taken thirty-seven more seconds. He looks in the coin return, and sees a dime in there. He drops it into the coin slot again, and it drops into the return box again. He tries this two more times and then notices that it is a Canadian dime, adding seventeen seconds to the ordeal. He then asks around for a "real" dime, finds one, and finally gets the tasty treat that he wanted to munch on after thirty-five more seconds. Total time to get the goods from start to finish: two minutes and sixteen seconds.

Now, let's rewind these two minutes and sixteen seconds and see what was happening at the exact moment Superman started to look through his desk for loose change: a few blocks away on the Clinton Bridge in Metropolis, a car cut off a school bus, causing the driver to lose control and crash into the West River. The impact resulted in some injuries and recent rains have filled the river causing the swift current to quickly pull the bus under the water, putting the lives of many children in danger.

Superman was not planning on spending the next minute or so working already at this point. He may have the heard the crash, and if he did not, he didn't because he was choosing not to listen. Changing his clothes, flying to the bus, rescuing the children, and returning to his desk would not take Superman more than two-minutes and ten seconds—a whole six seconds shorter than it would end up taking him to get his small chocolate treat and return to his desk to enjoy it. In those extra six seconds, he probably could have also obtained the mini baked good using his super speed if he wasn't worried about people seeing him, but even then he probably could have been so fast about no one would have seen him grab it. So Superman could have saved everyone, gotten his cake, and eaten it, too. What would be the cost here for him? Paying a little more attention to others? Working a little faster doing the mundane things in life? I'm not really finding a real cost here, except a little bit of effort.

If you could save someone's life by simply giving that person a penny, do you *have* to do it? Let's assume that you had enough money to buy this book. If you had enough money to buy this book, then you could certainly afford a penny to save someone's life. You can give them that penny and it will cost you just one cent. That's almost nothing—in fact, if you just found a penny, it cost you the amount of time it took to bend down and pick it up. If it took such little effort and cost to yourself to save a life, then you are obligated to do it.

Solve this math problem without a calculator: $23 \times 6 = ???$. What if solving that saved someone's life? You'd have to expend just a little bit of brain power to do it. Similarly, it would seem wrong for Superman to let someone die just so he could get a mini chocolate cake. It's not that hard for Superman to save lives if he just puts a little bit of effort into it, so doing so is not supererogatory, it's obligatory. Now, what if I tell you that every time you do a math problem like this, someone is saved? Don't do the problem, and someone dies. Every few seconds you don't do it, someone dies. It's not that it will be never-ending–do enough of them, and the amount you have to keep doing greatly slows down. You become so good at doing the equations that you can almost do them in your sleep. Let's say that you can do hundreds of thousands in just a few hours. All of the work adds up, and it's very taxing, but you can do it. Do you have to?

I would like to say you have to do a lot of them, at least up to a point. If you have to do this once, then you should have to do it repeatedly, within reason. However, you don't really *have* to do them. You can choose not to, since it's your time and you can do with your time what you want. But you can do it, a lot. If you don't do it, you're pretty much a dick, since you chose not to do something small for you, but so important for another person. I'll just have to tell little Timmy's mommy that you were too busy to solve 67 × 22 and save his life. No, you had to go and read a philosophy book for fun instead.

Superman can clearly save more people than he does, but Batman might be at his people-saving peak since he's limited by stupid things like mortality and non-super abilities. Let's say that Superman takes the bus to work and it takes him fifteen minutes. Instead, he could have flown to work and used the other fourteen minutes and fifty-nine seconds to save *at least* one person. Would this even cost him anything? Instead of taking the bus, he'd actually save money by flying. He would get to work at the same time and have the same total commute time, only he'd take a little detour to do some good. His opportunity cost by flying to work and saving someone on the way is not taking the bus and paying money. From someone who regularly rides the bus (myself), that doesn't really sound like a cost. If I could fly to work and save money, time, and a person on the way, then I'd rather do that—I'd *better* do that. And Superman should, too. Any time that he can save someone at little or no cost to himself, then he really ought to do it. But how much good does he really have to do?

How Much Is Too Much? How Little Is Too Little?

To save people, Superman does have to do a bit more than just solve some math problems. Batman certainly has to do a lot more than that. But how much can we expect them to do? How much is *too* much to expect from them? We need to find the right balance of their moral obligations, lest I be rash in calling Superman a dick. If he is doing what we can reasonably expect of him, then I'd be the dick for calling him a dick. And I don't want to be a dick.

Let's look at ourselves first. How much do we normal, non-heroic types have to do for others? There is a moral problem that the philosopher Peter Singer first brought to everyone's attention that is often called "the problem of famine and affluence." The problem raises a question about the disparate qualities of living people have around the world, and amounts to this: Is it morally consistent for many people in the world to enjoy high levels of affluence while many other people are famished and might not even have the basic goods necessary for a minimally happy life? For example, we have comic books and superhero movies while others do not have basic vaccines. While it's difficult to put exact numbers on what it costs to provide services to impoverished children in need of clean water, food, and vaccines, the cost of a polio vaccine dose for UNICEF is as little as ten cents. Let's just assume that obtaining, shipping, and administering that dose more than doubles the base cost of that vaccine, then it would cost less than a quarter to immunize a child for polio, potentially saving its life. Other vaccines don't cost much more—you could search your couch cushions for enough money to provide most of the vaccines any child in the world needs to be protected from some of the most deadly diseases. For the cost of money we didn't even know we had, we could be saving some lives, but we usually don't, and instead buy ice cream, watch movies, and buy books.

The fact that you're reading this book means that you enjoy a certain level of affluence, and it's safe to say that you're quite better off than more than half of the people in the world. You have regular access to clean water, toilets, food, and health care, and don't have to worry too much about dying in a war or from diarrhea (which is a really crappy way to go). You also have money to spend on things unnecessary for living, like cell phones, computers, books, and lattes. Other people in the world (perhaps even those just a few blocks from where you live) have to seriously worry about where they'll get their next mouthful of water and whether or not it's safe to drink. What do we, the affluent, owe to these other people, the famished?

We might not owe them anything, but it seems morally wrong that we might enjoy such luxuries while others are starving *if* foregoing those luxuries will alleviate the suffering of other people. We certainly can help those less fortunate than us rather easily and go without all sorts of things we enjoy, but we don't want to. We also don't have to, as we're still generally morally allowed to do whatever we want with whatever properly earned money and goods that we have.

Why can't I do what I want with what I got? Because, unfortunately, we do have to help other people if we're to be morally good. Perhaps it's fine to purchase a thousand-dollar TV if it will bring you a good amount of satisfaction to your life, but what about spending twenty thousand on your own home theater system complete with a concessions stand, while other people die from lack of water, food, and basic shelter? We can be self-centered to a point, but enjoying too many unnecessary things might be morally repugnant if others are dying so that we can consume those luxuries. We can maintain some level of affluence for ourselves, but we can't just completely ignore those in need. We ought to give them what we can afford while still being able to go to the movies.

How many times have you dropped change on the dark, sticky floor at a theater and decided not to pick it up since it's just too gross? That money you just threw away could have saved a life. We don't have to give those in need too much, but we also can't give too little. It will vary across people for what we all will have to do, but we ought to give what we can, especially if we can do it at little or no real cost to ourselves.

Batman and Superman are the "affluent" heroes and we are the "famished" non-heroes. They have the means to help us average citizens. Just as we're obligated to help those less-fortunate than ourselves if we can do so at little or no cost, they are obligated to help us in a similar fashion. It is unfortunate (or fortunate) for them that they are capable of doing things to help those in need, and because they have the ability to do so, they must do so—to an extent. They can't do nothing, but they may not have to do everything. They just really have to do what they can, given their abilities and limitations.

Superman does not have to rush into a building full of kryptonite gas and kryptonite rose bushes. Batman may not have to run into a burning fireworks factory to save the arsonist that set the fire. Superman *does* have to catch a baby falling out of a building. Batman *does* have to stop the mugging at knifepoint. Superman doesn't have to stop all parents from spanking their children too hard. Batman doesn't have to throw himself in front of a grenade, but if he can, he should stop the guy from pulling the pin in the first place. Batman doesn't have to stay up all day every day to stop everything since he has to sleep sometimes. Superman, however, doesn't have to sleep. What can he do without disrupting his life or sanity too much? A lot, I'm guessing. Gotham, for example, is a mess—Superman, as SuperBat has proven, could help clean it up in no time. Certainly he could spend just five minutes and stop a human trafficking ring, like SuperBat did, without really costing him all that much.

So what's worth more than saving a few people from slavery? For Batman, almost nothing. Batman puts forth as much effort as he can do what he can, and when he is SuperBat, there is a whole lot of good he does. For Superman, what is worth more than saving a few people from slavery? Chilling in his arctic fortress and making decorating decisions. Pretending to nap at his desk at work. Going shopping. Searching for change and buying a candy bar. I'll allow him to do these things to an extent, but he could certainly do more, stop more crimes, and save more people than he does.

Unless in between every panel in every comic and in every scene that he's absent from in a movie he is actually saving the world, then he can do more. He doesn't have to do everything, but with how messy the world is, he could certainly do more. But he doesn't. Superman does less than he ought to because he's just a selfish dick. He places an unhealthy value on his personal pursuits when compared to the good that he can do. Batman, however, does do what he can, at an even greater cost to himself. That makes him not a dick and a real hero.

Superman, the Super Dick

Sorry, Superman, not everything is super: saving people when you can at little or no cost to yourself is not *super*erogatory, it's obligatory. Batman seeks out complete strangers to save all the time *because* they need him, even when he might die doing it. We even expect normal people to save others when they can, assuming it is not dangerous to do so. The responsibility might weigh heavily on Superman and take its toll on him psychologically, but Superman, being *Super*, does have a real obligation to do more than he does for the good of mankind.

Yes, Batman is quite flawed and *just* a really badass (and rich) dude with a lot of sweet gear, but at least I know he'd save me if he could, and Superman, the Super Dick, probably would not. Batman doesn't win this fight, but Superman loses it superbly.

I'm not necessarily saying Superman's *wrong* for choosing not to save everyone that he can, but he's definitely a dick. A Super Dick.

19

Overpower versus Empowerment

Sébastien Hock-Koon

Superman is close to being the ultimate superhero: he can fly, he's strong, fast, pure-hearted, nearly invincible . . . Sadly for us gamers, some of these very qualities also make him a very bad video game hero.

Superman and Batman have appeared in roughly the same number of movies. There are six *Superman* movies, seven if you include the *Supergirl* spin-off, and seven *Batman* movies. However, when you consider video games, if you include the different platforms, there are almost a hundred *Batman* video games while you can't find fifteen of their *Superman* counterparts.

Quantity is not the only differentiating factor; while the *Batman:Arkham* series is both critically and publically acclaimed, it's hard to come up with one good *Superman* video game. If game developers were entirely responsible for this, it would mean that *Superman* is just unlucky with video games. As a player, a game designer, and a game design teacher, I consider that it's harder to create a good *Superman* video game than to create a good *Batman* video game because Superman is stronger than Batman. It may be hard to admit, but *Superman* video games suck because their main character is far too powerful. Batman, a mere human, makes a far better video game hero.

Kryptonian Superpowers versus Human Tricks and Training

Let's start by comparing the two characters' abilities. In the red corner, we present to you Superman, a.k.a. Clark Jerome Kent, a.k.a. Kal-El, a.k.a. the Man of Steel. He was born on the planet Krypton and sent to Earth as a baby by his father Jor-El before their planet's destruction. Discovered and adopted by a couple of Kansas farmers, he has been raised as Clark Jerome Kent. From early childhood, he has been displaying superhuman abilities which he decided to use for the benefit of humanity. His favorite colors seem to be blue, red, and yellow. He traditionally likes to wear blue costumes with red trunks held by a yellow belt, red boots, and a long flowing red cape, recently his trunks disappeared and the belt turned red. His chest bears a characteristic red and yellow "S" symbol. His alter-ego, Clark Kent, is a journalist for the *Daily Planet*, a Metropolis newspaper. Superman does not wear a mask; all he needs to hide his secret identity is a pair of glasses.

In the (dark) blue corner, we present to you Batman, a.k.a. Bruce Wayne, a.k.a. the Dark Knight. He's an American billionaire, industrialist, and philanthropist living in Gotham City. After witnessing the murder of his parents as a child, he swore to devote his life to fighting crime. Unlike many superheroes, Batman does not possess any superpower. He uses his intellect, detective skills, martial arts training, and technology against criminals. His favorite color is unknown; but whatever it is, it should be a fairly dark one. His outfit is modeled after a bat to frighten his enemies. A dark cowl with a pair of bat-like ears protects his secret identity. He usually wears a dark costume, a dark cape, dark gloves, dark boots, and a utility belt for his various gadgets.

Superman's powers and characteristics have evolved over several decades; here is a selection of the most common or notable ones:

- **Flight: originally, Superman was only able to jump over tall buildings. But the Superman we all know can fly in the air. In some cases, he can also fly in space and from planet to planet.**

- **Superhuman strength: simply put, Superman is really strong— strong enough to lift a bus, a plane, or a mountain, to make a planet move, or to crush diamonds with his bare hands.**

- **Superhuman speed: Superman is said to be faster than a bullet, however, in order to fly from planet to planet or reverse the Earth's rotation, one's speed should be closer to the speed of light than to the speed of a bullet.**

- Invulnerability: the Man of Steel is immune to everything . . . well, almost everything. Somehow, his outfit seems to share this ability since it appears unharmed even after facing laser beams that could melt a building.

- Superhuman senses: these superhuman senses include, but are not limited to, x-ray, infrared, telescopic and microscopic visions, ultrasound, infrasound and ultrasensitive hearings, and heightened and highly accurate sense of smell.

- Heat vision: Superman's eyes can emit laser-like beams which are not only powerful enough to destroy steel or rocks but also precise enough to perform surgical interventions at microscopic levels.

- Freeze breath: with his breath Superman can cool things down to sub-zero temperatures and freeze air moisture solid. His freeze breath combines well with his ability to inhale or exhale enormous volumes of air.

- Vulnerability to Kryptonite: Superman's one and only weakness: exposure to a piece of rock from his birth planet makes him lose the aforementioned abilities and turn into a mere human being.

Arguably, vulnerability to Kryptonite makes Superman a more interesting character; without it the Man of Steel would be purely and simply invincible. It is harder to create tension with an invincible character.

In complete contrast, Batman does not have any inherent superpowers. But he compensates for what he lacks in superhuman gifts with human skills and abilities . . . and also state-of-the-art equipment:

- Investigation Skills: Batman is considered to be one of the world's greatest crime solvers. He is a very efficient interrogator and investigator familiar with law enforcement methods.

- Martial Arts Training: even though he uses his appearance to frighten his enemies, Batman is among the finest martial artists in the DC Universe. Among the martial arts he studied, ninjutsu makes him a stealth master.

- **Genius-level Intellect:** along with his physical abilities, Batman benefits from one of the most brilliant minds of the planet; his mind has allowed him to defeat Superman at least once before ... with a little help from an alien green stone.

- **The Batsuit:** While the cape allows Batman to glide in the air, the latest versions of the Dark Knight's costume also include armor that protects him from bullets, impacts, heat, cold, blades ...

- **Utility Belt:** this belt is supposed to be quite normal—not super natural; however its exact content is unknown. It gives him an uncanny ability to carry exactly the appropriate tool for a given situation.

- **Many other Bat-Things:** in the Batcave, Batman stores many useful devices and vehicles to fight crime. These include the famous Batmobile, the Batplane a.k.a. the Batwing, and the Batboat.

It seems that Superman and Batman could hardly be more different. On the one hand, we have a humanoid coming from another planet who seems to have limitless or almost limitless superpowers, while on the other hand we have a mere human who has to make up for his limitations with his brain, training, and equipment. This has consequences for the way they face challenges. Superman's approach is pretty straightforward: the menace is often clearly identified and all he has to do is to end it. When he faces difficulties, it does not mean that the Man of Steel is not strong enough but that he is not using his unlimited superpowers enough. Usually, the only thing required from him is the force of will necessary to get back up, withstand the pain, and unleash his powers.

However, the approach is not so clear for Batman: he has to find a way. This may mean finding evidence in order to find the right person and the right way to make him or her talk in order to find the culprit of a crime. When he faces opponents stronger than himself, the Dark Knight has to find a way to defeat them, whether by discovering their weakness, learning the right technique, or using the right tool. At first sight, it might seem that Superman would be a much more enjoyable character to play than Batman. However, ...

Invincibility Sucks . . . Among Other Things

Dear reader, if you have ever played a video game in your life, let me ask you a couple of questions. We can argue that Superman is both (almost) invincible and almighty. Have you often played a character that was invincible? I am not talking about the temporary invincibility given by a magic potion, but about a character being permanently or almost permanently insensible to all the threats he or she could encounter in a video game.

Have you often played a character that was almighty? Once again, I am talking about a character being permanently so powerful that he or she could destroy any enemy or obstacle faced in the game with one punch. If you're an experienced player, the answers to these two questions should be "No." The reason for this is simple: video games are far more about getting stronger than about being strong.

There is a particular state that game designers try to make players reach called "flow." The original concept was created by Mihály Csikszentmihaly, who stated that flow lies between boredom and anxiety. Designers consider that flow is reached when there is a balance between the challenges offered by an activity and the skills of the person performing the activity. If this person is too skilled, he or she might get bored; if he or she is not skilled enough, he or she might be anxious. There is a very appropriate expression in the English language to describe flow: when one player is far stronger than his or her opponent, one might say that the second is "no match" for the first. Flow refers to the exact opposite of this situation; it is what happens when the strength of the two opponents is balanced, when there is a match between them. One might wonder about the difficulty to find a match for Superman.

Let's assume that, at a given empoment, a given player has reached flow with a game. It means that the difficulty of the game offers a proper challenge to his or her skills. The most enjoyable video game experience does not occur when the player is stronger than necessary but when there a balance between his or her skills and the challenge offered by the game. If difficulty does not evolve, the player will get better, sooner or later, and the game might get boring. Maintaining this balance while the player evolves through the game is not easy. Instead of considering flow between the player and the game, let us consider it between the "player + played character" and the game's obstacles. In our case, the played characters are obviously Superman and Batman. Both the player and the played character can get stronger, but they do so in different ways.

On the Played Character's Side

Video game researcher Jonas Linderoth has explained that it's possible to make the playable character stronger so that learning, which means developing your skills, isn't necessary to succeed in a game. To make the character stronger, designers have many means at their disposal such as more powerful equipment, capacity upgrades, and bonuses. Does this sound familiar?

Batman can train or acquire new equipment or vehicles when it's needed. He can become stronger, so he offers many possibilities for designers to create difficult obstacles as well as the solutions that make them easier to overcome. In addition to that, equipment may easily be lost or destroyed. In the *Metroid* series, Samus Aran spends her time finding new equipment to make her Power Suit more powerful. The fewer items the player collects, the more difficult the game will be. At the end of a *Metroid* game, the played character is usually far more powerful than at the beginning. But at the beginning of every *Metroid* game, Samus also loses all of her upgrades and goes back to the basic Power Suit. In the early games, the loss was not justified, but in the later ones, an explanation, or an excuse, is given to the player.

Resetting the played character's capacities is a way to avoid an escalade in powers. In *Dragon Ball,* this trick was not used by Akira Toariyama and this led to a rather extreme consequence—Goku going over the years from "I can cut wood with my bare hands" to "I can destroy entire planetary systems." Just like Samus Aran, the Dark Knight may gain new equipment throughout a given game and lose it for the one after. By contrast, it's hard for Superman to gain or to lose abilities, as he has built-in superpowers. He acquired them and trained in order to master them while he was growing up.

Of course, it would be possible to make the game start during Superman's childhood. When Clark Kent was young and forced to master his powers so that he did not kill anybody, he was not Superman yet. Using Kryptonite to make him lose these powers is also possible but not doable every time. However, Kryptonite neutralizes *all* of Superman's superpowers, which means he cannot, unlike Batman, recover them one by one.

Losing abilities is not an issue with the *Metroid* franchise because the main interest of the game is to be alone in a hostile environment and to look for ways to eliminate the main threat and to get off the planet alive. There's a substantial difference between what it means to play Batman and what it means to play Superman. The main thrill about playing Superman is being the Man of Steel, using his overwhelming powers. Losing them makes the player miss a part of the core experience. The main thrill about playing Batman is to be the Dark Knight, a crusader fighting crime in the shadows. Even without equipment, the experience is not altered.

There are two main issues a game designer has to deal with when the playable character is the Man of Steel. Firstly, a fully grown Superman is either overpowered or completely powerless because of Kryptonite. There is nothing in between, he does not use any device, weapon, or equipment, nor learn any technique. It's difficult to create a proper challenge for this type of character.

Secondly, being overpowered is a part of the experience of playing Superman. Almost by definition, he is the most powerful superhero of the DC Universe. A too powerful playable character can easily make a game boring. On the other hand, Batman can acquire new skills or equipment, making it easier to design a more varied and challenging experience. Losing or gaining abilities is independent of the essence of the Dark Knight. It offers designers a great plasticity without betraying the original character.

On the Player's Side

If we were to compare video games and movies or comics, what would be the main difference? From a game designer's point of view, one of the most crucial differences is that the author of a comic book or movie choses what the main character will do or what he or she will think. In a video game, the player decides what the main character will do most of the time. It implies that designers have to create a space with many possible paths instead of just drawing and describing one of them. Since the player is in control of the main character, we might say that he or she would basically play Superman's or Batman's brain. The player is the one giving order to the superhero and it leads to some problems in terms of design.

When a character is stronger than another or becomes stronger than before, it's rather easy to represent it in a video game. Instead of destroying a wall with one punch, he or she could wipe out an entire building. The consequences in the game are obvious and immediately noticeable. How can one show that a character is smarter than another or that this character is getting smarter? I mean in the game itself, not during in-game cinematics. Essentially, it is really hard because cleverness is a helpful quality when one has to understand how something works, find solutions or take decisions.

In a video game, these very tasks are performed by the player instead of the played character. When the player orders Batman or Superman to punch a wall, it's actually the character that punches it and the consequences on the wall should be quite different. When Superman or Batman has to find a solution to a problem in a video game, it's actually the player who is in charge of the problem. He or she has to find the solution that will be applied by the played character.

We've seen that Batman has a brilliant mind and is an expert investigator. He uses these qualities to solve crimes. While Superman is also said to be highly clever, he uses his muscles or any other power more often than his exceptional brain. Once again, the main element of the *Superman* experience is to use superpowers, while investigation and reflection are fully legitimate parts of the *Batman* experience. This is one more task that the player can be charged with when playing the Dark Knight. As the character also co-operates with the police, designers have an easy way to provide help when the player takes too much time to find a solution, be it a call from Jim Gordon to provide additional information or a police intervention. Once again, *Batman* offers more possibilities to designers than *Superman*.

On the Heart's Side

With the player being the brain and the played character being the body, there's still an element missing. Even with Superman's powers, the right understanding of the situation, and the choice of the right thing to do, an individual would need something more to accomplish it, especially if the right thing is difficult to do. The same thing goes for Batman as his training, his skills, and his equipment are not what make him a superhero.

The difference between someone with superpowers and a superhero lies in the desire to devote these powers to good, the motivation to fight for justice. We might say that these qualities reside in the heart of the character. It takes the heart of a hero to turn someone with superpowers into a superhero and this very heart may also turn a person without any superpowers into a superhero. Their hearts are what allows both Superman and Batman to withstand pain and keep fighting until victory. This element is extremely difficult to introduce in a video game.

Video game journalist Nicolas Verlet has studied a similar issue with the manga series entitled *Saint Seiya* a.k.a. *Knights of the Zodiac* . In *Saint Seiya*, every hero has access to an infinite power called Cosmo, the only thing required to harness this power is the heart of a hero. Every single one of them is basically a Superman, it is their heart that gives them the strength to get up and keep fighting even after being beaten to a pulp. Nicolas Verlet considers that this is one of the elements making the series very difficult to adapt into a video game. Indeed, not a single *Saint Seiya* game is considered a good game. No video game can require from the player the force of will necessary to come back from the verge of death in order to save your comrades. The only thing a video game can ask the player is to do the right action on the controller at the right moment. It can put the player's dexterity, speed, or sagacity to the test but not his or her will, at least not directly. Willpower may be necessary to train in order to get the skills required by the game, but it will never be tested directly by the game.

I'm not saying that either Superman or Batman is more heroic than the other; they both share the same heart of a hero. However, the way their heart is put to use is different. Superman has almost unlimited power at his disposal and his will allows him to use the full potential of his powers. A normal Kryptonian punch would be destructive in any situation on a human scale, but no supervillains would be glad to take a punch in which Superman put all his heart. This mechanism is really hard to transfer accurately into a video game. Batman has very limited powers but almost unlimited money and free time. His commitment to fighting crime makes him keep fighting even when at disadvantage or in pain. Designers cannot make players feel physical pain (yet) and being outnumbered and out powered is almost necessary to make a video game interesting. However, Batman also investigates himself, trains to be able to fight criminals, and looks for tools to defeat powerful enemies. These are things that a player can be put in charge of or that designers can provide him or her in a video game.

Rigid Steel and Flexible Dark

The differences between Superman and Batman regarding game design boils down to a question of flexibility: the Man of Steel is too rigid while the Dark Knight is flexible. Superman is either overpowered or powerless. When facing difficulties, his heart allows him to get the best out of his powers. Unfortunately, this mechanism is extremely difficult to transfer into a video game.

By contrast, Batman can obtain new possibilities through training or by acquiring new equipment. So, designers have a wide range of possibilities to create various interesting game situations. Being powerful, or even too powerful, is a defining element of *Superman* stories, making the character too rigid to easily adapt to the needs of the video game medium.

You might wonder whether or not there is a way to make up for this rigidity. I will purposely focus on action games. A *Superman* adventure game is of course conceivable, but the main challenge would be to make the player feel the character's might. Similarly to what was done in *Metroid: Other M*, Superman could be given objectives and orders that limit the use of his powers. However, it might be hard to create a believable situation in which a character could give orders to Superman.

Is there an overlooked part of the *Superman* character that could be used to make him a better video game hero? I would tend to think that there is one; this overlooked part is Clark Jerome Kent the journalist. At the end of the *Man of Steel* movie, Superman is asked what he intends to do when he is not saving the world and answers "I gotta find a job where I can keep my ear to the ground, where people will not look twice when I want to go somewhere dangerous and start asking questions." It shows that no matter how powerful he might be, he still needs information to know who and where to fight. As for me, it could be a very interesting starting point for a good *Superman* video game.

When playing Clark Kent, the player would have to collect information and investigate in order to know where Superman's powers are the most needed. He or she could also be presented with dilemmas where the Man of Steel cannot intervene at the two different points at the same time. Sometimes, the player would have to find a way to save people without catching the media's attention which means using the hero's superpowers discreetly or making his interventions look like favorable turns of events.

When the player has successfully identified a powerful hidden enemy, he or she may be rewarded with the possibility of unleashing the full extent of Superman's might on his enemy without any restriction. It's easier said than done, but it could be a way to create an interesting game in which the player actually plays an almighty hero. This kind of challenge would be particularly exciting.

For now, Batman obviously makes for a better video game character than Superman. However, if designers manage to overcome the difficulty to create a good Superman game, the comparison might become less obvious and more interesting.

20
What It Takes

Trip McCrossin

"He's the hero Gotham deserves, but not the one it needs right now," Gordon explains to his son James, about Batman, in the closing moments of *The Dark Knight*. "Why's he running?," James naturally wonders, given that Batman's just risked his life to rescue him from Harvey Dent's evil alter ego, Two Face.

Unaware of his dad's secret pact with Batman to attribute his rescue to Dent, and Dent's death to Batman, in order that the people of Gotham not learn from Dent's true identity to "lose hope," James is understandably confused by the idea that Batman's running "because we have to chase him," all the more so that it's "because he's *not* a hero."

Gordon reiterates here Batman's own denial of his heroism only moments early, contrasts himself with Dent as Gotham's "true hero," and concludes by telling James, and us, that he's rather "a silent guardian, a watchful protector, a dark knight." But to James, and to us, it seems Batman's acted quite to the contrary—quite *heroically*.

The tension's ultimately resolved in the closing moments of *The Dark Knight Rises*. Batman's about to save Gotham from nuclear annihilation, sacrificing himself in the process it seems. "Shouldn't the people know the hero who saved them?" Gordon pleads. "Anyone can be a hero," Batman counters, accepting finally his own heroism, albeit with admirable modesty. A hero can be "even a man doing something as simply and reassuring," he says, referring to Gordon himself, "as putting a coat around a young boy's shoulders to let him know the world hadn't ended."

Fellow Justice League member Superman has a complicated relationship with heroism as well. Compare, for example, Lois Lane's early appraisal of Superman in *Man of Steel* with what his foster mom, Martha, urges him to remember in *Batman v Superman*. "The only way you could disappear for good is to stop helping people altogether," Lois speculates, upon finally tracking him down, "and I sense that's not an option for you." Martha's sense, on the other hand, is a different one, born of a parent's natural frustration with their child's mistreatment. "People hate what they don't understand," she complains, so "be their hero, Clark, be their angel, be their monument, be anything they need you to be. Or be none of it. You don't owe this world a thing. You never did." Superman's look in response is one of appreciation, but also consternation.

Batman and Superman share a complicated relationship with heroism, but also *differ* in how they reflect it—or don't, as it were, in light of the idea that Batman leaves Gordon with above: that essential to *being* a hero is the business of *making* new ones.

More or Less Heroic Superheroes

As members of the Justice League, however different their origin stories, Superman and Batman are both officially "superheroes." As such, we naturally assume that they're *heroes* in the first place, and so share at least three characteristics conventionally associated with their less super counterparts.

First, heroes act to keep those around them safe from harm and injustice—in the case of Batman and Superman, the citizens of Metropolis and Gotham City respectively, which in *Batman v Superman* are newly adjacent sister cities. But as *Man of Steel* makes clear, the hero's focus extends out from the local as need be, and ability allows. However locally or globally, though, one's not much of a hero if one's never done the basic safekeeping thing.

Second, they do so in a manner that's morally upright and generally beneficial, even if the benefit's not always immediately recognized and appreciated, or becomes unintentionally problematic over time. In the case of Superman, for example, his defense of humanity against General Zod's proposed genocide, as portrayed in *Man of Steel*, is later condemned in *Batman v Superman* for its collateral damage.

Finally, they do so *atypically*, in ways that the unheroic are unwilling or unprepared—though not necessarily unable—to act.

In addition to the above three characteristics, David Rand and Ziv Epstein have recently proposed a fourth. In their 2014 study of over fifty Carnegie Hero Medal recipients, given broad popular exposure in an op-ed article co-authored by Rand for *The New York Times* entitled "The Trick to Acting Heroically," they found that when subjects "explain why they decided to help, the cognitive processes they describe are overwhelming intuitive, automatic and fast"—more unreflective, that is, than reasoned. Granted, storylines in which Batman and Superman act in this additional way are readily available—Batman instinctively rescuing James, for example. Still, in keeping with the various "challenges" and possible "biases" and "disconnects" that the study's authors admit to, their finding seems less like *the* trick, than *a* trick to acting heroically, however interesting and productive it may be. We would otherwise rule out, that is, it would seem, more reflective instances of heroism just as readily available—Batman saving Gotham from nuclear annihilation, for example.

Sticking with the three previous characteristics of heroism, then, what makes heroes "super"? What makes them super is of course the conventional exaggeration of the first and the third characteristic. On the one hand, heroes act to safeguard others around them from harm and injustice not in a one-off or even occasional way, but *systematically*. On the other hand, they act in a manner not just atypical, but *radically* so.

While there are similarities between Batman and Superman as supposed heroes, there are also important differences, two in particular, which appear to make Batman considerably more heroic than Superman.

The Hero and the Samaritan

In addition to heroic acts consisting of the systematic, morally upright, radically atypical safekeeping of others, don't we also want them to be *supererogatory*—performed, that is, without obligation? Put another way, if a Good Samaritan is someone who acts to promote another's welfare, *on purpose*, but *not out of obligation*, then we can think of a hero in the same spirit, but not as just a *Good* Samaritan, but an *Extraordinary* Samaritan.

Heroism is a function not only of acts, but also of actors. To get at the idea in a bit more detail—that heroism is a function not just of acts, but of actors—let's contrast two real-life figures from the real-life Gotham, New York City.

On the 2nd of January in 2007, Wesley Autrey jumped into the subway tracks at the 137th Street station in Harlem to save a young man, Cameron Hollopeter, who had fallen in as a result of a seizure, laying over him in between the tracks as the oncoming subway rolled over them. For this, he was dubbed, among other things, the "Hero of Harlem." When asked to account for what motivated him to act as he did, however, he resisted the language of heroism, saying simply, "I don't feel like I did something spectacular; I just saw someone who needed help. I did what I felt was right."

A little over two years later, on the 15th of January in 2009, Captain Chesley "Sully" Sullenberger piloted US Airways flight 1549, which had been disabled shortly after take-off, to a remarkable emergency water landing onto the Hudson River, saving not only all those aboard, but all those who would have been injured or killed if the plane had gone down most anywhere else on either side of the river. For this, the *New York Daily News* dubbed him the "Hero of the Hudson." While then Mayor Bloomberg was surely right, though, to praise him for having done "a masterful job of landing the plane in the river and then making sure everybody got out," why, in the midst of the "Great Recession," when he might well have been on the lookout for available heroes, did he choose not to take advantage of the occasion? Presumably for the same reason that Sullenberger himself, reflecting a modesty as laudable as Autrey's, appraised his actions as simply "what we're trained to do."

Both are surely to be praised for their modesty, in resisting being dubbed heroes. Still, there's reason to resist such resistance, in one of their cases in particular, which in turn sheds light on Batman's and Superman's respective heroisms.

There are, no doubt, a variety of things that we can say about Autrey's and Sullenberger's personal backgrounds, inclining them in this or that way toward public service. Both of them served, for example, in the military. But such background is, it seems, less relevant to understanding Sullenberger's actions on his fateful day in January of 2009, than they may be in understanding Autrey's two years earlier. It's hard to imagine Sullenberger turning to his co-pilot, Jeff Skiles, and saying, "I'm sitting this one out, so it's your call what to do," and not being judged unjust in the process. Autrey, on the other hand, if he'd turned to someone on the subway platform and spoken similarly, we might well be sorry for the sentiment, but we would not similarly condemn him. To train to sit in a captain's chair, and eventually sit there, is to accept certain obligations toward your passengers, but simply to stand on a subway platform is to accept few, if any such obligations toward your fellow commuters.

Autrey was not obligated to act as Sullenberger was, but acted rather as a Samaritan, and not just a good one, but it would seem an *extraordinary* one. It's not for nothing that he's more widely known as the "Subway Samaritan," and for precisely this reason he's also the "Hero of Harlem."

But isn't there a worry here, in finding Autrey more heroic than Sullenberger, for the reasons we have, which may go even so far as to undermine the latter's heroism altogether—though, again, not his masterfulness? Thinking about the real and fictional Gotham Cities, what would the police officers and fire fighters of, say, the NYPD, FDNY, GCPD, and FDGC think about all of this? Wouldn't they take issue with the idea that doing well what they're "trained to do," even while routinely labeled heroic, would nonetheless not be heroic, at least some, perhaps much, maybe even any of the time?

In response, and of course with all due respect, we might distinguish *becoming* a police officer or fire fighter, and continuing then to *be* one, in the sense of *taking on* and then routinely *accepting* the corresponding general duty to serve the public, from the various particular duties fulfilled as a result. Even if we're reluctant to attribute heroism to the latter, as we are above to Sullenberger's "it's what we train for" masterfulness on the Hudson, we needn't extend such reluctance to the former. We might also be able still to attribute heroism to *certain* of the latter, which are relatively conspicuously "above and beyond the call." So, along the lines currently contemplated, we might be reluctant to attribute heroism to the relatively routine business of rescuing the Joneses from fire or burglary, we needn't be so when it's a matter of trying to rescue them from the World Trade Center on that fateful day.

With the distinction between Autrey and Sullenberger still in place, then, how do Batman and Superman compare? And what does this tell us about their supposed heroism as super-heroes? Let's look to Alfred for help.

Alfred's Fantasy

"I had this fantasy," Alfred admits to Bruce Wayne in *The Dark Knight Rises*, that while on annual holiday in Florence, during the latter's self-imposed exile from Gotham, "I would look across the tables and I'd see you there, with a wife and maybe a couple of kids," and would "know that you'd made it, that you were happy." In the end, both happily and credibly, we see Alfred's fantasy realized. It seems not only possible, but plausible, that Bruce Wayne would ultimately survive Batman, to enjoy a happy, if not uncomplicated retirement. And this, even while we imagine not so easily that Gotham is no longer in need of Batman's services.

We find it more difficult to imagine, however, let alone enjoy, such a depiction of Superman's retirement. It seems that the only way we can, is to depict it as voluntary, but disastrous, leading inevitably to his return, as in the 1980 *Superman II*, or as compelled or unhappy or both, as for example in the 1996 *Kingdom Come* comic book series.

In this sense, Superman's actions aren't easily understood as supererogatory, while Batman's more clearly are. And so Batman appears to be the more heroic of the two, not so much in terms of the four conventional characteristics of superhero-ism—the systematic, morally upright, radically atypical safe-keeping of others—but in terms of supererogation as the proposed fifth characteristic, of heroism and superheroism alike. And the difference persists, even if we were to apply to Batman the above distinction between the heroism of becoming and being a police officer or fire fighter and the less obviously heroic fulfillment of resulting duties.

But how does this all square with the "what defines us" dialogue that Rachel and Batman share in *Batman Begins*? "It's not who you are underneath," Rachel chides Bruce, "it's what you do that defines you," which Batman later paraphrases in revealing himself as Bruce. It does square, because to empha-size the importance of acting on one's beliefs, instead of merely entertaining them, needn't be to assert that having them in the first place is irrelevant to who we are. What Rachel must mean, in other words, and what Batman must mean in heeding her warning, is that it's not *only* who we are underneath that defines us. If Batman's to aspire to be a hero, that is, and we're to aspire similarly, and what we do heroically in the process must be, among other things, supererogatory, then it's precisely "who we are underneath" that makes them so.

Heroes Begetting Heroes

Let's return for a moment to Officer Gordon's "simply and reassuring" gesture, as Batman describes it years later to Commissioner Gordon, of "putting a coat around a young boy's shoulders to let him know the world hadn't ended." However simple it may have been for Gordon, it was nonetheless extraordinary to Bruce, as a young boy and later on, given that it *is* extraordinary still to Batman. Their final exchange is in part Batman's simple gesture now of encouraging Gordon to think of heroism as something any truly caring person embodies, and as a subtle way to reveal his identity.

Judging from the look on Gordon's face, though, it urges something more as well—that heroism tends to beget *more heroism*. By revealing his identity to Gordon, and by doing so by sharing *that* moment in particular, Batman is *also* revealing to Gordon that *he helped make Batman.* Even if only because it prevented Bruce from losing himself in total despair, that little moment made it possible for Bruce to carry on and eventually save Gotham. When someone is a hero, they make it possible for others to be heroes. They make it possible for others *to be like them.*

In addition, that is, to heroic acts consisting of the systematic, morally upright, radically atypical, and supererogatory safekeeping of others, it would seem that we also want them to be *replicable*, at least in principle, even if in practice this may involve considerable difficulty. To get at the idea in a bit more detail, consider again for a moment Mr. Autrey, the "Subway Samaritan," but now with a superpower particularly helpful on that fateful day in January.

What if we were to learn that he'd acquired some special trait, or skill, or technology that came into play in safeguarding young Cameron? Perhaps it allows him to lie especially flat and so at a safe distance from train cars passing overhead, for example, or leaves him his usual shape and size, but allows the back of his body to harden into a protective shell. Its origins might be accidental, as those that gave us Flash, or learned, as those that gave us Aquaman, or gifted, as those that gave us Green Lantern, or inborn, with some help from circumstance, as those that gave us Superman. Whatever its origin, it didn't make it *easy* for Autrey to safeguard young Cameron, but it nonetheless shielded him from harm in the process, in a manner we would naturally understand as unavailable to us, making it difficult for us to imagine that we'd have acted as newfangled Autrey did, or would in the future, should the occasion arise.

The question is this. However *super* such a newfangled Autrey would be, and however grateful young Cameron would surely still be, would *we* still think of Autrey as a hero? Arguably, we wouldn't. We might suggest that he apply for admission to the Justice League—as, say, Pancakeman or Turtleman—kin as he would seem to be to the likes of the above members. But at the same time, we would likely experience a sense of loss in learning that he was in no real danger. The reason we value Autrey as a hero, that is, as he *actually* is, and value heroes in general—differently than we'd value the newfangled Autrey, that is, and value superheroes in general— is because we imagine that if *they* can do what they do, then *others* can as well—perhaps even *we* can.

In this sense Batman's actions, while extraordinary, are the result of abilities that are fundamentally human, and so replicable by the rest of us. Superman's, however, while also extraordinary, result from abilities that are otherworldly, and so not replicable, either in principle or in practice. Both work for and among us, but only Batman does so as fundamentally *of us*. While we can be grateful to both, we can only truly aspire to be one of them. Even if we find Superman's actions at least relatively supererogatory, that is, and it's not all that clear that we can, Batman would still appear the more *morally exemplary*, and so the more heroic of the two.

But isn't this at odds with what Batman tells Gordon in their final exchange? "Anyone can be a hero," he says, and so why would not *any*one include Superman? Literally speaking, yes, perhaps, but there's a less literal interpretation that's more suitable. "Any *one of us* can be a hero," is what he means, according to the present perspective. But *not* any one of us—as in *no one* among us—can be Superman, except Superman, and so *he* doesn't fit the bill in the end, as hero, even while he's still clearly a superhero.

The Importance of What We Are Underneath

Superman and Batman emerge out of the pages of DC Comics at more or less the same time, in the summer of 1938 and spring of 1939 respectively, at a time in world history when humanity was in dire need of superheroes. Such need having hardly abated since, they have thrived, both of them, and will likely continue to thrive for the foreseeable future. If Batman's more heroic than Superman, as we're contemplating here, then their joint appearance at such a crucial moment in history, and their continued popularity, begs the question as to what's important about having under such circumstances not only superheroes, such as Superman, but also super *heroes*, such a Batman.

There are undoubtedly many reasons, but among them is likely this. The world seems to many of us to be, since early in the twentieth century, more and more fatally precarious. And it seems that *we* are mostly to blame. And so we can't help but doubt that our rescue can come ultimately from our own ranks. And so we turn to superheroes, such as Superman. But we also want there to be super *heroes*, such Batman, because we want still to hold out hope that there may remain a few brave souls in our ranks, maybe just the one, willing to don a mask and lead us anonymously out of our self-imposed social and political wilderness. We also hope that in the process they may be able to inspire others to act heroically.

At the outset, we've indeed just the one—just *the* Batman. But we also know something of his origins, and so perhaps what to look for in ourselves. They lie in part in the senseless murders of Bruce's parents. More importantly, they lie in what makes Bruce into Batman, rather than merely a more vengeful version of himself. Perhaps in this too there's something that can animate us, even in the absence of such personal tragedy.

Ultimately, Batman is Bruce's response to the problem of evil, as we hear Rachel invoke it, in challenging Bruce to *be* more by *doing* more. This old problem is commonly phrased as the question, Why do bad things happen to good people, and good things to bad people? or, a bit more philosophically, Why in the world are virtue and happiness so often reflected in us so disproportionally? Very old indeed, it began life as a theological problem, as far back as the Book of Job—how, according to Milton's turn of phrase in *Paradise Lost*, do we "justify the ways of God" to humanity?—but it has also now a *secular* version, as Susan Neiman has proposed.

According to *this* version, more akin to what we hear from Rachel, we are again asked to worry about the extent to which human reason can cope with the conspicuous misery of the human condition, but without worrying about God's role in it—given all of the breathtaking ways in which reason has developed us in history, that is, philosophically and scientifically, how can we make reasonable sense of a world still teeming with suffering that would appear to defy reason?

In Rachel's version of the problem, what "keeps the bad people rich and the good people scared," when it's so clear *who* does—Carmine "The Roman" Falcone, of course. The problem, in other words, as she goes on to say, is this—how, knowing what we know, can "good people do nothing"? Batman's the result of Bruce emerging as a good person indeed—"that same great kid" she grew up with, Rachel muses—but also as more than just this. He emerges also, as Rachel hopes someone will eventually, as a good person who does *something* in response to the problem. In her mind, it would seem, even this much is already heroic, and it's also in Batman's, as we remember from what he says finally to Gordon.

But Batman does more than just *something*, and hence is not only heroic, but *super* heroic. *This* he does by marshalling in the service of goodness *not only* the power of wealth, social standing, and physical prowess. Just as importantly, if not more importantly, Bruce becomes Batman, and Batman thrives as a hero, because in the service of goodness he marshals also what he shares conspicuously with the rest of us, which is the power of *reason*. To cite just one example, from *The Dark Knight*, consider Batman marshalling the multitude of cell phones in Gotham, in order to defeat the Joker, but in a way that ensures that the means are not subsequently abused, and that Lucius Fox's faith in him is restored. By contrast, while Superman's power never fails to impress, it also makes a Batman-style reliance on reason largely superfluous, which makes him powerfully *un*like us, and so powerfully *un*able to inspire heroism.

The long conversation about the problem of evil, which Rachel nicely channels for us, has evolved since the Enlightenment, as Neiman has also proposed, into primarily two competing perspectives—one beginning with Jean-Jacques Rousseau, which insists that morality, based in reason, "demands that we make evil intelligible," the other beginning with Voltaire, which insists that it "demands that we don't." The challenge of the former perspective is the business of not just being, but *making ourselves be* virtuous in a world that so often frustrates our other primary pursuit, which is happiness, tempting us in the process with the apparently speedier path, which is wickedness. In this, we naturally look to our heroes for guidance, and so, it would seem, our superheroes. But in the case of Batman and Superman, we find importantly differently models.

"You're all some people have," Lois Lane reminds Superman in *Batman v Superman*, "all that gives them hope"—hope for their safety, that is, and so their happiness, at least in part. But can they similarly hope to embody whatever it is in him that satisfied their hope for safety and happiness, and so hope themselves to provide safety and happiness to those in more dire circumstances? They can't. Why? Because, without his "super" abilities, they simply can't do what he does. He's supposed to be a great hope for humanity, as Lois tells him, and us, a symbol of what we can be. The irony, however, is that by being not only who he is, but *what* he is, he's rather a symbol that reminds us of what we *can't* be—we can't be heroes, if being a hero means being like Superman.

Batman is a much darker symbol, designed to have his "enemies share his dread," and ours share ours. But he's also a symbol that reminds us that good people are willing to do more than meet their obligations. He gives us hope that we can be like him, can be heroic, whether we're saving whole populations from Armageddon, or comforting the suffering more modestly, one by one, simply to let them know the world hasn't ended.

There's hope, then, and also, thanks to Batman, a model. However lost we may feel without superheroes at the moment, in other words, he and his ilk allow us to hope for a time when we no longer need them, because heroes aplenty, super and otherwise, reasoning in response to the problem of evil, will be busy picking up the slack.[1]

───────

[1] Some of the material presented here I began to explore in essays in earlier volumes in the series, *Adventure Time and Philosophy* and *Girls and Philosophy*, and I'm grateful to their editors, Nicolas Michaud in the first instance and Richard Greene and Rachel Robison-Greene in the second, for their encouragement and assistance on these occasions. I'm also grateful to Susan Neiman for my interest in, and understanding of the related problems of heroism and evil, to whose work I owe the Wesley Autrey example in particular. I'm grateful as well to Erin Carlston and Carisa Showden for the Sully Sullenberger example, and what I believe is the helpful contrast it provides to Wesley Autrey's, and for their patience and assistance in helping me to sort this out. I'm additionally grateful to the folks in my Enlightenment Philosophy class, during the summer of 2015, for raising the worry involving police officers and fire fighters. Naturally, none of the above are responsible for what I've done with their insights and encouragement. Finally, I'm no less grateful to the current volume's editor for patience and assistance far above and beyond the call.

21
Batman Is Superman

Suzie Gibson

In Christopher Nolan's *The Dark Knight Rises* (2012) Bruce Wayne takes an impossible leap of faith in liberating himself from a subterranean prison. This act alone defines the extraordinary character of Wayne and his alter ego Batman.

In Nolan's epic trilogy, *Batman Begins* (2005), *The Dark Knight* (2008), and *The Dark Knight Rises* (2012) Christian Bale's Batman superbly encapsulates Friedrich Nietzsche's over-reaching *Übermensch* (commonly translated as superman) by constantly challenging his mortal limits. He's no ordinary man, and yet he's still a man.

His mortality is important since Nietzsche's superman has been misinterpreted as being superhuman. The *Übermensch* (from here on out the *Übermensch* and superman will be used interchangeably) might achieve the impossible but he's still a flesh and blood hero, and, moreover, one that is deeply flawed.

What further qualifies Batman as Nietzsche's superman is the idea that beneath his suit of armor lies a fragile and conflicted humanity. This duality of his identity as a man of big business by day and a caped crusader by night reveals a strained opposition between two worlds. Publically and superficially Wayne plays the role of the rich and selfish playboy but beneath all of the frivolity and glamour lies a seriousness and solemnity that is worthy of Nietzsche's troubled soul. Bale's intelligent and nuanced portrayal of Batman reveals a complex character who is at once vulnerable and strong, angry and reasonable. His mental and physical strength is founded upon these oppositions. Conflict and struggle are also central to

Nietzsche's thinking, and this is made clear in his concept of the superman.

In analyzing the creative potential of conflict, Nietzsche draws upon the ancient Greek gods of Dionysus and Apollo. Dionysus the god of wine, revelry and song is the opposite of Apollo the god of reason and rationality. Their struggle is ongoing. As warring gods, Dionysus and Apollo enact an ancient and contemporary quarrel between emotion and reason. Their conflict is perennial and embedded within the very mindset of the superman who cannot negotiate their agreement But the resolution of the two is not the ultimate goal of the *Übermensch* since his identity is forged in and through conflict. In fact, without struggle he would cease to be the ideal individual.

Batman and Nietzsche's superman are also rendered emotionally vulnerable by conflict in the sense that it has the capacity to open up an abyss of doubt and self-questioning. The *Übermensch* then is also an existential hero who is never quite at home within himself. Bale's memorable performance as the brooding and sometimes self-loathing protagonist brings out this dimension. Doubt and anxiety operate as essential elements in supporting the identities of both Nietzsche's superman and Bale's Batman.

The *Übermensch's* Birth at the Cost of God's Death

Nietzsche's famous (or perhaps infamous) rejection of God paved the way for a non-religious way of thinking. His concept of the *Übermensch* has been connected to his famous disavowal of the divine in operating as God's replacement. In popular culture there are all sorts of God-replacements that come in the form of superheroes. Take for instance the divine and semi-divine heroes in the recent Marvel franchise.

In a world without God, perhaps we need superheroes to gain strength, courage and comfort. Batman and Superman can be interpreted as surrogate Gods. Popular philosophy has certainly made the connection between Nietzsche's superman and the comic-book character of the same name. But Nietzsche's superman is not a divine being but a flawed and conflicted individual. Put more simply, Nietzsche's superman is not God's replacement. He never quite reaches perfection or divinity because he is anchored down by the very human emotions of doubt and anxiety. Nietzsche's *Übermensch* is a painfully mortal being, as is Bale's Batman.

Nietzsche excluded women from his concept of the *Übermensch*. At the time of his writing, women were hardly considered people. Only recently have they featured as superheroes in action movies. Modern narratives have tried to address the imbalance by introducing Batgirl and Catwoman, yet in comparison to Batman or Superman, they are marginal figures. Black Widow from the Marvel series provides a female complement to her male-Avenger colleagues, but she too is slighted by her overt sexualization. Superheroes and their narratives are male-centric. And so my repetition of "he" is not an affirmation of male power—it simply acknowledges the reality that female superheroes do not enjoy the same status as their male counterparts.

The Paradox of Identity

Bale brilliantly dramatizes Nietzsche's tormented hero. His interpretation of Batman captures the struggling dimension of superman, who is never quite settled within himself, and whose public battles parallel an inner and very private conflict. What's striking about Bale's Batman is his loneliness, which is essential to his individuality and identity. Nietzsche's superman is also a lonely figure whose identity is forged through the collision of oppositional forces: Dionysian and Apollonian urges that are never quite reconciled. Nietzsche relates Dionysus's madness (and love of partying) with a form of emotion that is creative and imaginative. The Greek god Apollo operates as Dionysus's foil in representing reason. Their conflict is what keeps Nietzsche's superman and Bale's Batman eternally at odds with themselves and the world at large.

The interior anguish of Batman involves competing and overlapping forces that mediate and moderate his desire for vengeance and justice. In fact, in *Batman Begins* vengeance and justice are represented as opposing forces—the former is associated with a violent Dionysian desire and the latter with Apollonian reason. The challenge for Batman in this first installment is to overcome his unfettered anger toward himself and the man who killed his parents, rendering him psychologically stable enough to restore law and order in the city of Gotham.

There is a tension and desire between loneliness and belonging that haunts both Nietzsche's superman and Bale's Batman. Their craving to reconcile their individuality with the wider world of others is in part what propels their actions. The difficult question of how to preserve our identity, while also being part of a larger society that may dilute or even eradicate the very distinguishing features that make us individuals, is an ongoing and unresolved issue. Such a conundrum lies at the heart of Batman's and the *Übermensch's* complex characters.

Paradox is essential to the identities of superman and Batman. The struggle of developing a unified self that successfully treads the fine line between sociality and singularity bedevils both characters. Their conflicting impulses between creativity and catastrophe, emotion and reason have the dual effect of threatening the status quo while also operating as a dynamic platform that suspends and supports their heroism.

All Too Inhuman

The Superman hero we have come to know and love from countless DC comic books, many TV shows—such as *The Adventures of Superman* (1952–1958), *Lois & Clark: The New Adventures of Superman* (1993–1997) and *Smallville* (2001–2011)—and innumerable big screen movies, is a character who is not of this world.

Superman comes from the distant planet of Krypton. Not belonging to the Earth means that his humanity cannot be threatened, since he is not human in the first place. Therefore, Superman cannot go beyond himself because he is already beyond himself: indeed, he is beyond everything that is mortal. Furthermore, as an alien being and not a full-blooded man, Superman cannot reach beyond his mortal limits. In order to come close to being Nietzsche's superman you must first be mortal.

However, in *Superman II*, the version played by Christopher Reeve decides to give up his divine status to marry Lois Lane and live as an ordinary human being. His decision is, of course, disastrous. Soon after surrendering his extraordinary powers he is beaten up by a truck driver in a tawdry diner. Mortality has a bitter taste. Such bitterness is intensified by the knowledge that the world is under threat by three vicious Kryptonians who have formed an alliance with his old foe Lex

Luthor. The only way in which Superman can protect the world from the megalomaniacal trio—led by General Zod, played by Terence Stamp—is to reverse his decision and thus return to his original condition of immortality.

What *Superman II* illustrates is the significance of Superman's immortality. It also highlights his freedom to choose. The liberty of being able to change from an immortal being into a mortal one and then back again reveals an extraordinary autonomy that is beyond the grasp of mere earthlings. This element of choice is a luxury that neither Batman nor Nietzsche's superman will ever know; they are weighed down by the gravity of a dark and messy Dionysian world. For a brief moment, though, the mortal Superman experiences the pain and suffering of being human—this is when he most resembles Nietzche's *Übermensch*.

But Superman can never be the *Übermensch* because he is not grounded in the Earth, and when he's temporarily made vulnerable he resorts to the safety of invincibility. In being superhuman he exempts himself from the very blood and guts agony of mortal fears that come to define Batman, and which are also essential to Nietzsche's *Übermensch*. Moreover, the otherworldliness of Superman's original home further distances him from the chaotic sphere of human suffering. Being a foreigner who comes from the distant planet of Krypton, Superman is an alien being.

Perhaps another crucial difference between Batman and Superman then is that Batman feels alien within himself, while Superman is a genuinely alien being. Batman's self-alienation enacts the very human struggle of needing to belong, and this aspect of his character provides another parallel to Nietzsche's anguished superman. There's nothing divine or immortal about the *Übermensch*, and Batman's mortality is further evidence of his resemblance.

The Agony and Ecstasy of Being Human

Nolan's *Batman Begins* provides a seriousness and solemnity to the comic-book character. This movie, which begins the trilogy, offers a dramatic and appealing alternative to the camp, witty, and intentionally parodic TV series *Batman* (1966–1968). We're presented with a quest journey where the hero, Bruce Wayne, has to confront and overcome what seems to be his greatest fear: bats. Yes these gliding mammals of the night are identified as his Achilles heel. He associates this fear with the murder of his parents.

In this first installment we learn of an early childhood trauma where the young Wayne falls down a well on the grounds of his family estate and is surrounded by bats. His first experience with these animals leaves a lasting and night-marish impression. Soon after the incident, while attending an opera with his mother and father, there is a moment on the stage when the characters resemble bats and his recent trau-matic memory is ignited. He asks his parents to leave the opera early and they do so immediately, because they care for him so much. The timing could not be worse for within moments of departing the theatre they are mugged and killed, leaving an orphaned Wayne to contemplate his fear of bats and the ensu-ing guilt of knowing that this one terror was unintentionally instrumental in his parents' deaths.

Batman Begins becomes a movie and an epic journey once the adult Bruce Wayne wanders strange lands in pursuit of knowledge, punishment, wisdom and courage. Far away from home, he is imprisoned in Bhutan only to be released by Henri Ducard, who trains him the dark arts of stealth and gladiator-ial combat. This coaching enables him to embrace his Apollonian capacity to be disciplined while also employing Dionysian theatrics that trick and deceive. His physical jour-ney into the abyss of pain and struggle involves impressive swordplay maneuvers and sleight of hand ninja moves.

Once Bruce Wayne transforms into a warrior, an interior world of suffering is allowed to emerge. This reveals him as a better man—not an immortal but a man capable of stretch-ing his mortality. The ordeal of training which enables a psy-chological awakening involves experiencing Nietzschean eternal recurrence, where traumatic memories of being attacked by bats, and worse still the murder of his parents, are relived.

Nietzsche's concept of eternal recurrence is about the repe-titious nature of our existence. Time is not a linear entity but a circular phenomenon that allows us to revisit over and over again events in our lives. Memory is crucial to this process. The reiteration of repressed childhood traumas leads to a form of reconciliation whereby Wayne is able to incorporate his past fears in forging a future back home in Gotham city.

Yet in this movie Batman is not created out of unconditional self-acceptance or self-knowledge, but rather guilt and anger. The agony and strange ecstasy of facing up to the truth of his guilt and anger enables his development as a conflicted *Übermensch* who experiences the paradoxical intertwining of passion and reason, rapture and discipline. Through harnessing and inhabiting his fear of bats, the caped crusader comes to embody Nietzsche's vision of man, who dangles like a "rope over an abyss," the abyss between animal and Superman.

Although bats are identified as the source of Wayne's fear, what is suggested throughout *Batman Begins* is that they represent far greater and unfathomable anxieties. Bats operate as a symbolic substitution of deeper fears—feelings that may or may not be overcome, or even known. Wayne's impersonation of a bat, achieved through donning his bulletproof costume and aerodynamic wings, is a way for him to control and own his fear, but not necessarily conquer it; there still needs to be the element of tension that drives his actions. The Bat-Signal that lights up Gotham city's night sky is another important symbol in signifying hope and justice. All of this is done in an effort to extend Wayne's mortal limits. But his mortality remains. And this is what makes him like Nietzsche's noble and suffering hero. Without the fragile reality of his humanity, his courage to meet, control, and ultimately embody his fears would mean nothing.

Enter the Dark Knight

The second installment of Nolan's trilogy—*The Dark Knight*—best captures the frightening paradox of the *Übermensch*. The foe is the Joker, who is the most malevolent of forces because he is the embodiment of chaos and madness. As a villain who has no rules or boundaries, he threatens to tip the delicate balance between Batman's Dionysian and Apollonian impulses. The Joker is an extremely difficult enemy to reckon with because his anarchy exposes the thin veil of civilization. His crimes are social experiments that seek to reveal the devil within us all.

This idea is dramatically enacted through his devious plot of booby-trapping two ships with bombs. While one ship carries convicted criminals, the other carries Gotham's law-abiding citizens. The challenge is to test the moral fiber of both groups by giving them the option of blowing up the other ship and thereby preserving their lives. He believes that the survivalist principle will trump ethics, but is proven wrong.

What's really interesting about the plan and its unraveling is the fact that the ship full of convicts comes off as the most socially responsible. This makes us question the goodness of people and how those outside of jail may not be all that different from those within its walls. In this way, the Joker knows how to cut through the veneer of social niceties and public displays of decency by appealing to the animal within us all. And he nearly succeeds.

The Joker's mockery of institutions and authority figures opens up a heart of darkness where there appears to be no limit to human violence and cruelty. He makes fun of those who try to surpass or better themselves because in the end he believes in nothing and the human race is merely "a laughing stock, a thing of shame." Heath Ledger's interpretation of the Joker threatens to undo the symbolic power of Batman by preying upon the most fundamental of human emotions: fear.

The anguish and paradox of identity is opened up again by the Joker's fear mongering. His embrace of the Dionysian urge to destroy and wreak havoc manages to keep Gotham's police force and citizens fearful and captive. His seemingly inhuman capacity to outwit the most experienced of policemen in Commissioner Gordon, as well as a shrewd and savvy district attorney, Harvey Dent, challenges belief and unsettles the nerves. But the most disturbing aspect of all is that the Joker knows Batman, not as a disguised Bruce Wayne but as a force whose existence and heroism is precariously dependent upon the belief and admiration for the people of Gotham city.

The Joker understands Batman as the antidote to his chaos. Batman's rules define his lack of rules. The Joker and Batman are the flipside of one coin, which disturbingly suggests that he too might be an *Übermensch*. Unlike the trickery of Harvey Dent's same-sided coin, the Joker and Batman are the Janus face of one another. The Joker's mission is in part to preserve Dent's same-sided coin, where the chaos and anarchy of Dionysus rules and reigns over Batman and the citizens of Gotham he has elected to protect. The challenge for Batman and Gotham City is to restore the balance between order and disorder, and part of this involves maintaining a belief in humanity's goodness. The conflict is difficult because the Joker has a talent for inciting Batman's violence that threatens to overshadow his reason. By murdering his childhood friend and adult sweetheart Rachel Dawes, the Joker temporarily unleashes Batman's primal Dionysian drives in seeking revenge.

The Joker's will to power involves rendering others powerless. His malevolence also brings to the fore the existential dimension of Nietzsche's superman as the crusader who wrestles with his personal demons in trying to remain the better man. The Joker's extraordinary creativity is devastating since it is not just about the violence of blowing up hospitals, banks and police stations—it's also about being the harbinger of despair. The challenge for Batman, then, is to win the psychological battle of the mind. What also makes the Joker a particularly worthy adversary is that he understands Batman's symbolic power as a figure of hope. It is his mission to extinguish this hope, and he almost succeeds.

Life's Eternal Recurrence

The trump card in the *Übermensch*'s psychological arsenal is his capacity to play the joker. The superman in Batman means that he can straddle Dionysian chaos with Apollonian reason. This is something that the superhero Superman cannot do. In echoing Batman's tragedy, the Joker villain in Superman's narrative also murders the love of his life, Lois Lane, and his unborn child, rendering him a revengeful tyrant who is blind to justice. Unlike Batman, Superman's anger cannot be tamed as he falls into an angry Dionysian abyss. What makes Batman worthy of being the *Übermensch* is that he's able to resist the impulse for excessive revenge. He is able to incorporate the conflicting emotions of revenge and reason and it is this attitude that can outplay any Joker. The weakness of the Joker is found in the idea that he has only one card to play. Harvey Dent may be, in the Joker's words, his "ace in the hole," but Batman manages to trump it by relinquishing his own heroic status.

In *The Dark Knight*, district attorney Dent succumbs to what the Joker calls the "gravity of madness" after losing the love of his life, as well as half of his face. Unlike the stoical Bruce Wayne, Dent wreaks havoc upon all those deemed responsible for Rachel's murder. He thus becomes the Joker's agent of vice. He also dies in pursuit of embracing the unfettered madness of revenge.

In death, the Joker's Ace becomes Batman's trump card as he convinces Commissioner Gordon to turn Dent into Gotham's new symbol of hope, giving the city a hero it "needs" but not one it "deserves." Batman's self-sacrifice means that he has achieved a form of temporary wholeness where the competing drives between emotion and reason are suspended. Inadvertently, through being Batman's adversary, the Joker restores some order to his conflicted identity.

By acting the Joker and embodying all that is wrong with unfettered emotion, Batman learns to keep his feelings in check. His belief in justice above all things separates him from a herd mentality that is bent on violence and revenge. But the price paid in remaining true to his belief in justice and the good in people means that he is metaphorically again cast out of his home city and left to wander the earth alone.

Nietzsche's concept of eternal recurrence is enacted in Nolan's final chapter, *The Dark Knight Rises*. Once more Bruce Wayne finds himself trapped within a well-like prison that requires a great deal of self-belief and physical prowess to escape. The weeks and months of blood and bone training are reminiscent of his time in Bhutan when Henri Ducard taught him to become an elite warrior. Bruce Wayne is again subjected to enormous suffering and self-doubt where he tries to scale the impossibly high walls of his cell. The hero's quest for wholeness is re-enacted where the challenge is not just a physical feat but also a psychological test. In fact the psychological dimension becomes the deciding factor in ultimately liberating Nolan's hero. In making the impossible leap of faith out of his prison chamber, a confinement echoing his childhood entrapment, Wayne is propelled once more into the chaotic world of Dionysian monsters.

The great threat is again about preventing the destruction of Gotham City as a metropolis of hope and justice and physical space of industrial beauty. It is appropriate that the weapon of choice for its annihilation is an atomic bomb. The villains behind the scheme are clever and deceitful but they do not come near to threatening the *Übermensch's* equilibrium, as the borders between chaos and order remain intact. But there is another tricky figure in the mix, one that is difficult to read because she is a criminal with a conscience. Catwoman makes an appearance in this last installment and she becomes Batman's unwilling and unlikely ally. Her complexity as a villain with morals makes her the best and perhaps only companion for an embattled and complicated Bruce Wayne.

Batman and Catwoman are isolated beings who strike up a dynamic friendship in overcoming the schemes of Ra's al Ghul and his daughter Tahlia. The movie ends in the rescue of Gotham City by its two masked crusaders and once more the heroes exit the stage once they have restored order. Batman and Bruce Wayne are presumed dead which allows them to disappear from the public realm of rumor and scrutiny. The *Übermensch* is left again to wander the Earth. Except this time he is not alone.

Batman Is Superman

Batman in Nolan's trilogy embodies the conflicted nature of Nietzsche's superman, whose existence is divided between being a creative force of justice and an ordered man of big business. Christian Bale's Batman reveals a very mortal hero whose struggles are multiple and often seemingly overwhelming. His private inner demons are the source of his strength as well as his weakness. The inner and repetitious journey of seeking self-acceptance is constantly compromised and threatened by villainous foils and dangerous plots. Thus the external dangers Batman confronts come to exemplify an internal turmoil that just might be resolved in *The Dark Knight Rises*.

Significantly, the neo-gothic and existential character of Batman dramatizes Nietzsche's conceptualization of a superman who is never quite perfect, but comes close to it in extending and challenging the boundaries of his mortality. Unlike the immortal Superman, the ordinary person has the opportunity to imagine himself or herself as Batman who has it within themselves the capacity to extend their mortal limits.

Batman is superman because he relentlessly strives for virtue in the face of great vice and personal suffering. As a free-spirited being he never succumbs to the herd mentality, or in Joker's words, to the "gravity of madness," which means that he is the consummate individual whose mortality is both his weakness and his strength.

Superhero Truthers Speak Out!

22

Unmasking the World and Its Heroes

MATTHEW TABIZON AND ERIK JACKIW

Theatricality and deception are powerful agents.

—RA'S AL GHUL (*Batman Begins*)

While fans and philosophers debate the age old question of Superman vs. Batman, we take the question to be almost silly. Yes, it's true that Superman and Batman literally come from different planets. Yet they face similar problems as they struggle to find their way in the world. First, they must learn to see beyond mere appearances. A failure to understand the world can lead to failed actions. Then, they try to inspire others to do the same. But it's not easy. So, they turn to masks to protect those they care about, while also allowing themselves a private life and break from the demands on a hero. Worrying about who does more or who is better kinda misses the point. They both face challenges to make the world a better place. Even their masks can be dangerous, so heroes must walk a fine line between hiding their identity and losing it.

Allegory of the Batcave

Hope. Every man who has rotted here over the centuries has looked up to the light and imagined climbing to freedom. So simple. So easy. And, like shipwrecked men turning to sea water from uncontrollable thirst, many have died trying.

—BANE (*The Dark Knight Rises*)

The world isn't what we think it is. Plato (429?–347 B.C.E.) made this point with a famous allegory—a story in which prisoners see only shadows and so come to believe that it is the shadows that are real. Could we be stuck in a cave, unknowingly relying on misperceptions to guide our judgments and behavior? It's like the moment Bruce Wayne targets the man responsible for his parents' murder. Killing a murderer might seem a judicious way of "evening the score" and Bruce is willing to risk his life to make it happen. The citizens of Gotham would seem to fare no better, for they are trapped in the cave with Bruce and lack a sense of the true nature of their world. Like Bruce, the people of Gotham have become apathetic. But unlike Bruce, that apathy has led them to inaction— to accepting or ignoring their circumstances. Bruce soon sees through the shadows, to realize that another murder would do nothing to restore justice to Gotham. Instead, he has to do something to change the nature of justice in Gotham. But this isn't easy, since it would also require getting others to change the way they view the world.

Clark Kent has his own cave to escape, as he begins to discover that he has "powers and abilities far beyond those of mortal men." Not being immune to the pressures of fitting in and standing out, young Clark uses his powers to impress Lana Lang (*Superman: The Movie*). Of course he could do so much more. "Every time I get the ball, I can make a touchdown . . . is it showing off if somebody's doing the things he's capable of doing? Is a bird showing off when it flies?" Without the right guidance, Clark could have been forever imprisoned in the cave. Fortunately, his father was understanding and ready to tell Clark what he needed to hear. "There's one thing I do know, son, and that is you are here for a *reason*. I don't know whose reason, or whatever the reason is . . . But I do know one thing. It's *not* to score touchdowns" (*Superman: The Movie*). By determining what would be a waste of his effort, Clark is able to focus on what is real.

Plato issues an important warning about just how dangerous the cave can be. For even if someone had managed to become free and look beyond the shadows, Plato warns he would not be greeted as helpful or heroic if he returned to help the other prisoners. "Wouldn't it be said of him that he'd returned from his upward journey with his eyesight ruined and that it isn't worthwhile even to try to travel upward? And, as for anyone who tried to free them and lead them upward, if they could somehow get their hands on him, wouldn't they kill him?" (*Republic*, 517). Change, no matter how well-intentioned, may be received as hostile and if the citizens of Gotham and Metropolis do not feel safe with either Batman or Superman then they will seek refuge with someone else, even if this means turning over Batman to the Joker or releasing Superman to Zod. Fear is at odds with justice; our heroes must nevertheless stand tall and serve as symbols of hope.

Escaping the Cave

> People need dramatic examples to shake them out of apathy. I can't do that as Bruce Wayne. As a man, I'm flesh and blood; I can be ignored, destroyed. But as a symbol . . . as a symbol, I can be incorruptible. I can be everlasting.
>
> —BRUCE WAYNE (*Batman Begins*)

If being in the cave means being a prisoner, then our heroes' greatest challenge may be helping the rest of us to escape. This is the predicament of Batman and Superman, who have come to see how dangerous the world can be . . . and how complacent some of us are who live in it. Bruce Wayne faces this challenge as Batman. How can you as a citizen of Gotham do the right thing when the entire city is wrapped around mobster Carmine Falcone's finger? Police, judges and other city leaders are only feeding the crime machine leading the people deeper and deeper into the cave. These people are so lost that the Joker uses the opportunity to seize control of Gotham by playing with their fears. The Joker threatens to blow up hospitals and marks people for death with the hopes that Gotham will tear itself apart. Fortunately, it is Batman's brazen acts and the hope he inspires that steers Gotham straight. Refusing to bend to the Joker's demands, Batman sends the message that his soul is not a bargaining chip and Gotham's isn't either. The Joker's plan culminates with a ferry filled with convicts pitted against a ferry filled with civilians. They're given an ultimatum: save yourselves or die at the hand of Gotham. Both the civilians and convicts come close to triggering the detonator, but ultimately refuse to play the Joker's game. This scene is a true turning point for the people of Gotham and marks their ascension from the cave. It shows that even in the most desperate times, people of completely opposite social classes can come together and stand up against evil. The Joker's sick social experiment proves there is still good left in Gotham.

Like the son of Gotham, Kal must discover what he can offer the people of Metropolis and more importantly, what is it he wants to represent. Although it would be easy to dismiss Superman and his godlike abilities as irrelevant to deciding human conduct, Kal's father, Jor-El, disagrees. He thinks very highly of human beings and believes his son can help guide them out of the cave. "They can be a great people, Kal-El; they wish to be. They only lack the light to show the way. For this reason above all, their capacity for good, I have sent them you... my only son (*Superman: The Movie*)." Jor-El even offers his son some advice on how best to serve humanity. "Live as one of them, Kal-El, to discover where your strength and your power are needed (*Superman: The Movie*)." This leads to Kal becoming "Clark Kent, mild-mannered reporter for a great metropolitan newspaper." In Superman's latest outing, *Man of Steel*, Jor-El notes that humans are different from Kryptonians. " . . . I believe that is a good thing. They won't necessarily make the same mistakes we did. But if you guide them, Kal, if you give them hope . . . Embodied within that hope is the fundamental belief in the potential of every person to be a force for good. That's what you can bring them (*Man of Steel*)."

Superman realizes that the best way to help us is through example. "I put my shield out there to inspire people to step up and be their own heroes." To those who would be his fans, he says, "Don't believe in me. Believe in the shield and what it represents. Most importantly, believe in yourselves." To the Wonder Twins, who helped stop a drug dealer and kept Superman's secret identity as the "Blur" from going public, he says, "Metropolis doesn't need more Blur fans. It needs people who are willing to do exactly what you did today (*Smallville*, Season 9, episode 8)." Heroes.

Masks for Protection

"...no man will survive who genuinely opposes you or any other crowd and prevents the occurrence of many unjust and illegal happenings in the city. A man who really fights for justice must lead a private, not a public, life if he is to survive for even a short time.

—SOCRATES (469?–399 B.C.E.), *The Apology*

The world can be a dangerous place. Lex Luthor is willing to use anything to gain everything, while the Joker is willing to risk everything for nothing. Even an honorable person might come to believe that "cities like Gotham are in their death throes—chaotic, grotesque. Beyond saving." Those who attempt to stop such villainy can become targets of some diabolical plan, but so can the people they care about. So, how is a hero to save the day, while protecting the people he cares about? It's a secret!

A secret identity, or mask, allows a hero to heed the warning of Socrates. Jonathan Kent was so convinced that the world wasn't ready to accept a powerful alien, he chose to die to protect his son's secret (*Man of Steel*). While some might simply fear what they don't understand, others might try to find ways to take advantage of it. What if Superman's powers could be transferred to a human (*Lois & Clark*)? Perhaps Superman would be studied in a lab. What if a criminal were to discover his weakness? Lex Luthor brutally stabs Superman with kryptonite, retaliating for his role in Luthor's prison sentence (*Superman Returns*). Even Superman's friends aren't safe. His childhood friend, Pete, is kidnapped and interrogated by a corrupt FBI agent (*Smallville*). A criminal gang threatens to kill Lois Lane if Superman interferes with their business. (*Lois & Clark*).

These concerns are not simply for the super-powered among us. As Gotham's protector, Batman must do battle while thwarting any form of retaliation aimed at the people he cares about. Alfred quickly realizes that Bruce's injuries and behavior can receive unwanted attention. "Strange injuries, a nonexistent social life. These things beg the question as to what exactly does Bruce Wayne do with his time and his money" (*Batman Begins*). Bruce agrees and risks ruining his family's good name, by acting like a shallow, billionaire playboy. They

even go to lengths to see that people don't figure out that Bruce
Wayne is buying all of Batman's "toys."

Problems with the Mask

"Well, I guess you either die a hero or you live long enough to see
yourself become the villain.

—HARVEY DENT, *The Dark Knight*

The greatest gift a mask can offer our heroes is refuge. But a
mask can work too well, blurring or blending identities and
leading to a loss of self. It can be so all-consuming, that it creates titanic-like confidence that will ultimately sink all the
good our heroes set out to accomplish.

Shallow, billionaire playboy. Concerned citizen and friend.
Will the real Bruce Wayne please stand up? And let's not forget
his other mask. Is Batman's fight for justice merely an orphan's
personal crusade? We see that vengeance is still ripe in Bruce
Wayne and even witness him nearly gun down Joe Chill in public (*Batman Begins*). After the murder of Rachel, Batman acti-
vates a surveillance system capable of spying on all of Gotham.
Research Head Lucius Fox worries that "this is too much power
for one person" and offers his resignation if the technology is
ever used again (*Dark Knight*). With the level of power
entrusted to our heroes, the temptation to violate that trust is
very much alive. There may be a point where the people of
Gotham have to worry if the mask is hiding Batman's identity
or merely covering his tracks.

It's no easier trying to understand Kal-El (aka Clark Kent
or Superman). Is "Clark Kent" the mask? If so, shouldn't he be
happy with Lois' love for Superman? But as he explains to Lois,
it's more complicated than that. "You think it was easy for me
sitting there, watching you swoon over Superman and at the
same time ignoring me . . . Superman is what I can do. Clark is
who I am" (*Lois & Clark*, Season 2, ep. 20).

Kal-El must wrestle with the idea that he deserves more
from his life or powers. After all, he could do more, get more, and
win more than his earthly neighbors. In a moment of weakness,
young Clark introduces another mask to numb the pain in his
life and take advantage of his powers. This mask is in the form

of a Red Kryptonite ring, which changes Kal-El into a self-absorbed version of himself, granting him the ability to commit acts he would normally never do. After abandoning Smallville and nearly killing his Earth father, Clark reflects on his time with the ring. In spite of his regrets, he's forced to admit that "it was like this huge weight had been lifted" (*Smallville*, Season 3, episode 2). This push and pull from his masks reveals Kal-El's struggle to reconcile his life as both Clark and Superman.

Heroes Unmasked

Bruce, deep down you may still be that same great kid you used to be. But it's not who you are underneath, it's what you do that defines you.

—RACHEL DAWES, *Batman Begins*

Most of the work our heroes do, they do blindly. There is no handbook on how to be a superhero, so perhaps they can be forgiven if they become fixated on one mask or another. But with so much power and so much at stake, it's important that they think about how to determine right from wrong.

One solution is for heroes to build their understanding of right and wrong from their experience, rather than strict moral guides. This is important because heroic actions do not always manifest themselves the same way. For instance, rushing to the aid of people trapped inside a burning building could be considered courageous, but so could speaking out against injustices in your community. Over time, and with enough experience, our heroes can eventually learn to trust in themselves to make the right moral decisions. Ultimately, the actions they perform may be less important than the reasons they choose to perform them.

Our heroes may be forced to take actions that seem cruel, cold, and out of character. Recall in their final showdown, Superman is forced to save human lives by killing General Zod (*Man of Steel*). What appears to be an act of desperation from Superman is really a conscious decision, an investment of trust, a solid contract with the people of Earth that they are worth saving. Now consider Ra's Al Ghul's last question to Batman, "Have you finally learned to do what is necessary?" To which Batman responds, "I won't kill you . . . but I don't have to save you." Up until that point Batman chugged along very much like that runaway train. His goals were straightforward: save the innocent, stop evil and don't kill. The choice not to save Ra's Al Ghul was an acknowledgment by Batman, that justice is not black and white. Batman's choice shows how impractical relying on moral absolutes can be.

This emphasis on freedom and choice can also be found in *Man of Steel*. Jor-El explains the use of genesis chambers, in which Kryptonians were conceived. "Every child was designed to perform a predetermined role in our society as a worker, a warrior, a leader, and so on. Your mother and I believed Krypton lost something precious, the element of choice, of chance. What if a child dreamed of becoming something other than what society had intended? What if a child aspired to something greater?" (*Man of Steel*). It turns out that Kal-El, the Superman, represents a shift back to natural birth and freedom.

While it would be easy to end this essay with a debate over Superman vs. Batman, the story of Socrates is much more helpful in understanding heroism. Just as we might compare one hero to another, there is a legend that in Socrates's time, someone asked an oracle if there was anyone wiser than Socrates. The answer was no. Socrates was dumbfounded by this response and set out to prove it false. His efforts to disprove the oracle failed, but he did not conclude that he was the wisest. Instead, he realized that he was not literally intended to be identified as the wisest person. The oracle was "only using my name by way of illustration, as if he said, O men, he is the wisest, who, like Socrates, knows that his wisdom is in truth worth nothing" (Socrates, *The Apology*). Just as anyone can be a Socrates, anyone can be a hero. Batman reminds us, "A hero can be anyone. That was always the point . . . Anyone. A man doing something as simple and reassuring as putting a coat around a little boy's shoulders to let him know that the world hadn't ended" (Batman, *The Dark Knight Rises*).

We, too, have choices and we can choose to be heroes.[1]

----

[1] This paper is written in memory of Roland, Noah, and Eunice, with thanks to my family. —EJ. To my family; the source of all my joy. —MT.

23
I Fight Crime in My Sleep

MARY GREEN AND RONALD S. GREEN

FOR IMMEDIATE RELEASE:
Man sent to Arkham after Two-Face-like Altercation over Buddhism

GOTHAM CITY, IL/NY. Police escorted a self-proclaimed "crime fighter" to Arkham Asylum yesterday after responding to a domestic disturbance call. Upon arrival at the scene they discovered only one man in a superhero costume rolling downstairs and whipping himself with a broken car antenna. Officer James Gordon told reporters that the man was ranting about whether Buddhism favored Superman or Batman. Gordon said, "As we led him away he kept asking frantically 'Which of the two is closer to awakening; what superpower is best for becoming enlightened; who is more able to see reality like the Buddha; what is the karmic connection and interconnectivity of Superman, Batman, and the criminals they fight?'" Upon admission to the asylum, the man was entrusted to the care of a resident psychiatrist who also understands Buddhism.

"With a Batarang Between Your Teeth, You Speak Only in Vowels. Its tip jabs at the back of your tongue as the serrated point of its wing presses into your palate. There are one hundred varieties of batarangs, the sonic batarang, the siren, the smoke emitting, the exploding, and the magnetic batarang made to disarm a criminal. I know this because he knows this. Superman knows this because Batman knows this and vice versa. Be glad this one wasn't Batarang X.

"People say you always hurt the one you love. Well, it works both ways. But it hadn't always been like this between us. For the longest time we had been super friends and the things we did together helped me sleep. Before that I was lost to night terrors about the orphaned children of murdered parents. This had made me as cold as the Joker's laugh.

"If you asked me now, I couldn't tell you why I called him or even how. It seems to me now that I just called out and he was there. Maybe he was waiting for that and shortly after arriving he said, 'I want you to do something for me. I want you to hit me as hard as you can.' I said, 'You just want me to hit you?' and he replied 'C'mon, do me this one favor.' When I hesitated at this absurd suggestion, he continued, 'I don't want to die without any scars.'

"Let me tell you about my extraordinary associate. He took a job as a book editor at a prominent company under the alias of Nicolas Michaud so he could remove lewd and lascivious scenarios from manuscripts. He also works as a waiter, whipping out his thermometer and plopping it into soup bowls before serving, cooling it with his breath to make sure no citizen gets burnt."

[*The doctor interrupts this narration.*]

"It sounds to me like your call was actually a cry for help, an attempt to escape from the fears that have always plagued humanity, those surrounding old age, sickness, and death. Even the Buddha said this around the sixth century B.C.E. Your friend's behavior amounts to attempts at imposing order on the world. That might make you feel better for a moment, but it won't last, as the Buddha said, because all things are impermanent and constantly changing. He called this one of the three marks of existence and said we have to come to grips with this if we're ever going to be happy."

"Maybe so, but quite to the contrary of trying to arrange orderliness like my friend, I was working at LexCorp and let me tell you, that wasn't helping me sleep either. But my friend brought me to something that changed all of that.

"If you punch someone as hard as you can in the skull you'll probably get a boxer's fracture and be turned in to the authorities by the x-raying doctor. I don't punch as hard as I can. It could kill someone. Still, I let go with a pretty good one and my friend took it better than I'd seen any man do before and then returned one that was at least equal to my own. Catching me by surprise,

I almost tripped over my own feet. Slowly, we traded blows like this until we began to attract onlookers. One, a brawny blond man who smelled like fish, asked, 'Can I be next?'. Without hesitation my friend answered, 'Lose the trident.'"

He Secretly Rented the Hall of Justice with My Credit Card

I don't know how he found that house but it looked like it was waiting to be torn down. Most of the windows were boarded up and none of the locks worked. "What are you reading?" he asked.

"Listen to this, there's a whole set of the Mad Monk series create by Bob Kane. The Mad Monk, wearing a red hood, is a vampire. He feeds blood to his assistant, Dala. She in turn lures other women to his lair."

"What is that, *Dracula and Philosophy*?"

"I am Bob Kane's bizarre creation . . ."

". . . as penned by others."

Once a week we would meet with the other aspiring heroes we were attracting to trade blows. Six days a week we were plagued by our own silent fears of old age, sickness, and death. But on that one day a week, we were titans. At our gatherings he started by giving talks about what we were all after, talking about "truth, justice, and the American way." Later he asked me, "If you could fight any philosopher, who would it be?"

"Descartes," I said, "for cutting cats in front of students to demonstrate they have no souls. You?"

"I'd fight Buddha."

[The doctor interrupts the narration again.]

"Okay, fair enough if you want to make fun of my previous suggestion. But since you brought it up along with justice and the American way, Buddhism defines truth, the provisional and the ultimate. The provisional truth has the three marks of existence as I mentioned, impermanence or *anicca* is one of them. The others are no self or *anatta* and perpetual dissatisfaction or *dukkha*. The ultimate truth is nirv a. I've already describe how your buddy can't deal with the truth of impermanence.

Now let me suggest that he also fails to understand that the individualism he conceives among the fighters is a construction, a "self" narrated by the brain and imposed on experience in terms of likes and dislikes, that is, desires for the world to be different. This is what perpetuates the third of these marks, dissatisfaction. As long as you and your friends engage the world with an 'us and them' attitude of conflict, you will always perpetuate dissatisfaction. The Buddha said that hostility is never appeased by hostility but only by the absence of hostility is it appeased. Buddhism holds non-hurting, *ahimsa*, as one of its highest qualities. Resist not evil. This is an essential part of the path to awakening and awakening others. Buddhism defines justice as karma. In order to awakening to the truth of the world, one must understand karma and take responsibility for action. Karma is at work in *anicca*, *anatta*, and *dukkha*. When dualistic illusions about reality are overcome, there can be no 'verses' in the scenario."

"You have more Zen tricks than a Palahniuk novel, doctor. Soon the others wanted to move into the dilapidated house with us so that they could continue their once-a-week experience . . . perpetually, as you say. But he wanted to test them first, to make sure they were serious and worthy. To do this, when one came to our front door, he'd make them stand outside for days, occasionally shouting something at them like. . . .

Your Ring Is Too Gaudy! Get Your Lantern off My Porch!

"Bad news friend. It's not gonna happen. Your wings are too big!' or 'Do you think this is a game? You're too green, Manhunter! I'm going inside to get some fire!' Finally, after three days of putting up with this, he walked up to the emerald knight and said, 'Do you have two skintight computer generated imagery suits?'"

"Projected only by my ring, sir!"

"Two green masks with no visible means of support?"

"Supported by my headstrong personality, sir!"

"Are you Parallax free?" Silence.

"Then, 'That hurt, sir!'"

"Go inside."

Inside he began to hand out homework assignments in sealed envelopes and started referring to the house as The Hall of Justice. He called the team he had assembled Project Justice. He sent Arthur Curry on assignment to protect the

seven seas, Hal Jordon to patrol the American western coast-
line with Ferris Air, and we were to take the ground in our city.
Each of us was to be vigilant in our watch for crime and break
it up should we witness one. Some were sent to spawn branches
of Project Justice like franchises not only in Metropolis and
Gotham, but in Coast City, Central City, Midway City and even
to the far reaches of Leesburg, South Carolina. But I also heard
that LexCorp was setting up Project Injustice at every one of
these turns and more.

Living in our neighborhood, it wasn't long before the two of
us stumbled upon what our assignment called for, an armed
robbery in progress at the local convenient store. We didn't
even break stride but walked in saying, "Put that gun down"
and "It's all over now."

He swung the gun around at us and laughed, saying, "What
are you cosplay geeks doing here, take a wrong turn to Comic-
Con?"

"You need to call a doctor about that ulcer. I can see it throb-
bing and about to burst from here. Hmmm, let's see what else
we have here . . . David Hume, 1739 Empirical Ave."

"Whha? How'd you know all that? Do I know you?"

"I can see it in your wallet."

"Since you know who I am, you must also know I don't back
down from an argument that easy."

"You're not going to win this one, David. Put that gun down.
Now there's no need for the police either. This is all just a huge
misunderstanding we can figure out according to natural law.
Let's give you a little guidance, using gravity." The would-be
robber was dragged by the arm from the store, his gun crushed
underfoot, destroying a piece of sidewalk public property in the
process. Then, with David Hume over one shoulder, we flew up
the fire escape ladder to the top of the building across the
street and stood on the ledge holding him there. "So, David, I
doubt you wanted to grow up to be a small time convenience
store robber. What *did* you want to be?"

"Ahh, ahh, let me down!"

"I don't think you want me to do that. It's what, four stories
down?"

"Answer him, David!"

"Let me down! Your idea of law and order isn't grounded on
what is, but on what you think it ought to be."

"Who are the people in those pictures in your wallet, your mom and dad? I hope they won't have to call up kindly doctor so-and-so to dig up your dental records, because there won't be much left of your face if I have to drop you down there. Then the details of my idea of law and order aren't going to matter so much to you."

"Hey! Hold up. This wasn't a part of our plan. Answer him, David!"

"A, a philosopher."

"Ahhh, hence the college ID and the attitude."

David looked over the side of the building, then said, "Just going along with accepted values is legal positivism!"

"Going along with accepted values is exactly what makes you the pale criminal you are, as Nietzsche said to your fellow philosophers. This separates you from the super criminals we usually deal with; you have a since of guilt. That's why I'm giving an option I don't give them. If you're not back in school studying philosophy in six months from now, I'm going to revisit this ledge with you and your sophist smarts."

"Okay, okay. I was planning to go back anyway, but I owe so much in student loans as it is . . . and bankruptcy won't help, you know! Hey, since it's illegal to torture prisoners, aren't you being a little Machiavellian yourself?"

"You don't want to stick around to find out the extent of it. Now, get out of here before the police arrive. Run David, run!"

As David ran off I said, "Come on! What are we doing here? I know we want to stop crime but I never knew what a jerk you could be."

"Then you haven't been keeping up with the New 52. Listen, all this is just Smallville. What I'm really after is the big global extorters and murders. I'm just assembling the crew now, and training you. Soon we'll be ready to bring down the largest evil in the world, LexCorp.'"

[*The doctor interrupts.*]

"Sooo, I'm going to entertain for a few moments that you actually believe as least some of these Action Comics stories you're telling and try to help you through them. But I really have my work cut out for me. Let me start with these super-powers you're so fixated on.

Buddhism has what's called the Wheel of Life. It's a drawing illustrating six types of existence. Among these we find one called the "realm of the titans."

"That's appropriate."

"I thought so. Those in the realm of the titans are not human, but possess superhuman powers. Unfortunately, these demi-gods are constantly fighting. They can't seem to help themselves; it's their nature to kill and be killed in wars. Some say there are six types of humanoid existences in the universe and others interpret the six as psychological states. According to any of the interpretations, the Buddha specified that it is far better to be human. Only as humans are we capable of reaching the ultimate, which is Buddhahood. Thus, in this view, Batman has an advantage over Superman because Superman is far more distracted by and is a slave to his own superpowers. For example, his "super-intellect" is self-defeating. According to the Buddha's Four Noble Truths, intellect is causing us perpetual dissatisfaction, *dukkha*, because it's through the intellect that we impose a self-identity and judgments on the world instead of just experiencing life.

In addition to self-identity being manufactured and imposed on experiences, the superheroes you seem to idolize have manufactured a second secret identity, twice removing themselves from the reality of pure experience. But this truth about their identities, that they are manufactured, is even secret from themselves. So, even though Superman seems to be able to experience various realms of space and various time periods, past, present and future, his understanding of ultimate reality is thereby reduced because all of these experiences are in the context of false perception, taking the illusion created in his mind as reality. I might even go as far as saying that because Superman has a self-defeating super-intellect, Bizzaro may even be more capable of enlightenment than either Superman or Batman, like a Zen lunatic of sorts."

"Oh yeah? What about the power to fly?"

"Buddha told his followers that if they happened to develop the ability to levitate through meditation, they should ignore it because it would only distract them from achieving the real goal."

"Well, what about heat vision?"

"External heat vision is not as good as internal ascetic heat, called *tapas*."

"What about x-ray vision?"

"X-ray vision is not as good as the Buddha-eye. The Buddha is able to see what people truly need and prescribe "medicines" according to their capacities. Superman and Batman are only able to beat people. But I'm intrigued. How has this story of yours played out so far?"

"Did I ever tell you about the time he burnt this kiss-shaped scar on the back of my hand with his heat vision and then cooled it with his Ice Breath Those cold lips felt as good as his hot eyes had felt bad.

My God! I Haven't Been Kissed Like That Since Robin

That aside, by the time I had figured out what he was ultimately up to and our real interconnection became clear to me, it was too late. He had already taken the Phantom Zone projector to the Fortress of Solitude, rewired it not as an arrow this time, but with an explosive charge that could propel an entire floor of a building into oblivion. He planted this charge over the ceiling tiles in one of the bathrooms of LexCorp's corporate office. Once I figured it out, I pleaded with him to stop. "Listen Blue, I'm truly grateful for everything that you've done for me, but this is way, way too far. I'm begging you, I don't want this. Please, you can't even send one person to the Phantom Zone, much less every senior employee of the LexCorp and anyone else who happens to be in the area. It's not ethical!"

"Not ethical?! You wanna lecture me on ethics now? Setting aside the fact that you're in no position to do so, Masked Manhunter, you have to admit that these people are horrible global terrorists and their minion is Project Injustice."

"You're not judge, jury, and executioner! Let the legal system sort them out."

"I know what I'm doing. Haven't I brought us this far with super-intellect? No one dies; we're sticking to our vow."

"It's worse than death! They'll become disembodied spirits. They don't age, they can't touch anyone, they can only watch and communicate telepathically. It is a living hell and you don't have the right to do that to any being, not even the vilest murderer."

"What do you want?! Do you want to go back to insomnia, to reading Marvel to help you doze off? Forget it. I won't do it. So shut up. Sixty seconds. Can you see all right, Caped Crusader?"

"Just wait! I can figure this out. This isn't even real, just like Buddha says. You're not real. You're like my extreme superego unleashed. No one can fly around the world and spin it backwards to reverse time. Time isn't even like that. I'm just taking my own ambition to stop the crimes that killed my parents and supercharging them. You hear like I want to hear, you see like I want to see, you're fast like I want to be fast . . ."

"How do you know I'm not just projecting my desire to fit in as a human as the *you* that I'm creating in *my* mind. Maybe *you're* the one who's not real. If you're really convinced that I'm not real, then what are you so afraid of? But, if I *am* real, well, I'd like to see the world's greatest detective try to stop the Man of Steel. Forty-five seconds. What's that? A batarang? I wouldn't care if you affixed a nuclear warhead to it. Which of the one hundred is it?"

"It's none of them. You don't know it because I didn't know it. I know that you know at least everything I do. But this one I wouldn't even acknowledge to myself. I kept it out of my head with mindfulness meditation just in case you *were* a figment of my imagination, concentrating only on my breaths, I'm breathing in . . . I'm breathing out." [*He opens one eye after giving this meditation demonstration and says to the doctor*] Okay, just hear me out.

"Whichever batarang it is, don't make me stick it . . ."

Before he could finish his sentence, I stepped forward and saw Kal-El's right leg quiver slightly. It was working and that was my cue to clock him fully in the square of his jaw with the same fist I held the batarang. He fell back on one knee and was quickly back up, but humanly quick this time. He swung, I parried; he kicked, I deflected. Maybe on the sun or moon I'd be finished. But we both knew what was going to happen given equal footing in my city. My fists and elbows went around every swing and block he tried until I straddled him and forced it into his mouth panting, 'Say hello to the Kryptonite batarang. It's number 101 and is soon to become number 1002 of the *1001 Ideas That Changed the Way We Think*."

I think this is about where we came in. He asked in a muffled voice, "Where did you go, psycho boy?"

I answered, "I wanted to destroy something beautiful, our relationship."

"H-ow . . . ?"

"I've always kept a vial of Kryptonite for just this occasion. Knowing it would inevitably arrive, I just planted it in a batarang."

[*Ahmfff.*"

"I didn't catch that, Man of Tomorrow. Would you like to say a few words to mark the occasion?" I withdrew the batarang and saw a tiny stream of alien blood trickle from its tip as I helped him to his feet with my left hand. For all of his obsession and dictatorial insistences, I still could not help but love my longtime fellow-legionnaire. But as Gandhi said, there is no people on Earth who would not prefer their own bad government to the good government of an alien power.

As he stood swaying still under the influence of the Kryptonite and my fists, he smiled and managed in a hoarse whisper, "One second," collapsing into me fully. Suddenly there was a silent blast like at ground zero of the apocalypse. A ghastly flash of light spread from the center with a color I'd never witnessed, somehow sucking away all the oxygen in its wake. The last thing I saw out the window before losing consciousness was the top floor of the *Daily Planet* turning into an outline of itself, then dissolving completely, taking with it in the radiance the Metropolis Marvel, who had fallen over my body like an invulnerable shield."

[*The doctor was silent for a moment with the blunt tip of her pen touching her lips, as if still taking in the fantastic details of the story. Then she said the following.*]

"Well, I *was* hesitant to bring this up it, but you said it all for me. Like Superman, because Batman's mind is always engaged in conflict, he is barely capable of awakening and never will as long as he keeps up that lifestyle. But it's more, much more than that. Batman's mind is actually damaged. In short, as you say, he's a psycho boy. The combination of the two, the psychosis and the violence, inevitably leads here to Arkham Asylum. Just as Superman's super-intellect is matched with that of Lex Luthor's brain power, Batman is matched with the Joker in terms of insanity.

"If anyone ever portrays your Batman in a movie, it should be Christian Bale because he characterized Batman perfectly when he previously starred as Patrick Bateman in *American Psycho*. Ironically, not only is Bateman one letter away from Batman, but Batman is only one step away from being Bateman. Like Batman, Bateman wears a mask. But after peeling it off he still does not know who is behind it. Like Bruce Wayne, Patrick Bateman is an economically privileged, white, well educated, urban American male who refuses to let anyone become close to him. Much more tragic for both, they refuse to be mindful of themselves and are unaware of the interconnectedness of their personalities with those of their perceived antagonists. Both entertain as socialites who maintain a façade of affability while hiding a dark secret behind cold eyes.

"Like Batman, Bateman's inability to know the truth of himself or what he has done is not due to a failure in his memory. In fact, the memories and intellectual capacities of Bateman and Batman are greater than their peers. But in both cases their failure to know is a problem of false perception. This has always been the case with humanity, just as the Buddha explained. This trait manifests according to historic circumstances in different times. In our time and place, the personality manifests in post-industrial America as Bateman's obsession with Whitney Huston, horror porn, business cards, and cocaine, all of which shapes his view of others as meat and bones. Batman's worldview is no less degenerate.

"Again, the Buddha says in the *Dhammapada* that as long as we're led around by desires for something we don't have and desires to get rid of things we do have, we're not in control of ourselves but are like zombies, as good as dead. I'm afraid Bateman and Batman both demonstrate that theirs is just the American way, which, by the way, is the third element in the Boy Scout's trinity formula, along with truth and justice.

"In general, Superman and Batman are both victims of Mara, one's own internal deceiver and the greatest super villain in all history. Only a true conqueror can defeat Mara; everyone else is conquered in all they do. This is the only superpower worth having for oneself and for all humanity, far better than fighting and winning wars, wouldn't you agree?"

"What's that old saying about you always kill the one you love? Well that one works both ways too. Okay, okay. It's not that I completely disagree with everything about your Buddhist analysis of my situation, it's just that I can't help getting a strong impression that somehow you *personally* don't want to see me or the other members of Project Justice fighting crime anymore. Am I right, Dr. Quinzel?"

She leaned forward and whispered, "We look forward to getting you back. It's all going according to the plan, Mr. Kent."

24
The Fifty-Third Card

JACK NAPIER

W ell, wasn't that just fantastic? . . . All those philosophers working so hard to try to pick the winner of such a silly little made-up fight. There are just so many perspectives on it. Is Superman not working hard enough to do good? Is Bats too grumpy? Bla bla bla. Two psychos running around in their granny's old tights, and there wasn't a single laugh.

And that's such a shame! What's the point really? They worked so hard to prove which nutzo they thought was the winner, but they never really did crack the shell of the problem, did they? After all, these superclever authors never considered the possibility that both "heroes" are just big fat stinking losers. But if you're going to sit down to the game, you'd better be ready to play the hand you're dealt. And, well, maybe this is just me, but I don't think the game's really over until every card in the deck is put on the table.

A little hero-worship isn't such a bad thing. I'm just saying that we want a fair game. If we assume that the boy scout and the bat are heroes, then we haven't really considered every perspective. Maybe they are the villains of the story. Had we thought of that? Well then, shame on us! So many little minds working so hard to prove that the other guy is a loser and we never thought to ask, "Are they both losers?" I don't want to hurt anyone's feelings, but there has been a lot of effort put into showing not just who's better, but also why the other "hero" sucks. Really, they are both a bit of a tit. The big brawling super-brat with all that power and still the world burns, and the rat with wings . . . isn't he just a killing-spree waiting to happen? How surprised would we really be if we found out that little Brucey snapped and started drowning kittens because his neighbor's telepathic dog told him too? No, I don't think we've played fair at all. We need to take a closer look at how both of them fail us.

Now I can sense that I'm losing you here. But I haven't gotten to the punchline yet. And this is a pretty damn good joke these guys have played on us. We're all working so hard to prove who's a hero, but we completely ignored the fact that proving one guy is the better hero really meant tearing the other one down. Really. How many chapters showed one cape-wearing maniac was better by trashing the other? All that negativity just left me feeling down in the dumps. Do we really have to lift ourselves up by putting down others?

I don't know about you, but I think a real super-man wouldn't worry so much about what others thought about him and really do everything he could to make the world better. If we really look at him, he wants to be a hero. And it's a bit demeaning, all that saving the day. Oh boo-hooo "My fantastically powerful parents died saving my planet from destruction, and I was raised by the two most perfect, apple-pie-eating, Brady-Bunch-loving people on the planet, but I still want people to love me. So I'll flying around wearing a bit red 'S' on my shirt so that everyone will know how really awesome I am."

Stuperman is really just a wedgy in the ass-crack of our lives, always begging for our attention. He can move so fast that he could literally save all those pathetic little people without ever being seen. No, he wants the attention. Why? So he can be a "symbol" of what . . .? Of something the rest of us can never be! Not to be cheeky, but that just chafes doesn't it? He can't leave us to save ourselves? What is he, our super-mommy?

And Bat-fraud . . . All that money. Oh so much money. We could just put it all in a vault and go swimming naked it it. . . . And what a selfish way to use it. . . . He could be donating billions to charity around the world and literally save millions of lives. Instead, all that money goes to wonderful toys so he can pretend he is just like Superfreak . . . He's super looney. Wow. How much must it bother Batty that he can never, no matter how much money he has, be even close to Supertwit? But Bats does try, and pours all that money into his ego. Thousands of kids die every day, and he's at home washing his tights! What kind of hero would rather beat up two-bit thugs, who, let's be honest, probably just need a hug, a good home, and a talking too from their mommies, instead of doing real world-wide good? It's enough to make any old Memaw want to throw a smiling bunny-slipper at him. Seriously, I don't know why Brucey's own sainted mother puts up with it. . . . Oh right, well that explains a lot.

What, Too Soon?

All I'm saying is that a real super-man wouldn't need all that attention and wouldn't try to force other people to be like him. He would live a resentment-free life and do what he knows is best. What both of our little megalomaniacs are doing is self-indulgent weenie measuring. But I think they both come up short. The world isn't filled with good people trying to do right. It is filled with lots and lots of little people who are all trying to screw each other over.

We've got Philip over here stealing staples from work and Fanny over there who just "forgets" to report all of the money she makes to the IRS. What harm is there in that? Just a bit of fun, right? The fact is we are just all as moral as our circumstances. We make up all these rules, but then we don't follow them. Think about how many people truly believe that they will go to hell if they don't follow ten simple rules, and they don't even have them all memorized! It's just ten rules for heaven's sake! It's enough to make even Charlton Heston weep!

Oh the humanity! Aren't we just inconsistent bastards . . . ? Think about how we all would beat the gosh-darned tarnation out of anyone who hurt our little mutt Rover. Whoooeeeee would we just be as mad as a chicken with her beak cut off. But we have no trouble saying, "Please pass the bacon, Ma!" Ha! It is funny isn't it? Anyone who hurts our pet, they're a monster, but we will gladly torture little piggies who are far smarter than our Rover for whom the highlight of his day is licking his own butt. We applaud Superprude and Crackedman for saving little kids from burning buildings and lust over their eight-pack super-abs while shoving chocolate into our fat faces for which the cocoa was picked by little child slaves who are kept in cages and beaten every day. Don't believe me? Look it up. Joke's on you . . .

Now don't get your tights in a wad. It's just you and me here. We don't need to pretend. We all like to be a bit naughty now and then . . . I mean, sure we could give our money to the homeless, but they smell after all . . . and we like those new shoes. So what if they are made by kids in sweat-shops. That doesn't make us bad people. Those little kids are all the way over there. And it isn't like we're the ones torturing them. We just bought the shoes, and they just are just oh-so comfy. Little Lacey who made them, she'll be fine. After all we do need someone with fingers small enough to do all that fine stitching.

All I'm saying is that a real super-man would see all this, and puke. He wouldn't delude himself into believing that he needs to play by the world's rules. We aren't moral. We've never been. We pretend to follow the rules and then quietly slip the knife into the back of whoever we can, usually some poor kid in another country we never meet. We respond to people killing our people by killing their people and walk away pretending like our morality is still intact. You remember the movie *The Dark Knight* where all those people in those two boats were given a choice, "Either blow up the other boat or you all die . . ." That was the one thing in the film I couldn't believe . . . everyone raised themselves up and chose to "do the right thing" and *both* groups choose to not push the button. What a titanic mistake! In reality, in our world, we would have been climbing over each other to press the button.

What reason do we have to believe otherwise . . . that everyone would choose to die rather than kill people they don't know? We are the same people who would rather pay farmers to not farm to keep our economy strong than give the starving of the world food for free! Would we really, when thinking about our wife and kids at home, be willing to let the other guys push the button first? I don't think so. We would find a way to morally rationalize killing them all. "Well it's a boat full of prisoners" or "It's a boat full of affluent, white jerks." And we'd feel a little guilty now and then and then remind ourselves that we are good people and go back to eating our veal. The director decided that the people on those boats would all make the right decision because we are delusional, and he didn't want to be the one to burst our bubble . . . we kill every day. Killing is making a choice, and we chose not to help. Because we don't help them, people die.

But see, I'm not like Superlube and Batguano, I'm being honest. I'm not judging you. I'm not telling you, "Be a better person" while choosing to go out on a booty call with Lois Lane when I could be saving a life instead, or beating the snot out of a kid who likely needs to be in rehab getting real help instead of being pummeled by a guy with a bat-fetish . . . I'm just saying that we're all probably just as moral as our opportunities allow. Had we been born in the ghetto with a crack dealer father and a prostitute mother, we would probably engage in a little crime now and then too. In fact, we probably do anyways . . . I mean how many of us have shoplifted, or realized when we got home that the cashier never rang up something in our cart. Drat! . . . Well if her register comes up a little short . . . that's okay. It doesn't do her that much harm . . . Cha Ching! Free stuff!

In the Pale Moonlight

A real super-man would be the guy pointing out to us that we don't have to follow all these little rules that make our lives so mundane. No, we really don't have to be to work on time, and no, we really don't need to work harder so we can have more crap we don't need. Really, the thing that all these do-gooders forget is that everyone dies. There isn't any stopping that. So what really matters is what we do before we dance with the devil.

Every day we have a chance to say to the world, "Here's how I think we really should live." We can get up, and do the things that we feel are right. Instead, we let the world tell us what's right. So even if we think something's wrong, pick your cause, the treatment of children in sweatshops, torturing animals for food and fun, racism, sexism, the treatment of the disabled, carpet-bombing civilians, mistreatment of clowns, whatever. You really could do something about it. Think about people who come back after a war. How many of them literally had to pick off pieces of their best friends brains off of their uniform . . . how crazy must they think the rest of us are for screaming at our cell-phone because of bad reception? How important is all this crap, really?

I promise you, what shoes you own really doesn't matter to you that much if some psycho puts you in a little box with a dead rat as your only company, and, while humming "Frère Jacques," laughs about how he's going to slice your intestines out with his favorite knife and tells you how he looks forward to getting to know you better. You get a much sharper perspective on the things that really matter. Believe me, I know.

I'm sure you can see where I'm going with this . . . Maybe those two arrogant "Make me into another action figure" bastards aren't heroes at all. They both stand as shining examples to the rest of us that we can indulge our egos while failing to do the things we really believe are right. They both lets thousands die while claiming to be super and meeting their own arrogant ends. To me, the real hero would be the guy who just lives his life doing what he really thinks is right, not claiming to be moral at all, because he knew the real secret . . . that life's short, so you might as well have a laugh now and then.

He wouldn't pretend to be a hero at all. The kind of guy you would hate, really, because he would remind you that you can't be Superman, and that Batman is just a rich brat who isn't willing to give his money to do real good. He'd be the kind of guy who'd remind us that we all don't bother following the moralities that we say we love so much. He'd be like the fifty-third card in every deck that we throw out, because we just don't know how to deal with it. . . . He'd be the smiling face that reminds us that right under the skin . . . we're all clowns, pretending to be moral, laughing as we watch the world burn.

References

Acton, H.B., and John W.N. Watkins. 1963. Symposium: Negative Utilitarianism. *Proceedings of the Aristotelian Society, Supplementary Volumes* 37.

Aristotle. 1992. *The Art of Rhetoric*. Penguin.

Bakewell, Sarah. 2011. What It All Means. *New York Times* (January 23rd).

Brubaker, Ed. 2014. *Batman: Bruce Wayne—Murderer?* DC Comics

———. 2014. *Batman: Bruce Wayne—Fugitive*. DC Comics.

Busiek, Kurt. 2002. *Astro City*. Vertigo.

Contestabile, B. 2013 [2005]. Negative Utilitarianism and Justice. *Philosophy as Therapy*. <www.socrethics.com/folder2/justice.htm>.

Csíkszentmihályi, Mihály. 1991. *Flow: The Psychology of Optimal Experience*. Harper.

Eco, Umberto. 1972. The Myth of Superman. *Diacritics* 2:1 (Spring).

Gale, Bob, et al. 2012. *Batman: No Man's Land*. Volumes 1–4. DC Comics.

Griffin, J. 1979. Is Unhappiness Morally More Important than Happiness? *Philosophical Quarterly* 29:114.

Hamilton, Edith. 1969 [1940]. *Mythology*. Mentor/NAL.

Hine, David. 2011. *Batman: Imposters*. DC Comics.

Hobbes, Thomas. 1996. *Leviathan*. New York: Cambridge University Press.

Hume, David. 1897. Of the Original Contract. In David Hume, *Essays*, ed. Eugene F. Miller. Liberty Fund.

Jurgens, Dan, 1992. *The Death of Superman*. DC Comics.

———. 1993. *Doomsday! Superman*. Volume 2, #75. DC Comics.

Keen, Maurice.1984. *Chivalry*. New Haven, Yale University Press.

Landis, Max. The Death and Return of Superman. Video <www,youtube.com/watch?v=0PlwDbSYicM>.

Kant, Immanuel. 2012 [1785]. *Groundwork of the Metaphysics of Morals*. Cambridge University Press.

Linderoth, Jonas. 2010. Why Gamers Don't Learn More. *DiGRA Nordic 2010 Proceedings* <www.digra.org/dl/db/10343.51199 .pdf>.

Locke, John. 1988. *Two Treatises of Government*. Cambridge University Press.

Loeb, Jeph, and Ed McGuiness. 2005. *Superman/Batman: Public Enemies*. DC Comics.

Maggin, Elliot S. 1997. Introduction to *Kingdom Come* by Mark Waid. DC Comics.

Matheson, Mark, ed. 2012. *The Tanner Lectures on Human Values*. University of Utah Press, 2012

Mayerfeld, J. 1996. The Moral Asymmetry of Happiness and Suffering. *Southern Journal of Philosophy* 34.

———. 2002. *Suffering and Moral Responsibility*. Oxford University Press.

Mill, John Stuart. 2002 [1864]. *Utilitarianism*. Hackett.

Millar, Mark. 2014. *Superman: Red Son*. DC Comics.

Miller, Frank. 1997. *The Dark Knight Returns*. DC Comics.

Moore Alan. 1986. Whatever Happened to the Man of Tomorrow? Superman #423 and Action Comics #583. DC Comics.

———. 2006. *DC Universe: The Stories of Alan Moore*. DC Comics.

Morrison, Grant. 2011. *Supergods: What Masked Vigilantes, Miraculous Mutants, and a Sun God from Smallville Can Teach Us about Being Human*. Spiegel and Grau.

———. 2011. *All-Star Superman*. DC Comics.

———. 2013. *Batman Incorporated*. DC Comics.

Neiman, Susan. 2002. *Evil in Modern Thought: An Alternate History of Philosophy*. Princeton University Press.

———. 2011. What It All Means. *New York Times* (20th January).

———. 2012. Victims and Heroes. In Matheson 2012.

Nietzsche, Friedrich. 1974. *The Gay Science: With a Prelude in Rhymes and an Appendix of Songs*. Vintage.

———. 1995. *The Birth of Tragedy*. Dover.

———. 1999. *Thus Spake Zarathustra*, Dover.

———. 2006. *The Nietzsche Reader*. Wiley-Blackwell.

———. 2003, *The Genealogy of Morals*. Dover.

Nozick, Robert. 1974. *Anarchy, State, and Utopia*. Basic Books.

Plato. 2000. *The Trial and Death of Socrates*. Indianapolis: Hackett.

Popper, Karl R. 1971. *The Open Society and Its Enemies. Volume 1: The Spell of Plato*. Routledge.

Rand, David, and Ziv Epstein, 2014. Risking Your Life without a Second Thought: Intuitive Decision-Making and Extreme Altruism. <http://journals.plos.org/plosone/article?id=10.1371/journal.pone. 0109687>.

Raz, Joseph 1975. Permissions and Supererogation. *American Philosophical Quarterly* 12:2 (April).

Rozakis, Bob. 1987. *Superman IV: The Quest for Peace*. DC Comics.

Peter Singer, 1972. Famine, Affluence, and Morality. *Philosophy and Public Affairs* (Spring) 1:3.

Steinbeck, John. 1992 [1939]. *The Grapes of Wrath*. Penguin Classics.

Urmson, James Opie. 1958. Saints and Heroes. In *Essays in Moral Philosophy*, ed. A.I. Melden. University of Washington Press.

Verlet, Nicolas. 2014. Dossier: La Malédiction Saint Seiya, *Gamekult*, accessed December 11th, 2014, <www.gamekult.com/actu/dossier-la-malediction-saint-seiya-A99919.html>.

Waid, Mark. 2008. *Kingdom Come*. DC Comics.

———. 2008. *The Brave and the Bold*. DC Comics.

Wolf, Susan. 1982. Moral Saints. *Journal of Philosophy* 79.

Wolff, Robert Paul. 1970. *In Defense of Anarchism*. Harper and Row.

Yoeli, Erez. and David Rand. 2015 The Trick to Acting Heroically. *New York Times* (August 30th).

The Rogues Gallery

RAY BOSSERT earned his PhD in early modern literature, but frequently teaches college students to overanalyze popular culture and graphic media. Between researching Shakespeare and teaching comic books, he spends far too much time thinking about men in tights.

MARVIN LEE DUPREE is a PhD student at the University of Rijeka, and his main focus is ethics, aesthetics with a focus on philosophy of film, and cognitive science. He has been a passionate fan of Batman since reading ish #200 of *The Brave and the Bold*, and has never looked back. He also believes that many ethical matters and political issues could easily be solved simply by asking a single question: What would Batman do?

SCOTT FARRELL is the director of the Chivalry Today Educational Program, and producer/host of the award-winning Chivalry Today Podcast. Inspired by Adam West's TV series *Batman*, he spent much of his childhood years dressed in a black mask and cape—which may explain his ongoing fascination with extraordinarily chivalrous superhero characters. While the cape and mask have long since been retired, he can be found today dressed in a full suit of armor, giving talks on knighthood and the ideals of chivalry for conferences, schools, and professional groups throughout Southern California. His articles and short stories have appeared in dozens of print and online publications, including the *New York Times*, *Military History Quarterly*, and the Shakespeare Birthplace Trust blog.

MIRELA FUŠ is a PhD student at the University of Rijeka and has been a visiting scholar at the universities of St. Andrews, Graz, and Vienna. Her main interests are in philosophy of language, philosophy of mind, and cognitive science. In her free-time she enjoys exploring as many teahouses and cafés as is humanly possible, thus she is also quite hopeful she might catch a glimpse of the Dark Knight even though he retired recently.

Early, **CHRIS GAVALER** decided he must turn his titanic intellect into channels that would benefit mankind. As the years passed, he prepared himself for his career. He became a superhero scholar. He is the author of *On the Origin of Superheroes* (2015) and is now working with fellow Washington and Lee University professor Nathaniel Goldberg on a book titled *With Great Power: How Superhero Comics Channel and Challenge Philosophy*.

SUZIE GIBSON lectures in English Literature at Charles Sturt University in Australia. Her research examines literary, philosophical and popular culture texts. She is an avid fan of the Batman franchise, in particular Julie Newmar's seductive portrayal of Catwoman in the 1960s television series. In fact, she own costumes inspired by Newmar's sleek look and it has been suggested on more than one occasion that she is Catwoman. Batman wins because he is smart enough to hook up with Catwoman in Nolan's *The Dark Knight Rises*!

NATHANIEL GOLDBERG is an associate professor of philosophy at Washington and Lee University. He has written an academic book called *Kryptonian Conceptual Geography* (or thereabouts) and is finishing a popular book with Chris Gavaler called *With Great Power: How Superhero Comics Channel and Challenge Philosophy*.

MARY GREEN is an animation student in Eugene, Oregon. She once lived in the Southern region of the United States, but moved out West to pursue her education. Fear not, citizens, for she was able to find a stand-in named Linda Danvers to take over her prior duties while she is away at school.

RONALD S. GREEN has a PhD in Buddhist Studies. He currently teaches Asian Religions at Coastal Carolina University, having moved there from Leesburg after creating Linda Danvers from synthetic protoplasm when her first superhero incarnation, Mary Marvel, moved to Oregon.

SÉBASTIEN HOCK-KOON should very soon create a middle-school math teacher to cover the fact that he comes from another planet: he has a PhD in Education Science from the University of Paris-Nord but studies learning with video games. He used this soon-to-be hidden identity to conceal an even darker one: he is a former game designer, game design teacher and high level arcade player.

By day, **A.G. HOLDIER** is an ethics instructor for Colorado Technical University and a high-school theology teacher in Southern Idaho; by night, he's usually a much more tired version of that same thing. Though his work on the philosophy of religion, environmental ethics, and aesthetics might not lead to super strength or an empire the size of Wayne Industries, he's more than happy to have two living parents instead.

ERIK JACKIW is a lecturer at Metropolis Polytechnic, striving to save the day with powers of philosophy, logic, and ethics. His not-so-secret hope is that students will develop their own superpowers and share them with the world.

CHRISTOPHER KETCHAM earned his doctorate at the University of Texas at Austin. He teaches business and ethics for the University of Houston Downtown. His research interests are risk management, applied ethics, social justice, and east-west comparative philosophy. Buddha is a superhero. He goes around brandishing karma and enlightening folks. Wonder what he could do for old dour Batman.

TIM LABAUVE's origins are unknown. Rumors at Arkham Asylum are that he's been seen patrolling the dark alleys of Gotham's underbelly, stamping out ignorance with a precise and merciless use of the Socratic Method. The damned of the Phantom Zone swear that they've been changed for the better by his powerful lectures on Scriptural Theology. Regardless of the whisperings of Gotham and Metropolis, one thing about LaBauve is certain: he still sleeps in his Superman pajamas.

Dr. **NOAH LEVIN** (he didn't spend ten years in "evil" graduate school to be called "Mr.") is an Instructor of Philosophy at Golden West College in sunny Huntington Beach, California. When he's not fighting ignorance from a comfortable armchair, he is sitting in said armchair enjoying other activities. If he had superpowers, he'd be using them, and definitely not merely sitting in that same armchair, like that lazy dude in the red cape would do. And my costume would be way cooler and have no cape, as those things have been proven to be dangerous.

DANIEL P. MALLOY is a lecturer in philosophy at Appalachian State University who has made a variety of contributions to popular culture and philosophy, including chapters on Superman, Batman, Green

Lantern, Iron Man, Spider-Man, and the Avengers. One of the many confrontations between Batman and Superman was actually part of an elaborate scheme of Daniel's. Unfortunately, he got so caught up watching the fight that he forgot to set his further plans in motion. Foiled again!

TRIP MCCROSSIN teaches in the Philosophy Department at Rutgers University, where he works on, among other things, the nature, history, and legacy of the Enlightenment. He finds that students sometimes, in receiving their work back, channel Bruce Wayne. "All this," they plead, waving their hand over the pages, "it's not me." "Inside," they insist, ever so earnestly, "I *am* more." What better response than to say, just as earnestly, "But what would Rachel say?"

NICOLAS MICHAUD teaches philosophy and English in Jacksonville, Florida. He believes the supposedly never-ending question of "Who is better, Batman or Superman?" could easily be solved if Bruce would finally just beat the living snot out of the big blue bastard and be done with it. No worries though, in editing this book he was totally objective. Really.

JACK NAPIER wonders why we can't all just get along! Everyone is just so uptight . . . "Who's better? Batman or Superman?" . . . "I like chocolate. Well, I like vanilla!" . . . "I'd rather slit him open stem to sternum with a festive sock puppet. I'm more of a traditionalist and rather just beat him bloody with a crowbar." Argue, argue, argue! When really, does any of this matter? All those petty little lives worrying about such trivial things. It's a sad pursuit, really. If it didn't make Jack want to cry he would just have to laugh at how silly everyone was being . . . silly, silly, silly. That's why he'd rather spend his time dancing. Nothing like grabbing your partner for a midnight twirl and spinning her head around until she just can't ever stop smiling. Jack realizes that we could resolve so many of our problems if we'd just work together. For example, couldn't we just put the sock puppet on the crow bar? Nothing wrong with adding a bit of flavor to a traditional approach. See? Now everyone's happy. Problem licked.

PATRICK J. REIDER, PhD, teaches Philosophy at the University of Pittsburgh. He hopes to one day be awarded the title Dread Lord of Philosophy, upon which he will start a new career as a petty villain. He has aspirations of being a tyrant of a small island nation where he can promote anti-Superman sentiment. If his plans of tyranny fail, he would happily settle to be employed in HR for the planet Apocalypse or Luther Corp. Most of his days are spent sulking, because the title Grand Accuser is already taken.

BEN SPRINGETT is finishing his PhD on the nature of dreaming and is a teaching assistant at the University of Bristol. He only writes about dreams or superheroes. He's never saved anybody's life. Unfortunately.

As a library professional at the City of Commerce Public Library, MATTHEW TABIZON enjoys sharing his interests in books, comics, television, and movies with younger generations of superhero fans. As a tinkerer of all things tech it's no wonder Batman holds a special place in this fanboy's heart. Although it's hard to admit if you ask him which thrill coaster one ups the other, Six Flags Magic Mountain's Batman: The Ride, or Superman: Escape from Krypton, Escape from Krypton wins!

CRAIG VAN PELT is a PhD student at the University of Oregon. His sociological research focuses on environmental health, poverty, and food security. Although Superman clearly wins this time, Van Pelt is a bigger fan of Batman.

Index

POPULAR CULTURE AND PHILOSOPHY®

DOCTOR WHO

POLICE BOX

POLICE PUBLIC BOX

POLICE TELEPHONE

PULL TO OPEN

AND PHILOSOPHY
BIGGER ON THE INSIDE

EDITED BY COURTLAND LEWIS AND PAULA SMITHKA

Printed in the USA
CPSIA information can be obtained
at www.ICGtesting.com
JSHW012021140824
68134JS00033B/2802

9 780812 699180